THE RINEHART BOOK OF VERSE

The Rinehart Book of Verse

EDITED WITH A PREFACE AND NOTES BY

Alan Swallow

HOLT, RINEHART AND WINSTON
NEW YORK • CHICAGO • SAN FRANCISCO
TORONTO

Seventeenth Printing, December, 1962

28246-0112

Typography Design by Stefan Salter
Printed in the United States of America
Library of Congress Catalog Card Number: 52-5604

PREFACE

The Rinehart Book of Verse has been assembled as a source book for students and teachers—particularly for those students and teachers who, perhaps for the first time, are studying together seriously the mysteries and revelations, the difficulties and rewards, of accomplished poetry.

The editor's intention has been to bring together in a relatively small and usable book *some* of the fine poems of the English language. The defining perspective has been that of the classroom: to anthologize poems which the editor, and other teachers who have been kind enough to grant their advice, have found significant in the joint student-teacher activity which especially characterizes the introductory class in literature.

To issue an anthology is to challenge, to throw down the gauntlet. It is to say, "The devil take you!—this is *my* reading of the history of poetry, and you better well come along for the ride."

Each student of English and American literature has his own version of the "history" of that literature, a history which he will defend, naturally, with every facility he has. And to select some items from that literature—no matter what the purpose or intent—is to run the gauntlet indeed.

I hope that it is apparent from the contents of this book, selected on the chief principle indicated above, that I have wished to avoid as much as possible such controversy. This book does not embody, with thoroughness, my own version of the history of English and American poetry. Instead, I have endeavored to work with some of the standard anthology pieces; yet, that small "golden treasury" has been carefully reworked, with considered deletions and additions, generally to accord with contemporary critical feeling; and more particularly in view of the fact that close analysis of the poem is frequently used, today, as a study and teaching device in the classroom.

Certain principles of selection have seemed to be necessary in order to keep the main purpose in view:

1. The history of poetry in English is tremendously rich in *variety*: it is hoped that the selections give appropriate indication of that rich variety in accomplishment, tone, theme, and method.

2. The poems have been arranged chronologically—even in the chronology of birth of the known poets—not merely because, for the teacher who does not emphasize chronology such an arrangement is perhaps the simplest, but much more positively because, for many teachers—the editor included—the close reading of the poem is importantly affected by one's knowledge of the historical affairs, both in the broad and the specific senses, which conditioned the particular poem.

3. Without treating the history of English and American poetry exactly, the editor has desired to give, particularly to the newer student, some awareness of the chief poets, both major and minor; and awareness of some of the great moments in that poetry.

4. The need for a compact book—a book not wastefully equipped with much more material than can possibly be used—has prevented, in many cases, any effort to give a "fair" or "rounded" picture of individual poets; that is, an inclusive sampling of the variety of work a poet may have written. This has been particularly true of those poets who have a chief reputation for dramatic or narrative poems.

5. Space has not been sufficient to include any very long dramatic poems; this type of work being represented only by the brief dramatic lyric, the dramatic monologue, and similar work. Furthermore, no long narratives could be included; however, a considerable number of shorter narratives, from ballads to a complete tale by Chaucer, to "The Rape of the Lock" and "Rime of the Ancient Mariner," are included.

6. A principle of using no excerpts has been abandoned only to provide brief glimpses of some very large and important works too long for inclusion in their entirety.

7. A large emphasis, of necessity, has been placed upon the lyric—certainly one of the great accomplishments of poetry in English. The selection provides lyrics of many varying kinds and, in the loose classification of the "meditative lyric," emphasizes the great variety of themes and subjects, throughout our poetry, which have been used for the serious lyric. In addition, selection, in various periods, of work upon recurrent themes and juxtaposition reasonably close together of handlings of similar topics (for examples, the two poems by Ben Jonson and John Donne entitled "A Hymn to God the Father," and the several poems of religious doubt and enquiry of the recent periods) provide opportunities for comparative study where such is desired.

8. The poets of the twentieth century present a special problem. For this anthology I have chosen to represent, with sizable inclusion, only those poets who have without question established outstanding reputations—poets who have had long careers and published, certainly, a large proportion of their mature work. Of those represented, Mr. Frost, Mr. Stevens, and Mr. Eliot are still living, but their position as poets "to be known" by even the initiate to poetry will hardly be questioned.

Alan Swallow

Denver
June, 1952

TABLE OF CONTENTS

Page

THE PROLOGUE TO THE PARDONER'S TALE*

GEOFFREY CHAUCER

"Lordings," he said, "in churches when I preach
I try to have a high-resounding speech,
And ring it out as round as any bell;
I know by heart all of the things I tell;
My theme is always one, and ever was:
Radix malorum est Cupiditas.[1]
"The place that I have come from first I call,
And then my bulls I show them, one and all;
My letter, with our liege lord's signature,
I show them first, my body to secure, 10
That none may be so daring, priest or clerk,
As to disturb me in Christ's holy work.
And after that I say my say, and then
Show bulls from popes and cardinals again,
And patriarchs and bishops—not a few;
And then in Latin say a word or two
To give a flourish to my sermonizing,
And set the piety in men to rising.
I show my boxes, made of crystal stone,
Crammed full of bits of cloth and broken bone; 20
And all think these are relics. And I keep
A shoulder-bone in latten, from a sheep
In ancient times owned by a holy Jew.
'Good men, take heed,' I tell them, 'all of you;
For if this bone be washed in any well,
And cow, or calf, or sheep, or ox shall swell
Because a snake hath bitten it, or hath stung,
Take water from that well, and wash its tongue,
And it will soon be whole! And furthermore,
From pox or scab or any kind of sore 30

* This and the following selection are from *The Canterbury Tales* by Geoffrey Chaucer, done into Modern English Verse by Frank Ernest Hill. Copyright 1935 by Longmans, Green & Co., and used with their permission.

[1] Radix malorum est Cupiditas—*The love of money is the root of all evil,* I Timothy

Shall any sheep be healed that of this well
May drink a draught; take heed of what I tell.
And if the husbandman that owns the flock
Shall every week, ere crowing of the cock,
Fasting, drink from this well, I tell you, sirs,
As that same Jew did teach our ancestors,
He will increase in flocks and property.
And, sirs, it is a cure for jealousy;
For though a man fall into raging dotage
Of jealousy; if ye will make his pottage 40
With this same water, he will then mistrust
His wife no more, although he know her lust,
And she of priests had taken two or three.
"'Here is a mitten, too, that ye may see.
He that will put this mitten on his hand,
Shall have the grain grow thick upon his land
When he hath sown it, be it wheat or oats—
If he will pay his pennies here, and groats.
"'Good men and women, one fair word of warning:
If there be one within this church this morning 50
Hath done a sin so horrible to name
That he dare not be shriven of it, for shame,
Or a young woman, or an old and staid,
That of her husband hath a cuckold made,
Such people shall not have the power or grace
To pay me for my relics in this place.
And he that knows him free of all such blame,
May come and make his offering in God's name,
While I absolve him by the authority
Which has by bull been granted unto me.' 60
"By such tricks I have gathered, year by year,
A hundred marks since I was Pardoner.
There in my pulpit like a clerk I stand,
And see the lay folk sit on every hand,
And preach, as ye have heard, and tell a store
Of other yarns besides—a hundred more.
I take good pains to stretch my neck far out,
And east and west I thrust and nod about
As doth a dove upon a stable sitting.

So busily my hands and tongue go flitting 70
It is joy to see me work like this!
Of all such cursèd things as avarice
My preaching ever is, to make them free
In giving pence—especially to me!
For all my interest is in what I win,
And not in saving people from their sin.
When they are buried, why should I be worrying
Whether or not their souls have gone blackberrying?
For often preachments, if the truth be told,
Grow out of ill intentions men may hold. 80
Some, pleasing folk by wit and flattery,
Seek an advancement through hypocrisy;
Some spring from vanity, and some from hate.
For should I need thus to retaliate,
Then in my preaching I will lash a man
So he shall never—do the best he can—
Escape, if he have done some injury
To any of my brethren, or to me.
For though I never speak his proper name
Yet men shall recognize him just the same, 90
By many a hint or other sly allusion.
And thus I bring our foes to their confusion,
Thus I spit out my venom under hue
Of holiness, and seem devout and true.
"But briefly, my intention it is this:
I preach of nothing but of avarice;
Therefore my theme is this, and always was,
Radix malorum est Cupiditas.
Thus I can preach against the very vice
I have myself, and that is avarice. 100
And yet though I myself am guilty of it,
I can discourage other folk that love it
From avarice, and make them sore repent.
But that is not my principal intent.
I do no preaching but for that same vice;
Now this, as to that matter, should suffice.
"And then I tell them instances I know
From ancient stories many years ago,

For ignorant people love old stories well;
Such things they can remember and re-tell. 110
What? Do ye think while I am busy preaching,
And win good gold and silver from my teaching,
That I will gladly live in poverty?
Nay, nay, I never thought it, certainly.
For I will preach and beg in various lands,
And I will do no labor with my hands,
As, making baskets, that I need not go
In idleness a-begging, to and fro.
In no apostle's path I set my feet;
I will have money, wool, and cheese, and wheat, 120
Though from the poorest page I get my pillage,
Or from the poorest widow in a village,
Although her children from starvation pine,
Nay! I will drink good liquor of the vine,
And have a jolly wench in every town.
But lordings, if the end of this be shown,
Your liking is that I shall tell a tale.
And having drunk a draught of new-brewed ale,
I hope, by God, I have a thing to tell
That will, and that with reason, please you well. 130
For though a vicious man in much I do,
Yet I can tell a moral tale for you
Which I have preached, some profit thereby winning.
Now hold your peace, my tale is now beginning."

❡ THE PARDONER'S TALE

GEOFFREY CHAUCER

In Flanders once there dwelt a company
Of young folk, steeped in foolish revelry—
Who haunted brothels, feasts and games of chance;
And to the harp and lute they used to dance,
And they would cast at dice both day and night,
And also eat and drink beyond their might,
And in the devil's temple in this evil
Manner make sacrifices to the devil

By their abominable superfluity.
They swore so loudly and so damnably 10
It was a grisly thing to hear them swear.
They rent our blessèd Saviour's body there,
As if the Jews had not enough defiled
Those limbs, and at each other's sins they smiled.
And dancing girls would come, graceful and slender,
And after them, fruit-wenches, young and tender,
Singers with harps, bawds, and confectioners,
That are the very devil's officers
To kindle and fan the fire of lechery
That is so near allied to gluttony. 20
Let holy scripture witness that excess
And lust are born of wine and drunkenness.
  Lo, against nature did not drunken Lot
Lie with his daughters two, and knew it not?
He was too drunk to be responsible.
  And Herod, let him look it up who will,
When wine had made him sodden and unstable,
Gave his command, sitting at his own table,
That guiltless John the Baptist should be slain.
  Seneca says a word both wise and sane. 30
He says there is no difference he can find
Between a man that may have lost his mind
And one that's lost in drink, save that insanity,
Uniting with the evil in humanity,
Will persevere longer than drunkenness.
O gluttony, full of such vile excess,
The primal source of all our degradation,
The very origin of our damnation
Till Christ redeemed us with His blood again!
To put it in a word, how dearly then 40
This cursèd sin was paid for, when ye see
That all the world was lost through gluttony!
  Adam our father for that very vice
Was scourged to woe and toil from Paradise,
And Eve as well—there is no doubt, indeed;
For Adam, while he fasted, as I read,
Remained in Paradise; but instantly

When he had eaten of the forbidden tree,
He was cast out to pain and degradation.
Thou dost deserve our bitter accusation, 50
O gluttony! Ah, if a man could guess
The maladies that follow on excess
He would take care to be more moderate,
Sitting at table, in the things he ate.
Alas! The short throat and the tender mouth
They rule men East and West and North and South,
And make them slave in water, earth, and air
To get a glutton dainty drink and fare.
Of this, O Paul, the word thou sayst is good:
"Food unto belly, and belly unto food—" 60
As Paul has said, "God shall destroy them both!"
Alas, it is a foul thing, on mine oath,
More in the act, but foul when merely said,
When a man drinks so of the white and red
That of his throat, accursed with that excess,
He makes a privy in his wantoness.
The Apostle, weeping, cried out piteously:
"Many there go, described for you by me,
And now with piteous voice I say of these
That they of Christ's cross are the enemies, 70
And Belly is their god, their end is death."
O Belly, O thou bag of stinking breath,
Where dung and vile corruption do offend,
Foul is the sound of thee at either end!
What great expense for thee, what toilsome pain!
These cooks—see how they pound and grind and strain,
And thus turn "substance" into "accident,"
To make thy lecherous appetite content!
They crack the hard bones, taking out the marrow,
For they discard no thing that through the narrow 80
Mouth of the gullet soft and sweet can go;
With leaf and root and bark and spice they sow
The glutton's sauce, prepared for his delight,
To give him still a fresher appetite.
And yet the man whom such delight entices
Is dead while he is living in those vices.

Wine leads to lechery; drinking to excess
Promotes contentious ways and wretchedness.
O drunkard, all distorted is thy face,
Thy breath is sour, thou'rt loathsome to embrace; 90
And through thy drunken nose the sound comes playing
As "Samson, Samson!" thou wert always saying.
Yet Samson never tasted wine, God knows!
Like a stuck pig, thou tumblest on thy nose;
Thy tongue is lost, thy seemly ways forgot,
For drunkenness is the true burying plot
For man's discretion, wit, and moderation;
For he in whom drink has its domination
Can never, surely, hold a secret tight.
Then keep yourselves far from the red and white, 100
Especially from the white wine of Lepe
They have for sale in Fish Street or in Cheape.
This grape of Spain has such a subtle spirit
It creeps through others that are growing near it,
And from this mingling such strong fumes proceed
That when a man has had three drinks, indeed,
And thinks that he is still at home in Cheape,
He is in Spain, within the town of Lepe—
Not at Rochelle, in truth, nor at Bordeaux;
Then "Samson, Samson," will the fellow go. 110
But, lordings, listen to one word, I pray:
All of the sovereign acts, I dare to say,
Of victories in the Old Testament,
Through grace of God that is omnipotent
Were done in perfect abstinence and prayer.
Look in the Bible, ye shall find it there.
Look at the conqueror, Attila the great—
He died in sleep, meeting a shameful fate
Of nosebleed, caused by drinking to excess.
Let a great captain live in soberness. 120
And more than this, consider long and well
That was commanded unto Lemuel;
Not Samuel, but Lemuel, I say—
Read in the Bible, and find it plain as day—
That giving wine to judges was a vice.

But now no more, for this will well suffice.
  And now that I have preached of gluttony,
I will forbid you gambling equally.
Gambling is mother of deceitful scheming,
Cursèd forswearing, lies, and Christ's blaspheming, 130
And homicide. There comes great waste through it
Of gold and time. It is the opposite
Of honor—nay, it's shame and degradation,
To have a common gamester's reputation.
The higher that a man is in degree,
The more abandoned is he held to be,
For if a prince will play at games of chance,
In public policy and temperance
He will be held, by general opinion,
The less deserving of his high dominion. 140
  Stilbon, the wise ambassador, was sent
With great pomp by the Spartan government
To Corinth, an alliance there to bind.
When he arrived, he came by chance to find
All of the greatest men within that land
Playing at hazard there on every hand.
And for that cause, as soon as it could be,
He stole home to his country quietly,
And said: "I will not thus lose my good name,
Nor will I dare so greatly to defame 150
Your honor as with gamblers to ally you.
Send other envoys who may satisfy you;
For by my troth I would prefer to die
Than see you take such gamesters for ally.
Your honor stands so glorious and so fine,
Ye shall not thus be bound by will of mine,
Nor any treaty in which I concur."
Thus spoke to them this wise philosopher.
  See also how to King Demetrius,
The king of Parthians, as is writ for us, 160
Dispatched in scorn a pair of golden dice;
For gambling heretofore had been his vice,
For which the Parthians held his reputation
And glory at but little valuation.

Lords can discover other kinds of play
Honest enough to drive the time away.
  Now of false oaths and great I speak to you,
As old books deal with such, a word or two.
Great swearing is a plain abomination,
And to swear false more worthy reprobation. 170
High God forbade all swearing, as ye see
In Matthew, and still more particularly
The holy Jeremy speaks thus of swearing:
"Swear true oaths only, false oaths never daring,
And swear with judgment and in righteousness."
But idle swearing is a vile excess.
See in the table unto man first handed
Of all the noble things high God commanded,
How in the second rule He wrote this plain:
"Take ye my name not idly or in vain." 180
Lo, swearing thus is earlier denied
Than many a cursèd thing like homicide.
I say that, as to order, it stands so.
They understand, who God's commandments know,
The second one commands us as I say.
Further, I tell thee in the plainest way
That vengeance shall not leave his house that dares
To make his oaths outrageous when he swears.
"By God's own precious heart, and by his nails,
And by the blood of Christ, that is in Hales, 190
My chance is seven and thine is five and three;
By God's arms, if thou play it false with me
This dagger shall go through thy heart at once";
This is the fruit grown from the bitchèd bones:
False swearing, anger, falseness, homicide.
Now for the love of Christ that for us died,
Leave off your oaths, I pray, both great and small;
But, sirs, I tell my tale—let this be all.

Now these three rioters of whom I tell,
Long yet ere prime was rung by any bell, 200
Were seated in a tavern at their drinking.
And as they sat, they heard a death-bell clinking

Before a body going to its grave.
Then roused the one and shouted to his knave—
"Be off at once!" he cried. "Run out and spy
Whose body it may be that passeth by;
And look thou get his name aright," he cried.
"No need, sir—none at all," this boy replied.
"They told me that before ye came, two hours;
He was, God's name, an old fellow of yours. 210
By night, it seems, and sudden was his dying;
Flat on his bench, all drunken, was he lying,
When up there crept a thief that men call Death
(Who in this country all the people slay'th)
And smote his heart asunder with his spear
And all in silence went his way from here.
During the plague he hath a thousand slain,
And, master, ere ye meet him this is plain:
That it is wise and very necessary
To be prepared for such an adversary, 220
Have readiness to meet him evermore;
So taught my mother—now I say no more."
"Yea, by Saint Mary," said the taverner,
"The boy speaks true, for he hath slain this year
Woman and child and man in yonder town,
And page and villain he hath smitten down.
I hold his habitation must be there.
Great wisdom were it that a man beware—
Lest he some fearful injury incur."
"Yea, by God's arms," replied this rioter, 230
"Is he so perilous a knave to meet?
Now will I seek him both by way and street,
Upon the bones of God I make a vow!
Fellows, we three are one—then hear me now:
Let each of us hold up his hand to th' other,
And each of us become the other's brother;
And we will slay this faithless traitor Death—
He shall be slain, he that so many slay'th,
Yea, by God's dignity, ere it be night!"
And so all three together made their plight 240
To live and die each one of them for other,

As though he had been born the other's brother.
And in this drunken passion forth they started,
And toward that very village they departed
Of which the tavern-keeper spoke before.
And then full many a grisly oath they swore,
And rent the Saviour's body limb from limb—
Death should be dead if they discovered him!
When they had travelled hardly half a mile,
Just as they would have stepped across a stile, 250
They chanced to meet a poor and agèd man.
This old man meekly spoke, and thus began
To greet them: "May God look upon you, sirs!"
The greatest braggart of these rioters
Replied: "Now curse thee, churl! What, where apace?
Why all wrapped up and hidden save thy face?
How darest thou live so long in Death's defy?"
Straightway this old man looked him in the eye
And answered thus: "Because I cannot meet
A man, by country way or city street, 260
Though unto Ind I made a pilgrimage,
Willing to give his youth and take my age!
So must I have my age in keeping still,
As long a time, indeed, as God shall will.
"Nor Death himself will have my life, alas!
So like a wretch from place to place I pass,
And on the ground, which is my mother's gate,
Knock with my staff and cry both early and late,
'Mother, belovèd mother, let me in!
See how I wither, flesh and blood and skin; 270
Alas, my bones! When shall they be at rest?
Mother, how gladly would I change my chest
That in my room so long a time hath been—
Yea, for a hair-cloth I could wrap me in!'
But yet she will not do me this poor grace:
Wherefore all pale and withered is my face.
"But, sirs, ye lack in common courtesy
That to an agèd man speak villainy
When he hath sinned neither in word nor deed.
For well in holy writings may ye read, 280

'Before an agèd man, whose hair is gray,
Ye should arise'; and therefore thus I say:
To an old man no hurt or evil do,
No more than ye would have men do to you
In your old age, if ye so long abide.
And God be with you, where ye walk or ride—
I must be gone where I have need to go."
"Nay now, old rogue! By God, thou shalt not so!"
Answered another rioter anon;
"Thou partest not so lightly, by Saint John! 290
Thou spake right now of that same traitor Death
That in this country all our comrades slay'th;
Have here my word: thou art a spy of his!
Then take the worst, or tell us where he is,
By God and by the Holy Sacrament!
For truly, thou art of his covenant,
To slay young folk like us, thou false intriguer!"
"Now, sirs," he answered, "since ye be so eager
To find this Death, turn up that crooked way;
There in yon wood I left him, sooth to say, 300
Under a tree, and there he will abide.
Not for your boasting will he run and hide.
See ye that oak tree? Ye shall find him there.
God, that redeemed mankind, save you and spare,
And better you!" Thus spoke this agèd man;
And toward the tree these drunken rascals ran
All three, and there, about its roots, they found
Of golden florins, minted fine and round,
Well nigh eight bushels lying, as they thought.
No longer then the traitor Death they sought, 310
But each was made so happy by the sight
Of all those florins shining fair and bright
That down they sat beside the precious hoard.
The worst of them was first to speak his word.
"Brothers," he said, "take heed of what I say;
My wit is great, although I jest and play!
Fortune hath found it fit to give this treasure
That we may live our lives in lust and pleasure;
Lightly it comes—so shall it melt away!

God's dignity! Who would have dreamed today 320
That we should have so fine and fair a grace?
But could the gold be carried from this place
Home to my house, or else to one of yours—
For well we know that all this gold is ours—
Then were we in a high felicity!
But such a thing by day could never be;
Men would proclaim us thieves and cause our seizure;
Might even make us hang for our own treasure!
This gold must then be carried hence by night
With secrecy and cautious oversight. 330
Wherefore I say, draw lot among us all,
And let us mark the way the lot shall fall;
And he that draws it shall with willing heart
And nimble pace toward the town depart,
And fetch in secret wine and bread, and we
That stay behind shall guard full carefully
This gold; and if our comrade does not tarry,
When it is night we will this treasure carry
Wherever by agreement shall be planned."
The one held out the lots within his hand, 340
And bade them draw, and look where it would fall;
And it fell on the youngest of them all,
And so by compact toward the town he started.
And scarce a moment after he departed
The one of them spoke slyly to the other:
"Thou know'st well thou art sworn to be my brother;
Now something to thy profit will I say.
Thou see'st our fellow takes himself away;
And here is gold, and that great quantity,
That shall be portioned out among us three. 350
Nevertheless, if I could shape it so
That we should share it all between us two,
Had I not done a comrade's turn by thee?"
The other said: "But that could never be!
He knows we two are here and guard the gold;
What could we do? What wouldst thou have him told?"
"Shall what I say be secret?" asked the first;
"Then shortly shall the method be rehearsed

Whereby I think to bring it well about."
"Agreed," replied the other, "out of doubt 360
I will betray thee not, as God is true."
"Now," said the first, "thou know'st that we are two,
And two of us are stronger than is one.
Watch when he sits, then go as if in fun—
As thou wouldst play about with him, and grip him,
And with my dagger through his sides I'll rip him,
While thou art struggling with him, as in play;
And see thou use thy knife the self-same way.
Then all this treasure shall belong to none,
My dearest friend, but me and thee alone! 370
Then may we sate our lusts until we tire
And play at dice whenever we desire!"
And thus these rascals have devised a way
To slay the third, as ye have heard me say.
This youngest, he that journeyed to the town,
Within his heart rolled often up and down
The beauty of these florins new and bright.
"O Lord!" quoth he, "if it were so I might
Have all this treasure to myself alone,
There liveth no man underneath the throne 380
Of God, that might exist more merrily
Than I!" And so the fiend, our enemy,
Put in his head that he should poison buy
Wherewith to make his two companions die;
Because the fiend found him in such a state
That he had leave his fall to consummate,
For it was out of doubt his full intent
To slay them both, and never to repent!
So forth he goes—no longer will he tarry—
Unto the town, to an apothecary, 390
And prays for poison to exterminate
Some rats, and pole-cats that had robbed of late
His roosts—and he would wreak him, if he might,
On vermin that tormented him by night.
Then this apothecary, answering:
"God save my soul, but thou shalt have a thing
That, let a living creature drink or eat

No bigger portion than a grain of wheat,
And he shall die, and that in shorter while,
By God, than thou wouldst take to walk a mile— 400
This poison is so strong and violent."
  All on his cursèd wickedness intent,
This rascal ran as fast as he could fly,
Bearing the poison, to a street near by,
And got three bottles of a man he knew;
And then he poured his poison in the two,
But in the third, his own, put none at all.
For all the night he thought to heave and haul
Carrying gold—then would he slake his thirst.
And so this rascal (may he be accurst!) 410
Filled all his bottles full of wine; and then
Back to his fellows he repaired again.
  What need is there to sermon of it more?
For just as they had planned his death before,
They slew him now, and quickly. Then the one
Spoke to the other after it was done:
"Now let us eat and drink and make us merry,
And afterwards we will his body bury."
And so by chance he drank, that very minute,
Out of a bottle with the poison in it, 420
And gave his comrade drink when he was through.
From which in little while they died, the two.
  But truly Avicenna, I suppose,
Wrote never in his canons of such throes
And wondrous agonies of poisoning
As these two wretches had in perishing.
Thus died these murderers of whom I tell,
And he who falsely poisoned them as well.

O cursèd sin, too evil to express!
O treacherous homicide! O wickedness! 430
O gluttony, O lechery and gaming!
O thou blasphemer, Christ forever shaming
With insult, with habitual oaths and proud!
Alas, mankind! How can it be allowed
That to thy Maker, that of clay did knead thee,

And with His own dear precious heart's blood freed thee,
Thou art so false, and so unnatural!
  Good men, may God forgive you, one and all,
And guard you from the sin of avarice!
My holy pardon cures you all of this, 440
If sterling coin make up your offerings,
Or nobles, silver brooches, spoons, or rings.
Come, bow your head beneath this holy bull!
Come up, ye wives, and give your yarn or wool;
See, here I enter your name upon my roll;
Right to the bliss of heaven ascends your soul!
I will assoil you by my sovereign power
As clear and clean as at the very hour
When ye were born (this is the way I preach);
And Jesus Christ, that is our soul's true leech, 450
Graciously grant you pardon and receive you,
For that is best, sirs; I will not deceive you.
  But I forgot one word, sirs, it is clear;
I have indulgences and relics here
As fair as any man's on English land,
And these were given me by the Pope's own hand.
If any of you would come up piously,
Make offering, and be absolved by me,
Come up at once, and kneel, and meekly take
The pardon that I give you for Christ's sake; 460
Or, if ye like, receive it as ye ride,
At every town's end, newly sanctified,
If every time ye offer me anew
Nobles and pence, each ringing fair and true.
It is an honor to you, it is clear,
That, riding in the lonely country here,
Where accidents are likely to occur,
Ye can be served by such a pardoner!
For ye might tumble, one or more of you,
Off of your horses, and break your necks in two. 470
How fortunate, what great security
For all that I have joined your company,
Who can absolve you, be ye low or high,

What time the soul shall from the body fly.
And I advise our Host here shall begin,
For he is most of all enmeshed in sin.
Come up, Sir Host, and make thine offering,
And thou shalt kiss the relics—everything—
Yea, for a groat! Come up, unlock thy purse!"
"No," he replied; "first may I have Christ's curse! 480
Not I, as I may thrive in health or riches!
For thou wouldst make me kiss thy mouldy breeches
Swearing the rag upon some saint had hung,
Though it were all discolored with thy dung!
But by the cross, Saint Helen's sanctuary,
I would I had thy testicles to carry
Instead of relic or of halidom!
Let's cut them off! I'll help thee keep them—come!
We will enshrine them—yea, in a pig's turd!"
This Pardoner he answered never a word; 490
He was so angry, no word could he say.
"Now," said our Host, "I will no longer play
With thee, or any other angry man."
But all at once the worthy Knight began—
Seeing the people laugh on every side—
"No more of this! It is enough!" he cried.
"Sir Pardoner, be glad—cheer up," said he;
"And ye, Sir Host, that are so dear to me,
I pray you, cease, and kiss the Pardoner.
And Pardoner, come here, I pray you, sir, 500
And let us, as before, all laugh and play."
And soon they kissed, and rode upon their way.

LORD RANDAL

ANONYMOUS

"O where hae ye been, Lord Randal, my son?
O where hae ye been, my handsome young man?"
"I hae been to the wild wood; mother, make my bed soon,
For I'm weary wi hunting, and fain wald lie down."

"Where gat ye your dinner, Lord Randal, my son?
Where gat ye your dinner, my handsome young man?"
"I dined wi my true love; mother, make my bed soon,
For I'm weary wi hunting, and fain wald lie down."

"What gat ye to your dinner, Lord Randal, my son?
What gat ye to your dinner, my handsome young man?"
"I gat eels boiled in broo; mother, make my bed soon,
For I'm weary wi hunting, and fain wald lie down."

"What became of your bloodhounds, Lord Randal, my son?
What became of your bloodhounds, my handsome young man?"
"O they swelld and they died; mother, make my bed soon,
For I'm weary wi hunting, and fain wald lie down."

"O I fear ye are poisond, Lord Randal, my son!
O I fear ye are poisond, my handsome young man!"
"O yes! I am poisond; mother, make my bed soon,
For I'm sick at the heart, and I fain wald lie down."

⁋ BONNY BARBARA ALLAN

ANONYMOUS

It was in and about the Martinmas time,
When the green leaves were a falling,
That Sir John Graeme, in the West Country,
Fell in love with Barbara Allan.

He sent his man down through the town,
To the place where she was dwelling:
"O haste and come to my master dear,
Gin[1] ye be Barbara Allan."

O hooly, hooly rose she up,
To the place where he was lying,
And when she drew the curtain by,
"Young man, I think you're dying."

[1] gin—*if*

"O it's I'm sick, and very, very sick,
  And 'tis a' for Barbara Allan;"
"O the better for me ye's never be,
  Tho your heart's blood were a spilling."

"O dinna ye mind, young man," said she,
  "When ye was in the tavern a drinking,
That ye made the healths gae round and round,
  And slighted Barbara Allan?"

He turned his face unto the wall,
  And death was with him dealing:
"Adieu, adieu, my dear friends all,
  And be kind to Barbara Allan."

And slowly, slowly raise she up,
  And slowly, slowly left him,
And sighing said, she could not stay,
  Since death of life had reft him.

She had not gane a mile but twa,
  When she heard the dead-bell ringing,
And every jow that the dead-bell geid,
  It cry'd, Woe to Barbara Allan!

"O Mother, mother, make my bed!
  O make it saft and narrow!
Since my love died for me to-day,
  I'll die for him to-morrow."

SIR PATRICK SPENS

ANONYMOUS

The king sits in Dumferling toune,
  Drinking the blude-reid wine:
O quhar will I get guid sailor,
  To sail this schip of mine?

Up and spak an eldern knicht,
  Sat at the king's richt knee:
Sir Patrick Spens is the best sailor,
  That sails upon the sea.

The king has written a braid letter,
  And signed it wi' his hand; 10
And sent it to Sir Patrick Spens,
  Was walking on the sand.

The first line that Sir Patrick red,
  A loud lauch lauchèd he:
The next line that Sir Patrick red,
  The teir blinded his ee.

O quhar is this has don this deid,
  This ill deid don to me;
To send me out this time o' the yeir,
  To sail upon the sea? 20

Mak haste, mak haste, my mirry men all,
  Our good schip sails the morn.
O say na sae, my master deir,
  For I feir a deadlie storme.

Late late yestreen I saw the new moone
  Wi' the auld moone in hir arme;
And I feir, I feir, my deir master,
  That we will come to harme.

O our Scots nobles wer richt laith
  To weet their cork-heild schoone; 30
But lang owre a' the play were played,
  Their hats they swam aboone.

O lang, lang may the ladies stand
  Wi' their fans into their hand,
Or e'er they see Sir Patrick Spens
  Come sailing to the land.

O lang, lang, may the ladies stand
Wi' their gold kems in their hair,
Waiting for their ain deir lords,
For they'll see them na mair. 40

Have owre, have owre to Aberdour,
It's fifty fadom deip:
And thair lies guid Sir Patrick Spens,
Wi' the Scots lords at his feit.

THE WIFE OF USHER'S WELL

ANONYMOUS

There lived a wife at Usher's Well,
And a wealthy wife was she;
She had three stout and stalwart sons,
And sent them o'er the sea.

They hadna been a week from her,
A week but barely ane,
Whan word came to the carline wife[1]
That her three sons were gane.

They hadna been a week from her,
A week but barely three, 10
When word came to the carlin wife
That her sons she'd never see.

"I wish the wind may never cease,
Nor fashes[2] in the flood,
Till my three sons come hame to me,
In earthly flesh and blood."

It fell about the Martinmas,
When nights are lang and mirk,

[1] carline wife—*old woman* [2] fashes—*troubles*

The carlin wife's three sons came hame,
  And their hats were o' the birk.[3] 20

It neither grew in syke nor ditch,
  Nor yet in ony sheugh;[4]
But at the gates o' Paradise,
  That birk grew fair eneugh.

"Blow up the fire, my maidens,
  Bring water from the well;
For a' my house shall feast this night,
  Since my three sons are well."

And she has made to them a bed,
  She's made it large and wide, 30
And she's taen her mantle her about,
  Sat down at the bed-side.

Up then crew the red, red cock,
  And up and crew the gray;
The eldest to the youngest said,
  "'T is time we were away."

The cock he hadna crawd but once,
  And clapp'd his wings at a',
When the youngest to the eldest said,
  "Brother, we must awa." 40

"The cock doth craw, the day doth daw,
  The channerin worm doth chide;
Gin[5] we be mist out o' our place,
  A sair pain we maun bide.

"Fare ye weel, my mother dear!
  Fareweel to barn and byre!
And fare ye weel, the bonny lass
  That kindles my mother's fire!"

[3] birk—*birch* [4] sheugh—*furrow* [5] gin—*if*

⁅ "MAKE WE MERRY BOTH MORE AND LESS"

ANONYMOUS

Make we merry both more and less,
For now is the time of Christymas.

Let no man come into this hall,
Groom, page, nor yet marshall,
But that some sport he bring withal.
  For now is the time of Christmas.

If that he say, he can not sing,
Some other sport then let him bring.
That it may please at this feasting.
  For now is the time of Christmas.

If he say he can naught do,
Then for my love ask him no mo.
But to the stocks then let him go.
  For now is the time of Christmas.

⁅ "ALL THIS TIME THIS SONG IS BEST"

ANONYMOUS

All this time this song is best,
Verbum caro factum est.[1]

This night there is a child born
That sprang out of Jesse's thorn,
We must sing and say thereforn
  Verbum caro factum est.

Jesus is the child's name,
And Mary mild is his dame,
All our sorrow shall turn to game,
  Verbum caro factum est.

[1] Verbum caro factum est—*The Word was made flesh,* St. John

It fell upon high midnight,
The stars shone both fair and bright,
The angels sang with all their might
  Verbum caro factum est.

Now kneel we down on our knee
And pray we to the Trinity,
Our help, our succour for to be.
  Verbum caro factum est.

WHO SO LIST TO HUNT

SIR THOMAS WYATT

Who so list[1] to hunt, I know where is an hind;
But as for me, alas, I may no more.
The vain travail hath wearied me so sore,
I am of them that farthest come behind.
Yet may I by no means my wearied mind
Draw from the Deer; but as she fleeth afore
Fainting I follow. I leave off, therefore,
Since in a net I seek to hold the wind.
Who list her hunt, I put him out of doubt,
As well as I may spend his time in vain.
And graven with diamonds in letters plain
There is written, her fair neck round about,
Noli me tangere[2] for Caesar's I am
And wild for to hold, though I seem tame.

THEY FLEE FROM ME

SIR THOMAS WYATT

They flee from me, that sometime did me seek
With naked foot, stalking in my chamber.
I have seen them gentle, tame, and meek
That now are wild, and do not remember

[1] list—*desires*   [2] noli me tangere—*Do not touch me*

That sometime they put themselves in danger
To take bread at my hand; and now they range
Busily seeking with a continual change.

Thanked be fortune it hath been otherwise
Twenty times better; but once, in special,
In thin array, after a pleasant guise,
When her loose gown from her shoulders did fall,
And she me caught in her arms long and small,
Therewith all sweetly did me kiss
And softly said, "Dear heart, how like you this?"

It was no dream: I lay broad waking.
But all is turned, through my gentleness,
Into a strange fashion of forsaking;
And I have leave to go of her goodness,
And she also to use newfangleness.
But since that I so kindly am served,
I would fain know what she hath deserved.

BLAME NOT MY LUTE

SIR THOMAS WYATT

Blame not my lute! for he must sound
  Of these and that as liketh me;
  For lack of wit the lute is bound
  To give such tunes as pleaseth me.
  Though my songs be somewhat strange,
  And speaks such words as touch thy change,
    Blame not my lute!

My lute, alas, doth not offend,
  Though that perforce he must agree
  To sound such tunes as I intend — 10
  To sing to them that heareth me;
  Then though my songs be somewhat plain,
  And toucheth some that use to feign,
    Blame not my lute!

My lute and strings may not deny,
But as I strike they must obey;
Break not them then so wrongfully,
But wreak thyself some wiser way;
And though the songs which I indite
Do quit thy change with rightful spite, 20
Blame not my lute!

Spite asketh spite, and changing change,
And falsèd faith must needs be known;
The fault so great, the case so strange,
Of right it must abroad be blown;
Then since that by thine own desert
My songs do tell how true thou art,
Blame not my lute!

Blame but thyself that hast misdone
And well deservèd to have blame; 30
Change thou thy way, so evil begone,
And then my lute shall sound that same;
But if till then my fingers play
By thy desert their wonted way,
Blame not my lute!

Farewell, unknown! for though thou break
My strings in spite with great disdain,
Yet have I found out, for thy sake,
Strings for to string my lute again.
And if, perchance, this silly rhyme 40
Do make thee blush at any time,
Blame not my lute!

❡ WITH SERVING STILL

SIR THOMAS WYATT

With serving still
This have I won,

For my goodwill
To be undone.

And for redress
Of all my pain,
Disdainfulness
I have again.

And for reward
Of all my smart,
Lo, thus unheard
I must depart!

Wherefore all ye
That after shall
By fortune be
As I am, thrall,

Example take,
What I have won,
Thus for her sake
To be undone!

I LOATHE THAT I DID LOVE

THOMAS, LORD VAUX

I loathe that I did love,
In youth that I thought sweet;
As time requires, for my behove,
Methinks they are not meet.

My lusts they do me leave,
My fancies all be fled,
And tract of time begins to weave
Grey hairs upon my head.

For age with stealing steps
Hath clawed me with his crutch, 10

And lusty life away she leaps,
 As there had been none such.

My Muse doth not delight
 Me as she did before;
My hand and pen are not in plight,
 As they have been of yore.

For reason me denies
 This youthly idle rhyme;
And day by day to me she cries,
 "Leave off these toys in time." 20

The wrinkles in my brow,
 The furrows in my face,
Say, limping age will lodge him now
 Where youth must give him place.

The harbinger of death,
 To me I see him ride;
The cough, the cold, the gasping breath
 Doth bid me to provide

A pickaxe and a spade,
 And eke a shrouding sheet, 30
A house of clay for to be made
 For such a guest most meet.

Methinks I hear the clerk
 That knolls the careful knell,
And bids me leave my woeful work,
 Ere nature me compel.

My keepers knit the knot
 That youth did laugh to scorn,
Of me that clean shall be forgot,
 As I had not been born. 40

Thus must I youth give up,
  Whose badge I long did wear;
To them I yield the wanton cup,
  That better may it bear.

Lo, here the bared skull,
  By whose bald sign I know
That stooping age away shall pull
  That youthful years did sow.

For beauty with her band
  These crooked cares hath wrought, 50
And shipped me into the land
  From whence I first was brought.

And ye that bide behind,
  Have ye none other trust;
As ye of clay were cast by kind,[1]
  So shall ye waste to dust.

⸿ TO HIS LADY

HENRY HOWARD, EARL OF SURREY

Set me whereas the sun doth parch the green,
  Or where his beams may not dissolve the ice,
In temperate heat, where he is felt and seen,
  With proud people, in presence sad and wise;
Set me in base, or yet in high degree,
  In the long night, or in the shortest day,
In clear weather, or where mists thickest be,
  In lofty youth, or when my hairs be gray;
Set me in earth, in heaven, or yet in hell,
  In hill, in dale, or in the foaming flood,
Thrall, or at large, alive whereso I dwell,

[1] kind—*nature*

Sick, or in health, in ill fame, or in good;
  Yours will I be, and with that only thought
  Comfort myself when that my hap is nought.

❡ THE SEAFARER

HENRY HOWARD, EARL OF SURREY

O happy dames, that may embrace
  The fruit of your delight,
Help to bewail the woeful case
  And eke the heavy plight
Of me, that wonted to rejoice
The fortune of my pleasant choice;
Good ladies, help to fill my mourning voice.

In ship, freight with rememberance
  Of thoughts and pleasures past,
He sails that hath in governance 10
  My life while it will last;
With scalding sighs, for lack of gale,
Furthering his hope, that is his sail,
Toward me, the sweet port of his avail.

Alas! how oft in dreams I see
  Those eyes that were my food;
Which sometime so delighted me,
  That yet they do me good;
Wherewith I wake with his return,
Whose absent flame did make me burn: 20
But when I find the lack, Lord, how I mourn!

When other lovers in arms across
  Rejoice their chief delight,
Drowned in tears, to mourn my loss
  I stand the bitter night
In my window, where I may see
Before the winds how the clouds flee.
Lo! what a mariner love hath made me!

And in green waves when the salt flood
Doth rise by rage of wind, 30
A thousand fancies in that mood
Assail my restless mind.
Alas! now drencheth my sweet foe,
That with the spoil of my heart did go,
And left me; but, alas! why did he so?

And when the seas wax calm again
To chase fro me annoy,
My doubtful hope doth cause me plain;
So dread cuts off my joy.
Thus is my wealth mingled with woe, 40
And of each thought a doubt doth grow;
"Now he comes! Will he come? Alas, no, no!"

WESTERN WIND, WHEN WILL THOU BLOW

ANONYMOUS

Western wind, when will thou blow,
The small rain down can rain?
Christ, if my love were in my arms
And I in my bed again!

BACK AND SIDE GO BARE, GO BARE

ANONYMOUS

Back and side go bare, go bare,
Both hand and foot go cold,
But belly, God send thee good ale enough
Whether it be new or old!

But if that I may have truly
Good ale my belly full,
I shall look like one, by sweet Saint John,
Were shorn against the wool.

Though I go bare, take you no care,
I am nothing a-cold, 10
I stuff my skin so full within
Of jolly good ale and old.

I cannot eat but little meat,
My stomach is not good;
But sure I think that I could drink
With him that weareth an hood.
Drink is my life; although my wife
Some time do chide and scold,
Yet spare I not to ply the pot
Of jolly good ale and old. 20

I love no roast but a brown toast,
Or a crab in the fire;
A little bread shall do me stead;
Much bread I never desire.
Nor frost, nor snow, nor wind I trow,
Can hurt me if it would,
I am so wrapped within and lapped
With jolly good ale and old.

I care right nought, I take no thought
For clothes to keep me warm; 30
Have I good drink, I surely think
Nothing can do me harm:
For truly than I fear no man,
Be he never so bold,
When I am armed and throughly warmed
With jolly good ale and cold.

But now and then I curse and ban,
They make their ale so small;
God give them care and evil to fare!
They stry[1] the malt and all. 40
Such peevish pew,[2] I tell you true,
Not for a crown of gold,

[1] stry—*destroy* [2] peevish pew—*thin stuff*

There cometh one sip within my lip,
  Whether it be new or old.

Good ale and strong maketh me among[3]
  Full jocund and full light,
That oft I sleep and take no keep
  From morning until night.
Then start I up and flee to the cup;
  The right way on I hold; 50
My thirst to staunch, I fill my paunch
  With jolly good ale and old.

And Kit my wife, that as her life
  Loveth well good ale to seek,
Full oft drinketh she, that ye may see
  The tears run down her cheek.
Then doth she troll to me the bowl,
  As a good malt-worm should,
And say "Sweet-heart, I have take my part
  Of jolly good ale and old." 60

They that do drink till they nod and wink,
  Even as good fellows should do,
They shall not miss to have the bliss,
  That good ale hath brought them to.
And all poor souls that scour black bowls,
  And them hath lustily trolled,
God save the lives of them and their wives,
  Whether they be young or old!

SWEET LOVE, IF THOU WILT GAIN A MONARCH'S GLORY

ANONYMOUS

Sweet Love, if thou wilt gain a monarch's glory,
Subdue her heart who makes me glad and sorry;

[3] among—*at times*

Out of thy golden quiver,
Take thou thy strongest arrow
That will through bone and marrow,
And me and thee of grief and fear deliver:
But come behind, for, if she look upon thee,
Alas, poor Love, then thou art woe-begone thee.

MY GIRL, THOU GAZEST MUCH

GEORGE TURBERVILLE

My girl, thou gazest much
Upon the golden skies:
Would I were heaven! I would behold
Thee then with all mine eyes.

THE MERRY CUCKOO, MESSENGER OF SPRING

EDMUND SPENSER

The merry Cuckoo, messenger of spring,
His trumpet shrill hath thrice already sounded;
That warns all lovers wait upon their king,
Who now is coming forth with garland crowned:
With noise whereof the quire of birds resounded
Their anthems sweet devised of love's praise,
That all the woods their echoes back rebounded,
As if they knew the meaning of their lays.
But 'mongst them all, which did love's honour raise,
No word was heard of her that most it ought,
But she his precept proudly disobeys,
And doth his idle message set at nought.
Therefore O love, unless she turn to thee
Ere cuckoo end, let her a rebel be.

OFT WHEN MY SPIRIT DOTH SPREAD HER BOLDER WINGS

EDMUND SPENSER

Oft when my spirit doth spread her bolder wings,
In mind to mount up to the purest sky,
It down is weighed with thought of earthly things
And clogged with burden of mortality,
Where when that sovereign beauty it doth spy,
Resembling heaven's glory in her light,
Drawn with sweet pleasure's bait, it back doth fly,
And unto heaven forgets her former flight.
There my frail fancy, fed with full delight,
Doth bathe in bliss and mantleth most at ease:
Me thinks of other heaven, but how it might
Her heart's desire with most contentment please.
Heart need not with none other happiness,
But here on earth to have such heaven's bliss.

LIKE AS A HUNTSMAN

EDMUND SPENSER

Like as a huntsman after weary chase,
Seeing the game from him escape away,
Sits down to rest him in some shady place,
With panting hounds beguilèd of their prey;
So after long pursuit and vain assay,
When I all weary had the chase forsook,
The gentle deer return'd the self-same way,
Thinking to quench her thirst at the next brook;
There she beholding me with milder look,
Sought not to fly, but fearless still did bide,
Till I in hand her yet half trembling took,
And with her own goodwill her firmly tied.
Strange thing, me seem'd, to see a beast so wild
So goodly won, with her own will beguil'd.

PROTHALAMION

EDMUND SPENSER

Calm was the day, and through the trembling air
Sweet-breathing Zephyrus did softly play
A gentle spirit, that lightly did delay
Hot Titan's beams, which then did glister fair;
When I, (whom sullen care,
Through discontent of my long fruitless stay
In princes' court, and expectation vain
Of idle hopes, which still do fly away
Like empty shadows, did afflict my brain,)
Walked forth to ease my pain 10
Along the shore of silver-streaming Thames;
Whose rutty bank, the which his river hems,
Was painted all with variable flowers,
And all the meads adorned with dainty gems
Fit to deck maidens' bowers,
And crown their paramours
Against the bridal day, which is not long:
Sweet Thames! run softly, till I end my song.

There in a meadow by the river's side
A flock of nymphs I chancèd to espy, 20
All lovely daughters of the flood thereby,
With goodly greenish locks all loose untied
As each had been a bride;
And each one had a little wicker basket
Made of fine twigs entrailèd curiously,
In which they gathered flowers to fill their flasket,
And with fine fingers cropped full feateously
The tender stalks on high.
Of every sort which in that meadow grew
They gathered some; the violet, pallid blue, 30
The little daisy that at evening closes,
The virgin lily and the primrose true,
With store of vermeil roses,
To deck their bridegrooms' posies

Against the bridal day, which was not long:
  Sweet Thames! run softly, till I end my song.

With that I saw two swans of goodly hue
Come softly swimming down along the Lee;
Two fairer birds I yet did never see;
The snow which doth the top of Pindus strew 40
Did never whiter shew
Nor Jove himself, when he a swan would be
For love of Leda, whiter did appear;
Yet Leda was, they say, as white as he,
Yet not so white as these, nor nothing near;
So purely white they were
That even the gentle stream, the which them bare,
Seemed foul to them, and bade his billows spare
To wet their silken feathers, lest they might
Soil their fair plumes with water not so fair, 50
And mar their beauties bright,
That shone as Heaven's light,
Against their bridal day, which was not long:
  Sweet Thames! run softly, till I end my song.

Eftsoons the nymphs, which now had flowers their fill,
Ran all in haste to see that silver brood
As they came floating on the crystal flood;
Whom when they saw, they stood amazèd still
Their wondering eyes to fill;
Them seemed they never saw a sight so fair 60
Of fowls, so lovely, that they sure did deem
Them heavenly born, or to be that same pair
Which through the sky draw Venus' silver team;
For sure they did not seem
To be begot of any earthly seed,
But rather angels, or of angels' breed;
Yet were they bred of Somers-heat,[1] they say.
In sweetest season, when each flower and weed
The earth did fresh array;

[1] Somers-heat—*a pun on Somerset, their name*

So fresh they seemed as day, 70
Ev'n as their bridal day, which was not long:
  Sweet Thames! run softly, till I end my song.

Then forth they all out of their baskets drew
Great store of flowers, the honour of the field,
That to the sense did fragrant odours yield,
All which upon those goodly birds they threw
And all the waves did strew,
That like old Peneus' waters they did seem
When down along by pleasant Tempe's shore,
Scattered with flowers, through Thessaly they stream, 80
That they appear, through lilies' plenteous store,
Like a bride's chamber-floor.
Two of those nymphs meanwhile two garlands bound
Of freshest flowers which in that mead they found,
The which presenting all in trim array,
Their snowy foreheads therewithal they crowned,
Whilst one did sing this lay
Prepared against that day,
Against their bridal day, which was not long:
  Sweet Thames! run softly, till I end my song. 90

"Ye gentle birds! the world's fair ornament,
And heaven's glory, whom this happy hour
Doth lead unto your lovers' blissful bower,
Joy may you have, and gentle heart's content
Of your love's couplement;
And let fair Venus, that is queen of love,
With her heart-quelling son upon you smile,
Whose smile, they say, hath virtue to remove
All love's dislike, and friendship's faulty guile
For ever to assoil. 100
Let endless peace your steadfast hearts accord,
And blessèd plenty wait upon your board,
And let your bed with pleasures chaste abound,
That fruitful issue may to you afford,
Which may your foes confound,
And make your joys redound

Upon your bridal day, which is not long:
  Sweet Thames! run softly, till I end my song."

So ended she; and all the rest around
To her redoubled that her undersong, 110
Which said their bridal day should not be long:
And gentle Echo from the neighbour ground
Their accents did resound.
So forth those joyous birds did pass along,
Adown the Lee that to them murmured low,
As he would speak but that he lacked a tongue,
Yet did by signs his glad affection show,
Making his stream run slow.
And all the fowl which in his flood did dwell
Gan flock about these twain, that did excel 120
The rest, so far as Cynthia doth shend[1]
The lesser stars. So they, enrangèd well,
Did on those two attend,
And their best service lend
Against their wedding day, which was not long:
  Sweet Thames! run softly, till I end my song.

At length they all to merry London came,
To merry London, my most kindly nurse,
That to me gave this life's first native source,
Though from another place I take my name, 130
An house of ancient fame:
There when they came whereas those bricky towers
The which on Thames' broad agèd back do ride,
Where now the studious lawyers have their bowers,
There whilome wont the Templar-knights to bide,
Till they decay'd through pride;
Next whereunto there stands a stately place,
Where oft I gainèd gifts and goodly grace
Of that great lord, which therein wont to dwell,
Whose want too well now feels my friendless case 140
But ah! here fits not well

[1] shend—*shame*

Old woes, but joys to tell
Against the bridal day, which is not long:
Sweet Thames! run softly, till I end my song.

Yet therein now doth lodge a noble peer,
Great England's glory and the world's wide wonder,
Whose dreadful name late through all Spain did thunder,
And Hercules' two pillars standing near
Did make to quake and fear:
Fair branch of honour, flower of chivalry! 150
That fillest England with thy triumphs' fame,
Joy have thou of thy noble victory,
And endless happiness of thine own name
That promiseth the same;
That through thy prowess and victorious arms
Thy country may be freed from foreign harms,
And great Eliza's glorious name may ring
Through all the world, filled with thy wide alarms,
Which some brave Muse may sing
To ages following, 160
Upon the bridal day, which is not long:
Sweet Thames! run softly, till I end my song.

From those high towers this noble lord issuing,
Like radiant Hesper when his golden hair
In the ocean billows he hath bathèd fair,
Descended to the river's open viewing,
With a great train ensuing.
Above the rest were goodly to be seen
Two gentle knights of lovely face and feature,
Beseeming well the bower of any queen, 170
With gifts of wit and ornaments of nature
Fit for so goodly stature,
That like the twins of Jove they seemed in sight
Which deck the baldric of the heavens bright;
They two, forth pacing to the river's side,
Received those two fair brides, their love's delight;
Which, at the appointed tide,
Each one did make his bride

Against their bridal day, which is not long:
Sweet Thames! run softly, till I end my song. 180

THE DANCE OF THE GRACES

EDMUND SPENSER

It was an hill placed in an open plain,
That round about was bordered with a wood
Of matchless height, that seemed th' earth to disdain,
In which all trees of honour stately stood,
And did all winter as in summer bud,
Spreading pavilions for the birds to bower,
Which in their lower branches sung aloud;
And in their tops the soaring hawk did tower,
Sitting like king of fowls in majesty and power.

And at the foot thereof, a gentle flood 10
His silver waves did softly tumble down,
Unmarred with ragged moss or filthy mud,
Ne mote[1] wild beasts, ne mote the ruder clown
Thereto approach, ne filth mote therein drown:
But nymphs and fairies by the banks did sit,
In the wood's shade, which did the waters crown,
Keeping all noisome things away from it,
And to the water's fall tuning their accents fit.

And on the top thereof a spacious plain
Did spread itself, to serve to all delight, 20
Either to dance, when they to dance would fain,
Or else to course about their bases[2] light;
Ne aught there wanted, which for pleasure might
Desirèd be, or thence to banish bale:
So pleasantly the hill with equal height
Did seem to overlook the lowly vale;
Therefore it rightly clepèd[3] was mount Acidale.

[1] mote—*might* [2] bases—*lines in a game* [3] cleped—*named*

They say that Venus, when she did dispose
Herself to pleasance, used to resort
Unto this place, and therein to repose 30
And rest herself, as in a gladsome port,
Or with the Graces there to play and sport;
That even her own Citheron, though in it
She usèd most to keep her royal court,
And in her sovereign majesty to sit,
She in regard hereof refused and thought unfit.

Unto this place when as the Elfin Knight
Approached, him seemèd that the merry sound
Of a shrill pipe he playing heard on height,
And many feet fast thumping th' hollow ground, 40
That through the woods their echo did rebound.
He nigher drew, to wit what mote it be;
There he a troop of ladies dancing found
Full merrily, and making gladful glee,
And in the midst a shepherd piping he did see.

He durst not enter into th' open green,
For dread of them unwares to be descried,
For breaking of their dance, if he were seen;
But in the covert of the wood did bide,
Beholding all, yet of them unespied. 50
There he did see, that pleasèd much his sight,
That even he himself his eyes envied,
An hundred naked maidens lily white,
All rangèd in a ring, and dancing in delight.

All they without were rangèd in a ring,
And dancèd round; but in the midst of them
Three other ladies did both dance and sing,
The whilst the rest them round about did hem,
And like a garland did in compass stem[4]:
And in the midst of those same three was placed 60
Another damsel, as a precious gem,

[4] stem—*surround*

Amidst a ring most richly well enchased,
That with her goodly presence all the rest much graced.

Look how the crown, which Ariadne wore
  Upon her ivory forehead that same day,
That Theseus her unto his bridal bore,
  When the bold Centaurs made that bloody fray,
  With the fierce Lapithes, which did them dismay,
Being now placèd in the firmament,
  Through the bright heaven doth her beams display, 70
And is unto the stars an ornament,
Which round about her move in order excellent:

Such was the beauty of this goodly band,
  Whose sundry parts were here too long to tell:
But she, that in the midst of them did stand,
  Seemed all the rest in beauty to excel,
  Crowned with a rosy garland, that right well
Did her beseem. And ever, as the crew
  About her danced, sweet flowers, that far did smell,
And fragrant odours they upon her threw; 80
But most of all, those three did her with gifts endue.

Those were the Graces, daughters of delight,
  Handmaids of Venus, which are wont to haunt
Upon this hill, and dance there day and night:
  Those three to men all gifts of grace do grant,
  And all, that Venus in herself doth vaunt,
Is borrowèd of them. But that fair one,
  That in the midst was placèd paravaunt,[5]
Was she to whom that shepherd piped alone,
That made him pipe so merrily, as never none. 90

She was to wit that jolly shepherd's lass,
  Which pipèd there unto that merry rout;
That jolly shepherd, which there pipèd, was
  Poor Colin Clout (who knows not Colin Clout?);

[5] paravaunt—*foremost*

He piped apace, whilst they him danced about.
Pipe jolly shepherd, pipe thou now apace
Unto thy love, that made thee low to lout:
Thy love is present there with thee in place,
Thy love is there advanced to be another Grace.

The Faerie Queene, VI. x. 6-16.

THE NYMPH'S REPLY TO THE SHEPHERD[1]

SIR WALTER RALEGH

If all the world and love were young,
And truth in every shepherd's tongue,
These pretty pleasures might me move
To live with thee and be thy Love.

Time drives the flocks from field to fold,
When rivers rage and rocks grow cold;
And Philomel becometh dumb;
The rest complains of cares to come.

The flowers do fade, and wanton fields
To wayward winter reckoning yields:
A honey tongue, a heart of gall,
Is fancy's spring, but sorrow's fall.

Thy gowns, thy shoes, thy beds of roses,
Thy cap, thy kirtle, and thy posies
Soon break, soon wither, soon forgotten,
In folly ripe, in reason rotten.

Thy belt of straw and ivy buds,
Thy coral clasps and amber studs,
All these in me no means can move
To come to thee and be thy Love.

[1] See p. 62.

But could youth last, and love still breed,
Had joys no date, nor age no need,
Then these delights my mind might move
To live with thee and be thy Love.

¶ WHAT IS OUR LIFE?

SIR WALTER RALEGH

What is our life? A play of passion,
Our mirth the music of division.
Our mothers' wombs the tiring-houses be,
Where we are dressed for this short comedy.
Heaven the judicious sharp spectator is,
That sits and marks still who doth act amiss.
Our graves that hide us from the searching sun
Are like drawn curtains when the play is done.
Thus march we, playing, to our latest rest,
Only we die in earnest, that's no jest.

¶ EVEN SUCH IS TIME

SIR WALTER RALEGH

Even such is time, that takes in trust
  Our youth, our joys, our all we have,
And pays us but with earth and dust;
  Who, in the dark and silent grave,
When we have wandered all our ways,
Shuts up the story of our days.
But from this earth, this grave, this dust,
My God shall raise me up, I trust.

¶ THE LIE

SIR WALTER RALEGH

Go, soul, the body's guest,
  Upon a thankless arrant;

Fear not to touch the best;
  The truth shall be thy warrant.
    Go, since I needs must die,
    And give the world the lie.

Say to the court, it glows
  And shines like rotten wood;
Say to the church, it shows
  What's good, and doth no good: 10
    If church and court reply,
    Then give them both the lie.

Tell potentates, they live
  Acting by others' action,
Not loved unless they give,
  Not strong but by their faction:
    If potentates reply,
    Give potentates the lie.

Tell men of high condition
  That manage the estate, 20
Their purpose is ambition,
  Their practice only hate:
    And if they once reply,
    Then give them all the lie.

Tell them that brave it most,
  They beg for more by spending,
Who, in their greatest cost,
  Seek nothing but commending:
    And if they make reply,
    Then give them all the lie. 30

Tell zeal it wants devotion;
  Tell love it is but lust;
Tell time it is but motion;
  Tell flesh it is but dust:
    And wish them not reply,
    For thou must give the lie.

Tell age it daily wasteth;
  Tell honour how it alters;
Tell beauty how she blasteth;
  Tell favour how it falters: 40
    And as they shall reply,
    Give every one the lie.

Tell wit how much it wrangles
  In tickle points of niceness;
Tell wisdom she entangles
  Herself in over-wiseness:
    And when they do reply,
    Straight give them both the lie.

Tell physic of her boldness;
  Tell skill it is prevention; 50
Tell charity of coldness;
  Tell law it is contention:
    And as they do reply,
    So give them still the lie.

Tell fortune of her blindness;
  Tell nature of decay;
Tell friendship of unkindness;
  Tell justice of delay:
    And if they will reply,
    Then give them all the lie. 60

Tell arts they have no soundness,
  But vary by esteeming;
Tell schools they want profoundness,
  And stand too much on seeming:
    If arts and schools reply,
    Give arts and schools the lie.

Tell faith it's fled the city;
  Tell how the country erreth;
Tell, manhood shakes off pity;
  Tell, virtue least preferreth: 70

And if they do reply,
Spare not to give the lie.

So when thou hast, as I
Commanded thee, done blabbing,
Although to give the lie
Deserves no less than stabbing,
Stab at thee he that will,
No stab the soul can kill.

❡ WITH HOW SAD STEPS, O MOON

SIR PHILIP SIDNEY

With how sad steps, O Moon, thou climb'st the skies,
How silently, and with how wan a face!
What! may it be that even in heav'nly place
That busy archer his sharp arrows tries?
Sure, if that long-with-love-acquainted eyes
Can judge of love, thou feel'st a lover's case.
I read it in thy looks; thy languisht grace
To me, that feel the like, thy state descries.
Then, ev'n of fellowship, O Moon, tell me,
Is constant love deem'd there but want of wit?
Are beauties there as proud as here they be?
Do they above love to be lov'd, and yet
Those lovers scorn whom that love doth possess?
Do they call virtue there ungratefulness?

❡ LEAVE ME, O LOVE

SIR PHILIP SIDNEY

Leave me, O Love, which reachest but to dust;
And thou, my mind, aspire to higher things;
Grow rich in that which never taketh rust,
Whatever fades but fading pleasure brings.
Draw in thy beams, and humble all thy might
To that sweet yoke where lasting freedoms be;

Which breaks the clouds and opens forth the light,
That doth both shine and give us sight to see.
O take fast hold; let that light be thy guide
In this small course which birth draws out to death,
And think how evil becometh him to slide,
Who seeketh heav'n, and comes of heav'nly breath.
Then farewell, world; thy uttermost I see;
Eternal Love, maintain thy life in me.

¶ A LITANY

SIR PHILIP SIDNEY

Ring out your bells, let mourning shows be spread;
For Love is dead.
All Love is dead, infected
With plague of deep disdain;
Worth, as nought worth, rejected,
And Faith fair scorn doth gain.
From so ungrateful fancy,
From such a female franzy,
From them that use men thus, 10
Good Lord, deliver us!

Weep, neighbours, weep! do you not hear it said
That Love is dead?
His death-bed, peacock's folly;
His winding-sheet is shame;
His will, false-seeming holy;
His sole executor, blame.
From so ungrateful fancy,
From such a female franzy,
From them that use men thus,
Good Lord, deliver us! 20

Let dirge be sung and trentals[1] rightly read,
For Love is dead.
Sir Wrong his tomb ordaineth

[1] trentals—*masses for the dead*

My mistress Marble-heart,
Which epitaph containeth,
"Her eyes were once his dart."
From so ungrateful fancy,
From such a female franzy,
From them that use men thus,
Good Lord, deliver us! 30

Alas! I lie, rage hath this error bred;
Love is not dead.
Love is not dead, but sleepeth
In her unmatchèd mind,
Where she his counsel keepeth,
Till due desert she find.
Therefore from so vile fancy,
To call such wit a franzy,
Who Love can temper thus,
Good Lord, deliver us! 40

THE NIGHTINGALE

SIR PHILIP SIDNEY

The nightingale, as soon as April bringeth
Unto her rested sense a perfect waking,
While late bare earth, proud of new clothing, springeth,
Sings out her woes, a thorn her song-book making;
And mournfully bewailing,
Her throat in tunes expresseth
What grief her breast oppresseth
For Tereus' force on her chaste will prevailing.
O Philomela fair, O take some gladness,
That here is juster cause of plaintful sadness.
Thine earth now springs, mine fadeth;
Thy thorn without, my thorn my heart invadeth.

Alas, she hath no other cause of anguish
But Tereus' love, on her by strong hand wroken,[1]

[1] wroken—*imposed*

Wherein she suffering, all her spirits languish;
  Full womanlike complains her will was broken.
  But I, who daily craving,
Cannot have to content me,
Have more cause to lament me,
  Since wanting is more woe than too much having.
O Philomela fair, O take some gladness,
That here is juster cause of plaintful sadness.
    Thine earth now springs, mine fadeth;
    Thy thorn without, my thorn my heart invadeth.

¶ WHO HATH HIS FANCY PLEASED

SIR PHILIP SIDNEY

Who hath his fancy pleased
  With fruits of happy sight,
Let here his eyes be raised
  On Nature's sweetest light;
A light which doth dissever
  And yet unite the eyes;
A light which, dying never,
  Is cause the looker dies.

She never dies, but lasteth
  In life of lover's heart;
He ever dies that wasteth
  In love his chiefest part.
Thus is her life still guarded
  In never-dying faith;
Thus is his death rewarded,
  Since she lives in his death.

Look, then, and die; the pleasure
  Doth answer well the pain;
Small loss of mortal treasure
  Who may immortal gain.
Immortal be her graces,
  Immortal is her mind;

They, fit for heavenly places;
  This, heaven in it doth bind.

But eyes these beauties see not,
  Nor sense that grace descries;
Yet eyes deprived be not
  From sight of her fair eyes;
Which as of inward glory
  They are the outward seal,
So may they live still sorry,
  Which die not in that weal.

But who hath fancies pleased
  With fruits of happy sight,
Let here his eyes be raised
  On Nature's sweetest light!

❡ CYNTHIA

FULKE GREVILLE, LORD BROOKE

Away with these self-loving lads,
Whom Cupid's arrow never glads!
Away, poor souls, that sigh and weep
In love of those that lie asleep!
  For Cupid is a meadow-god,
  And forceth none to kiss the rod.

Sweet Cupid's shafts, like destiny,
Do causeless good or ill decree;
Desert is born out of his bow;
Reward upon his wing doth go.
  What fools are they that have not known
  That Love likes no laws but his own!

My songs they be of Cynthia's praise,
I wear her rings on holy days;
In every tree I write her name,
And every day I read the same.

Where Honour Cupid's rival is,
There miracles are seen of his.

If Cynthia crave her ring of me,
I blot her name out of the tree.
If doubt do darken things held dear,
Then well fare nothing once a year!
For many run, but one must win;
Fools, only, hedge the cuckoo in.

The worth that worthiness should move
Is love, that is the bow of Love.
And love as well the foster[1] can
As can the mighty nobleman.
Sweet Saint, 'tis true you worthy be,
Yet without love nought worth to me.

❰ YOU LITTLE STARS THAT LIVE IN SKIES

FULKE GREVILLE, LORD BROOKE

You little stars that live in skies,
And glory in Apollo's glory,
In whose aspects conjoinèd lies
The Heaven's will and Nature's story,
Joy to be likened to those eyes,
Which eyes make all eyes glad or sorry;
For when you force thoughts from above,
These overrule your force by love.

And thou, O Love, which in these eyes
Hast married Reason with Affection,
And made them saints of Beauty's skies,
Where joys are shadows of perfection,
Lend me thy wings that I may rise
Up not by worth but thy election;
For I have vowed, in strangest fashion,
To love, and never seek compassion.

[1] foster—*forester*

YOUTH AND MATURITY

FULKE GREVILLE, LORD BROOKE

The nurse-life wheat, within his green husk growing,
Flatters our hope, and tickles our desire,
Nature's true riches in sweet beauties showing,
Which set all hearts, with labour's love, on fire.
No less fair is the wheat when golden ear
Shows unto hope the joys of near enjoying;
Fair and sweet is the bud, more sweet and fair
The rose, which proves that time is not destroying.
Caelica, your youth, the morning of delight,
Enamelled o'er with beauties white and red,
All sense and thoughts did to belief invite,
That love and glory there are brought to bed;
And your ripe years love none; he goes no higher,
Turns all the spirits of man into desire.

O FALSE AND TREACHEROUS PROBABILITY

FULKE GREVILLE, LORD BROOKE

O false and treacherous *Probability,*
Enemy of truth, and friend to wickedness;
With whose blear eyes opinion learns to see,
Truth's feeble party here, and barrenness.

When thou hast thus misled Humanity,
And lost obedience in the pride of wit,
With reason dar'st thou judge the Deity,
And in thy flesh make bold to fashion it.

Vain thought, the word of Power a riddle is,
And till the veils be rent, the flesh newborn,
Reveals no wonders of that inward bliss,
Which but where faith is, every where finds scorn;

Who therefor censures God with fleshly sprite,
As well in time may wrap up infinite.

❡ CHORUS SACERDOTUM

FULKE GREVILLE, LORD BROOKE

Oh wearisome Condition of Humanity!
Born under one Law, to another bound:
Vainly begot, and yet forbidden vanity;
Created sick, commanded to be sound:
What meaneth Nature by these diverse Laws?
Passion and Reason, self-division cause:
Is it the mark of majesty of Power
To make offenses that it may forgive?
Nature herself doth her own self deflower,
To hate those errors she her self doth give.
For how should man think that he may not do,
If Nature did not fail, and punish too?
Tyrant to others, to her self unjust,
Only commands things difficult and hard;
Forbids us all things which it knows is lust,
Makes easy pains, unpossible reward.
If Nature did not take delight in blood,
She would have made more easy ways to good.
We that are bound by vows, and by Promotion,
With pomp of holy Sacrifice and rites,
To teach belief in good and still devotion,
To preach of Heaven's wonders, and delights:
Yet when each of us in his own heart looks,
He finds the God there, far unlike his Books.

❡ TRICO'S SONG

JOHN LYLY

What bird so sings, yet so does wail?
O! 'tis the ravished nightingale.
Jug, Jug, Jug, Jug, Tereu, she cries,
And still her woes at midnight rise.
Brave prick song! who is't now we hear?
None but the lark so shrill and clear;
How at heaven's gates she claps her wings,

The morn not waking till she sings.
Hark, hark, with what a pretty throat
Poor Robin Redbreast tunes his note;
Hark how the jolly cuckoos sing
Cuckoo, to welcome in the spring,
Cuckoo, to welcome in the spring.

CONTENT

ROBERT DEVEREUX, EARL OF ESSEX

Happy were he could finish forth his fate
  In some unhaunted desert, most obscure
From all societies, from love and hate
  Of worldly folk; then might he sleep secure;
Then wake again, and give God ever praise,
  Content with hips and haws and bramble-berry;
In contemplation spending all his days,
  And change of holy thoughts to make him merry;
Where, when he dies, his tomb may be a bush,
Where harmless robin dwells with gentle thrush.

WHAT THING IS LOVE?

GEORGE PEELE

What thing is love? for sure love is a thing.
It is a prick, it is a sting,
It is a pretty, pretty thing;
It is a fire, it is a coal,
Whose flame creeps in at every hole;
And as my wit doth best devise,
Love's dwelling is in ladies' eyes,
From whence do glance love's piercing darts,
That make such holes into our hearts;
And all the world herein accord,
Love is a great and mighty lord;
And when he list to mount so high,
With Venus he in heaven doth lie,

And evermore hath been a god,
Since Mars and she played even and odd.

A VOICE SPEAKS FROM THE WELL
from *The Old Wife's Tale*

GEORGE PEELE

Fair maiden, white and red,
Comb me smooth, and stroke my head,
And thou shalt have some cockell-bread.
Gently dip, but not too deep,
For fear thou make the golden beard to weep.
Fair maiden, white and red,
Comb me smooth and stroke my head,
And every hair a sheaf shall be,
And every sheaf a golden tree.

MUSES THAT SING LOVE'S SENSUAL EMPERY

GEORGE CHAPMAN

Muses that sing Love's sensual empery,
And lovers kindling your enraged fires
At Cupid's bonfires burning in the eye,
Blown with the empty breath of vain desires;
You that prefer the painted cabinet
Before the wealthy jewels it doth store ye,
That all your joys in dying figures set,
And stain the living substance of your glory:
Abjure those joys, abhor their memory,
And let my love the honoured subject be
Of love, and honour's complete history;
Your eyes were never yet let in to see
The majesty and riches of the mind,
But dwell in darkness; for your God is blind.

SHADOWS

SAMUEL DANIEL

Are they shadows that we see?
And can shadows pleasure give?
Pleasures only shadows be,
Cast by bodies we conceive,
And are made the things we deem
In those figures which they seem.

But these pleasures vanish fast
Which by shadows are exprest.
Pleasures are not if they last;
In their passage is their best;
Glory is most bright and gay
In a flash, and so away.

Feed apace, then, greedy eyes,
On the wonder you behold:
Take it sudden as it flies,
Though you take it not to hold:
When your eyes have done their part,
Thought must length it in the heart.

CALLING TO MIND SINCE FIRST MY LOVE BEGUN

MICHAEL DRAYTON

Calling to mind since first my love begun,
  Th' incertain times oft varying in their course,
How things still unexpectedly have run,
  As please the Fates, by their resistless force,
Lastly, mine eyes amazedly have seen
  Essex great fall, Tyrone his peace to gain,
The quiet end of that long-living Queen,
  This King's fair entrance, and our peace with Spain,
We and the Dutch at length ourselves to sever.
  Thus the world doth, and evermore shall reel,

Yet to my goddess am I constant ever,
Howe'er blind Fortune turn her giddy wheel.
Though heaven and earth prove both to me untrue,
Yet am I still inviolate to you.

HOW MANY PALTRY, FOOLISH, PAINTED THINGS

MICHAEL DRAYTON

How many paltry, foolish, painted things,
That now in coaches trouble every street,
Shall be forgotten, whom no poet sings,
Ere they be well wrapped in their winding-sheet?
Where I to thee eternity shall give,
When nothing else remaineth of these days,
And Queens hereafter shall be glad to live
Upon the alms of thy superfluous praise.
Virgins and matrons reading these my rhymes,
Shall be so much delighted with thy story,
That they shall grieve they lived not in these times,
To have seen thee, their sex's only glory.
So shalt thou fly above the vulgar throng,
Still to survive in my immortal song.

SINCE THERE'S NO HELP, COME LET US KISS AND PART

MICHAEL DRAYTON

Since there's no help, come let us kiss and part.
Nay, I have done; you get no more of me,
And I am glad, yea, glad with all my heart,
That thus so cleanly I myself can free;
Shake hands for ever, cancel all our vows,
And when we meet at any time again,
Be it not seen in either of our brows
That we one jot of former love retain.
Now at the last gasp of Love's latest breath,

When, his pulse failing, Passion speechless lies,
When Faith is kneeling by his bed of death,
And Innocence is closing up his eyes,
Now if thou wouldst, when all have given him over,
From death to life thou mightst him yet recover.

TO THE VIRGINIAN VOYAGE

MICHAEL DRAYTON

You brave heroic minds,
Worthy your country's name;
That Honour still pursue,
Go, and subdue,
Whilst loitering hinds
Lurk here at home, with shame.

Britons, you stay too long,
Quickly aboard bestow you,
And with a merry gale
Swell your stretch'd sail, 10
With vows as strong
As the winds that blow you.

Your course securely steer,
West and by south forth keep,
Rocks, lee-shores, nor shoals,
When Aeolus scowls,
You need not fear,
So absolute the deep.

And cheerfully at sea,
Success you still entice, 20
To get the pearl and gold,
And ours to hold,
Virginia,
Earth's only paradise.

Where nature hath in store
Foul, venison, and fish,
  And the fruitful'st soil,
  Without your toil,
Three harvests more,
All greater than your wish. 30

And the ambitious vine
Crowns with his purple mass
  The cedar reaching high
  To kiss the sky,
The cypress, pine,
And use-full sassafras.

To whom, the golden age
Still nature's laws doth give,
  No other cares that tend
  But them to defend 40
From Winter's rage,
That long there doth not live.

When as the luscious smell
Of that delicious land,
  Above the seas that flows,
  The clear wind throws,
Your hearts to swell
Approaching the dear strand.

In kenning of the shore
(Thanks to God first given) 50
  O you the happiest men,
  Be frolick then,
Let cannons roar
Frighting the wide heaven.

And in regions far
Such heroes bring ye forth,

As those from whom we came,
And plant our name
Under that star
Not known unto our north. 60

And as there plenty grows
Of laurel every where,
Apollo's sacred tree,
You may it see,
A poet's brows
To crown, that may sing there.

Thy voyages attend
Industrious Hackluit,
Whose reading shall inflame
Men to seek fame, 70
And much commend
To after-times thy wit.

THE PASSIONATE SHEPHERD TO HIS LOVE[1]

CHRISTOPHER MARLOWE

Come live with me and be my love,
And we will all the pleasures prove
That hills and valleys, dales and fields,
And all the craggy mountains yields.

There will we sit upon the rocks
And see the shepherds feed their flocks,
By shallow rivers, to whose falls
Melodious birds sing madrigals.

There will I make thee beds of roses
And a thousand fragrant posies,
A cap of flowers, and a kirtle
Embroider'd all with leaves of myrtle.

[1] See p. 44.

A gown made of the finest wool,
Which from our pretty lambs we pull,
Fair linèd slippers for the cold,
With buckles of the purest gold.

A belt of straw and ivy buds
With coral clasps and amber studs:
And if these pleasures may thee move,
Come live with me and be my love.

The shepherd swains shall dance and sing
For thy delight each May-morning:
If these delights thy mind may move,
Then live with me and be my love.

❡ WHO IS SILVIA?

WILLIAM SHAKESPEARE

Who is Silvia? what is she,
  That all our swains commend her?
Holy, fair, and wise is she;
  The heaven such grace did lend her,
That she might admirèd be.

Is she kind as she is fair?
  For beauty lives with kindness.
Love doth to her eyes repair,
  To help him of his blindness,
And, being helped, inhabits there.

Then to Silvia let us sing,
  That Silvia is excelling;
She excels each mortal thing
  Upon the dull earth dwelling:
To her let us garlands bring.

TELL ME WHERE IS FANCY BRED

WILLIAM SHAKESPEARE

Tell me where is fancy bred,
Or in the heart or in the head?
How begot, how nourishèd?
  Reply, reply.

It is engender'd in the eyes,
With gazing fed; and fancy dies
In the cradle where it lies.
  Let us all ring fancy's knell:
  I'll begin it,—Ding, dong, bell.

FEAR NO MORE THE HEAT O' THE SUN

WILLIAM SHAKESPEARE

Fear no more the heat o' the sun,
  Nor the furious winter's rages;
Thou thy worldly task hast done,
  Home art gone and ta'en thy wages.
Golden lads and girls all must,
As chimney-sweepers, come to dust.

Fear no more the frown o' the great;
  Thou art past the tyrant's stroke;
Care no more to clothe and eat;
  To thee the reed is as the oak.
The sceptre, learning, physic, must
All follow this, and come to dust.

Fear no more the lightning-flash,
  Nor the all-dreaded thunder-stone;
Fear not slander, censure rash;
  Thou hast finish'd joy and moan.
All lovers young, all lovers must
Consign to thee, and come to dust.

No exorciser harm thee!
Nor no witchcraft charm thee!
Ghost unlaid forbear thee!
Nothing ill come near thee!
Quiet consummation have,
And renownèd be thy grave!

(SONNETS

WILLIAM SHAKESPEARE

18

Shall I compare thee to a summer's day?
Thou art more lovely and more temperate:
Rough winds do shake the darling buds of May,
And summer's lease hath all too short a date;
Sometime too hot the eye of heaven shines,
And often is his gold complexion dimm'd;
And every fair from fair sometime declines,
By chance, or nature's changing course untrimm'd:
But thy eternal summer shall not fade,
Nor lose possession of that fair thou ow'st,
Nor shall Death brag thou wander'st in his shade,
When in eternal lines to time thou grow'st;
So long as men can breathe, or eyes can see,
So long lives this, and this gives life to thee.

19

Devouring Time, blunt thou the lion's paws,
And make the earth devour her own sweet brood;
Pluck the keen teeth from the fierce tiger's jaws,
And burn the long-lived phoenix in her blood;
Make glad and sorry seasons as thou fleets,
And do whate'er thou wilt, swift-footed Time,
To the wide world and all her fading sweets;
But I forbid thee one most heinous crime:

O! carve not with thy hours my Love's fair brow,
Nor draw no lines there with thine antique pen;
Him in thy course untainted do allow
For beauty's pattern to succeeding men.
  Yet, do thy worst, old Time: despite thy wrong,
  My Love shall in my verse ever live young.

33

Full many a glorious morning have I seen
Flatter the mountain-tops with sovereign eye,
Kissing with golden face the meadows green,
Gilding pale streams with heavenly alchemy;
Anon permit the basest clouds to ride
With ugly rack on his celestial face,
And from the forlorn world his visage hide,
Stealing unseen to west with this disgrace:
Even so my sun one early morn did shine
With all-triumphant splendour on my brow;
But out, alack! he was but one hour mine;
The region cloud hath mask'd him from me now.
  Yet him for this my love no whit disdaineth;
  Suns of the world may stain when heaven's sun staineth.

53

What is your substance, whereof are you made,
That millions of strange shadows on you tend?
Since every one hath, every one, one shade,
And you, but one, can every shadow lend.
Describe Adonis, and the counterfeit
Is poorly imitated after you;
On Helen's cheek all art of beauty set,
And you in Grecian tires are painted new:
Speak of the spring and plenty of the year,
The one doth shadow of your beauty show,
The other as your bounty doth appear;

And you in every blessèd shape we know.
  In all external grace you have some part,
  But you like none, none you, for constant heart.

73

That time of year thou mayst in me behold
When yellow leaves, or none, or few, do hang
Upon those boughs which shake against the cold,
Bare ruin'd choirs, where late the sweet birds sang.
In me thou see'st the twilight of such day
As after sunset fadeth in the west,
Which by and by black night doth take away,
Death's second self, that seals up all in rest.
In me thou see'st the glowing of such fire,
That on the ashes of his youth doth lie,
As the death-bed whereon it must expire,
Consum'd with that which it was nourish'd by.
  This thou perceiv'st, which makes thy love more strong,
  To love that well which thou must leave ere long.

77

Thy glass will show thee how thy beauties wear,
Thy dial how thy precious minutes waste;
The vacant leaves thy mind's imprint will bear,
And of this book this learning mayst thou taste.
The wrinkles which thy glass will truly show
Of mouthèd graves will give thee memory;
Thou by thy dial's shady stealth mayst know
Time's thievish progress to eternity.
Look, what thy memory cannot contain
Commit to these waste blanks, and thou shalt find
Those children nurs'd, deliver'd from thy brain,
To take a new acquaintance of thy mind.
  These offices, so oft as thou wilt look,
  Shall profit thee and much enrich thy book.

116

Let me not to the marriage of true minds
Admit impediments. Love is not love
Which alters when it alteration finds,
Or bends with the remover to remove.
O, no! it is an ever-fixed mark
That looks on tempests and is never shaken;
It is the star to every wand'ring bark,
Whose worth's unknown, although his height be taken.
Love's not Time's fool, though rosy lips and cheeks
Within his bending sickle's compass come;
Love alters not with his brief hours and weeks,
But bears it out even to the edge of doom.
  If this be error, and upon me proved,
  I never writ, nor no man ever loved.

129

Th' expense of spirit in a waste of shame
Is lust in action; and till action, lust
Is perjur'd, murd'rous, bloody, full of blame,
Savage, extreme, rude, cruel, not to trust:
Enjoy'd no sooner but despisèd straight;
Past reason hunted, and no sooner had,
Past reason hated, as a swallowed bait
On purpose laid to make the taker mad:
Mad in pursuit and in possession so;
Had, having, and in quest to have, extreme;
A bliss in proof, and prov'd, a very woe;
Before, a joy propos'd; behind, a dream.
  All this the world well knows; yet none knows well
  To shun the heaven that leads men to this hell.

146

Poor soul, the center of my sinful earth,
Rebuke these rebel powers that thee array!

Why dost thou pine within and suffer dearth,
Painting thy outward walls so costly gay?
Why so large cost, having so short a lease,
Dost thou upon thy fading mansion spend?
Shall worms, inheritors of this excess,
Eat up thy charge? Is this thy body's end?
Then, soul, live thou upon thy servant's loss,
And let that pine to aggravate thy store;
Buy terms divine in selling hours of dross:
Within be fed, without be rich no more.
So shalt thou feed on Death, that feeds on men,
And Death once dead, there's no more dying then.

IN PLAGUE TIME

THOMAS NASHE

Adieu, farewell earth's bliss,
This world uncertain is;
Fond are life's lustful joys,
Death proves them all but toys,
None from his darts can fly.
I am sick, I must die.
Lord, have mercy on us!

Rich men, trust not in wealth,
Gold cannot buy you health;
Physic himself must fade, 10
All things to end are made,
The plague full swift goes by;
I am sick, I must die.
Lord, have mercy on us!

Beauty is but a flower
Which wrinkles will devour:
Brightness falls from the air,
Queens have died young and fair,
Dust hath closed Helen's eye.
I am sick, I must die. 20
Lord, have mercy on us!

Strength stoops unto the grave,
Worms feed on Hector brave,
Swords may not fight with fate.
Earth still holds ope her gate;
Come! come! the bells do cry.
I am sick, I must die.
  Lord, have mercy on us!

Wit with his wantonness
Tasteth death's bitterness; 30
Hell's executioner
Hath no ears for to hear
What vain art can reply.
I am sick, I must die.
  Lord, have mercy on us!

Haste, therefore, each degree,
To welcome destiny.
Heaven is our heritage,
Earth but a player's stage;
Mount we unto the sky. 40
I am sick, I must die.
  Lord, have mercy on us!

⁋ AUTUMN

THOMAS NASHE

Autumn hath all the summer's fruitful treasure;
Gone is our sport, fled is poor Croydon's pleasure.
Short days, sharp days, long nights come on apace,
Ah! who shall hide us from the winter's face?
Cold doth increase, the sickness will not cease,
And here we lie, God knows, with little ease.
  From winter, plague, and pestilence, good Lord, deliver us!

London doth mourn, Lambeth is quite forlorn;
Trades cry, woe worth that ever they were born.
The want of term is town and city's harm;

Close chambers we do want, to keep us warm.
Long banishèd must we live from our friends;
This low-built house will bring us to our ends.
  From winter, plague, and pestilence, good Lord, deliver us!

❡ ROSE-CHEEKED LAURA, COME

THOMAS CAMPION

  Rose-cheeked Laura, come;
Sing thou smoothly with thy beauty's
Silent music, either other
  Sweetly gracing.

  Lovely forms do flow
From concent divinely framed;
Heaven is music, and thy beauty's
  Birth is heavenly.

  These dull notes we sing
Discords need for helps to grace them;
Only beauty purely loving
  Knows no discord;

  But still moves delight,
Like clear springs renewed by flowing,
Ever perfect, ever in them-
  selves eternal.

❡ FOLLOW THY FAIR SUN, UNHAPPY SHADOW

THOMAS CAMPION

Follow thy fair sun, unhappy shadow.
  Though thou be black as night,
  And she made all of light,
Yet follow thy fair sun, unhappy shadow.

Follow her whose light thy light depriveth.
  Though here thou livest disgraced,

And she in heaven is placed,
Yet follow her whose light the world reviveth.

Follow those pure beams whose beauty burneth,
That so have scorchèd thee,
As thou still black must be,
Till her kind beams thy black to brightness turneth.

Follow her, while yet her glory shineth.
There comes a luckless night,
That will dim all her light;
And this the black unhappy shade divineth.

Follow still, since so thy fates ordained.
The sun must have his shade,
Till both at once do fade,
The sun still proved, the shadow still disdained.

FOLLOW YOUR SAINT

THOMAS CAMPION

Follow your saint, follow with accents sweet;
Haste you, sad notes, fall at her flying feet.
There, wrapped in cloud of sorrow, pity move,
And tell the ravisher of my soul I perish for her love.
But if she scorns my never-ceasing pain,
Then burst with sighing in her sight, and ne'er return again.

All that I sung still to her praise did tend.
Still she was first, still she my songs did end.
Yet she my love and music both doth fly,
The music that her echo is, and beauty's sympathy.
Then let my notes pursue her scornful flight;
It shall suffice that they were breathed, and died for her delight.

⸿ THOU ART NOT FAIR, FOR ALL THY RED AND WHITE

THOMAS CAMPION

Thou art not fair, for all thy red and white,
For all those rosy ornaments in thee.
Thou art not sweet, though made of mere delight,
Nor fair nor sweet, unless thou pity me.
I will not soothe thy fancies. Thou shalt prove
That beauty is no beauty without love.

Yet love not me, nor seek thou to allure
My thoughts with beauty, were it more divine
Thy smiles and kisses I cannot endure,
I'll not be wrapped up in those arms of thine.
Now show it, if thou be a woman right,
Embrace and kiss and love me in despite.

⸿ WHEN THOU MUST HOME TO SHADES OF UNDERGROUND

THOMAS CAMPION

When thou must home to shades of underground,
And there arrived, a new admirèd guest,
The beauteous spirits do engirt thee round,
White Iope, blithe Helen and the rest,
To hear the stories of thy finished love
From that smooth tongue, whose music hell can move:

Then wilt thou speak of banqueting delights,
Of masks and revels which sweet youth did make,
Of tourneys and great challenges of knights,
And all these triumphs for thy beauty's sake.
When thou hast told these honours done to thee,
Then tell, O! tell, how thou didst murder me.

THERE IS A GARDEN IN HER FACE

THOMAS CAMPION

There is a garden in her face,
Where roses and white lilies grow;
A heav'nly paradise is that place,
Wherein all pleasant fruits do flow.
There cherries grow which none may buy
Till cherry-ripe themselves do cry.

Those cherries fairly do enclose
Of orient pearl a double row,
Which when her lovely laughter shows,
They look like rosebuds filled with snow.
Yet them nor peer nor prince can buy,
Till cherry-ripe themselves do cry.

Her eyes like angels watch them still;
Her brows like bended bows do stand,
Threat'ning with piercing frowns to kill
All that attempt with eye or hand
Those sacred cherries to come nigh,
Till cherry-ripe themselves do cry.

WEEP YOU NO MORE, SAD FOUNTAINS

ANONYMOUS

Weep you no more, sad fountains;
What need you flow so fast?
Look how the snowy mountains
Heaven's sun doth gently waste.
But my sun's heavenly eyes
View not you weeping,
That now lies sleeping
Softly, now softly lies
Sleeping.

Sleep is a reconciling,
A rest that peace begets.
Doth not the sun rise smiling
When fair at even he sets?
Rest you then, rest, sad eyes,
Melt not in weeping,
While she lies sleeping
Softly, now softly lies
Sleeping.

❨[E'EN AS THE FLOWERS DO WITHER

ANONYMOUS

E'en as the flowers do wither
That maidens fair do gather,
So doth their beauty blazing,
Whereon there is such gazing.

As day is dimmèd with the night,
So age doth vade the red and white,
And death consumes e'en in an hour
The virgin's weed, that dainty flower.

And unto them it may be told,
Who clothe most rich in silk and gold,
Ye dames, for all your pride and mirth,
Your beauty shall be turned to earth.

❨[LOVE ME NOT FOR COMELY GRACE

ANONYMOUS

Love me not for comely grace,
For my pleasing eye or face,
Nor for any outward part,
No, nor for a constant heart:
For these may fail or turn to ill,
So thou and I shall sever:

Keep, therefore, a true woman's eye,
And love me still but know not why—
So hast thou the same reason still
To dote upon me ever!

TOM O' BEDLAM'S SONG

ANONYMOUS

From the hag and hungry goblin
That into rags would rend ye,
And the spirit that stands by the naked man
In the book of moons, defend ye,
That of your five sound senses
You never be forsaken,
Nor wander from yourselves with Tom,
Abroad to beg your bacon.
While I do sing: Any food,
Any feeding, drink, or clothing? 10
Come, dame or maid, be not afraid,
Poor Tom will injure nothing.

Of thirty bare years have I
Twice twenty been enragèd,
And of forty been three times fifteen
In durance soundly cagèd
On the lordly lofts of Bedlam,[1]
With stubble soft and dainty,
Brave bracelets strong, sweet whips, ding-dong,
With wholesome hunger plenty. 20
And now I sing: Any food,
Any feeding, drink, or clothing?
Come, dame or maid, be not afraid,
Poor Tom will injure nothing.

With a thought I took for Maudlin,
And a cruse of cockle pottage,

[1] Bedlam—*Bethlehem hospital for the mental patient*

With a thing thus tall, sky bless you all,
  I befell into this dotage.
I slept not since the Conquest,
  Till then I never wakèd, 30
Till the roguish boy of love where I lay
  Me found and stripped me naked.
    And now I sing: Any food,
      Any feeding, drink, or clothing?
    Come, dame or maid, be not afraid,
      Poor Tom will injure nothing.

When I short have shorn my sour-face,
  And swigged my horny barrel,
In an oaken inn I pound my skin,
  As a suit of gilt apparel. 40
The moon's my constant mistress,
  And the lowly owl my morrow;
The flaming drake and the night-crow make
  Me music to my sorrow.
    While I do sing: Any food,
      Any feeding, drink, or clothing?
    Come, dame or maid, be not afraid,
      Poor Tom will injure nothing.

The palsy plagues my pulses,
  When I prig your pigs or pullen, 50
Your culvers take, or matchless make
  Your chanticleer or sullen.
When I want provant, with Humphry
  I sup, and when benighted,
I repose in Powles with waking souls,
  Yet never am affrighted.
    But I do sing: Any food,
      Any feeding, drink, or clothing?
    Come, dame or maid, be not afraid,
      Poor Tom will injure nothing. 60

I know more than Apollo,
  For oft when he lies sleeping,

I see the stars at bloody wars
  In the wounded welkin weeping,
The moon embrace her shepherd,
  And the queen of love her warrior,
While the first doth horn the star of morn,
  And the next the heavenly Farrier.
    While I do sing: Any food,
      Any feeding, drink, or clothing? 70
    Come, dame or maid, be not afraid,
      Poor Tom will injure nothing.

The gipsy Snap and Pedro
  Are none of Tom's comradoes.
The punk I scorn, and the cutpurse sworn,
  And the roaring boys' bravadoes.
The meek, the white, the gentle,
  Me handle, touch, and spare not;
But those that cross Tom Rhinoceros
  Do what the panther dare not. 80
    Although I sing: Any food,
      Any feeding, drink, or clothing?
    Come, dame or maid, be not afraid,
      Poor Tom will injure nothing.

With an host of furious fancies
  Whereof I am commander,
With a burning spear and a horse of air
  To the wilderness I wander.
By a knight of ghosts and shadows
  I summoned am to tourney 90
Ten leagues beyond the wide world's end,
  Methinks it is no journey.
    Yet will I sing: Any food,
      Any feeding, drink, or clothing?
    Come, dame or maid, be not afraid,
      Poor Tom will injure nothing.

BEWARE FAIR MAID

ANONYMOUS

Beware fair maid of musky courtiers' oaths,
Take heed what gifts and favors you receive,
Let not the fading gloss of silken clothes
Dazzle your virtue, or your fame bereave.
For lose but once the hold you have of grace,
Who'll e'er respect your fortune or your face?

Each greedy hand will strive to catch the flower
When none regards the stalk it grows upon,
Each creature seeks the fruit still to devour
But leave the tree to fall or stand alone.
Yet this advice, fair creature, take of me,
Let none take fruit, unless he take the tree.

Believe no oaths, nor much protesting men,
Credit no vows, nor no bewailing songs,
Let courtiers swear, forswear, and swear again;
Their hearts do live ten regions from their tongues.
For when with oaths they make thy heart to tremble
Believe them least, for then they most dissemble.

Beware lest Caesar do corrupt thy mind
Or fond Ambition sell thy modesty.
Say though a king thou ever courteous find
He cannot garden thy virginity.
Begin with king, to subject you will fall,
From lord to lackey, and at last to all.

SLOW, SLOW, FRESH FOUNT

BEN JONSON

Slow, slow, fresh fount, keep time with my salt tears;
Yet slower, yet; O faintly, gentle springs;
List to the heavy part the music bears,
Woe weeps out her division when she sings.

Droop herbs and flowers,
Fall grief in showers,
Our beauties are not ours,
O, I could still,
Like melting snow upon some craggy hill,
Drop, drop, drop, drop,
Since Nature's pride is now a withered daffodil.

TO CELIA

BEN JONSON

Drink to me only with thine eyes,
And I will pledge with mine;
Or leave a kiss but in the cup,
And I'll not look for wine.
The thirst, that from the soul doth rise,
Doth ask a drink divine.
But might I of Jove's nectar sup,
I would not change for thine.

I sent thee, late, a rosy wreath,
Not so much honoring thee,
As giving it a hope, that there
It could not wither'd be.
But thou thereon did'st only breathe,
And sent'st it back to me.
Since when, it grows, and smells, I swear,
Not of itself, but thee.

EPITAPH ON ELIZABETH L.H.

BEN JONSON

Would'st thou hear what man can say
In a little? Reader, stay.

Underneath this stone doth lie
As much beauty as could die:

Which in life did harbor give
To more virtue than doth live.

If at all she had a fault,
Leave it buried in this vault.
One name was Elizabeth,
The other, let it sleep with death:
Fitter, where it died, to tell,
Than that it lived at all. Farewell!

INVITING A FRIEND TO SUPPER

BEN JONSON

To-night, grave sir, both my poor house and I
Do equally desire your company;
Not that we think us worthy such a guest,
But that your worth will dignify our feast
With those that come, whose grace may make that seem
Something, which else could hope for no esteem.
It is the first acceptance, sir, creates
The entertainment perfect, not the cates.
Yet shall you have, to rectify your palate,
An olive, capers, or some better salad 10
Ush'ring the mutton; with a short-legged hen,
If we can get her, full of eggs, and then
Lemons and wine for sauce; to these, a coney
Is not to be despaired of for our money;
And though fowl now be scarce, yet there are clerks,
The sky not falling, think we may have larks.
I'll tell you of more, and lie, so you will come;
Of partridge, pheasant, woodcock, of which some
May yet be there; and godwit, if we can,
Gnat, rail, and ruff too. Howsoe'er, my man 20
Shall read a piece of Virgil, Tacitus,
Livy, or of some better book to us,
Of which we'll speak our minds amidst our meat;
And I'll profess no verses to repeat;
To this, if aught appear which I not know of,

That will the pastry, not my paper, show of.
Digestive cheese, and fruit there sure will be;
But that which most doth take my muse and me
Is a pure cup of rich Canary wine,
Which is the Mermaid's now, but shall be mine; 30
Of which had Horace or Anacreon tasted,
Their lives, as do their lines, till now had lasted.
Tobacco, nectar, or the Thespian spring
Are all but Luther's beer to this I sing.
Of this we will sup free, but moderately,
And we will have no polly, or parrot by;
Nor shall our cups make any guilty men,
But at our parting we will be as when
We innocently met. No simple word
That shall be uttered at our mirthful board 40
Shall make us sad next morning, or affright
The liberty that we'll enjoy to-night.

IT IS NOT GROWING LIKE A TREE

BEN JONSON

It is not growing like a tree
In bulk, doth make men better be;
Or standing long an oak, three hundred year,
To fall a log at last, dry, bald, and sear:
A lily of a day
Is fairer far in May;
Although it fall and die that night,
It was the plant and flower of light.
In small proportions we just beauties see,
And in short measures life may perfect be.

TO HEAVEN

BEN JONSON

Good and great God! can I not think of thee,
But it must straight my melancholy be?

Is it interpreted in me disease,
That, laden with my sins, I seek for ease?
O be thou witness, that the reins dost know
And hearts of all, if I be sad for show;
And judge me after, if I dare pretend
To aught but grace, or aim at other end.
As thou art all, so be thou all to me,
First, midst, and last, converted One and Three!
My faith, my hope, my love; and, in this state,
My judge, my witness, and my advocate!
Where have I been this while exiled from thee,
And whither rapt, now thou but stoop'st to me?
Dwell, dwell here still! O, being everywhere,
How can I doubt to find thee ever here?
I know my state, both full of shame and scorn,
Conceived in sin, and unto labor born,
Standing with fear, and must with horror fall,
And destined unto judgment, after all.
I feel my griefs too, and there scarce is ground
Upon my flesh t' inflict another wound;
Yet dare I not complain or wish for death
With holy Paul, lest it be thought the breath
Of discontent; or that these prayers be
For weariness of life, not love of thee.

A HYMN TO GOD THE FATHER

BEN JONSON

Hear me, O God!
A broken heart
Is my best part:
Use still thy rod
That I may prove
Therein, thy Love.

If thou hadst not
Been stern to me,
But left me free,

I had forgot
Myself and thee.

For sin's so sweet,
As minds ill bent
Rarely repent,
Until they meet
Their punishment.

Who more can crave
Than thou hast done:
That gav'st a Son
To free a slave?
First made of nought;
With All since bought.

Sin, Death, and Hell,
His glorious Name
Quite overcame,
Yet I rebel
And slight the same.

But, I'll come in,
Before my loss
Me farther toss,
As sure to win,
Under his Cross.

THE CANONIZATION

JOHN DONNE

For God's sake hold your tongue and let me love,
Or chide my palsy or my gout,
My five gray hairs or ruin'd fortune flout,
With wealth your state, your mind with arts improve,
Take you a course, get you a place,
Observe His Honour, or His Grace,
Or the King's real, or his stamped face

Contemplate, what you will, approve,
So you will let me love.

Alas, alas, who's injur'd by my love? 10
What merchant's ships have my sighs drown'd?
Who says my tears have overflow'd his ground?
When did my colds a forward spring remove?
When did the heats which my veins fill
Add one more to the plaguey Bill?
Soldiers find wars, and Lawyers find out still
Litigious men, which quarrels move,
Though she and I do love.

Call us what you will, we are made such by love;
Call her one, me another fly, 20
We are tapers too, and at our own cost die,
And we in us find th' Eagle and the Dove.
The Phoenix riddle hath more wit
By us, we two being one, are it.
So to one neutral thing both sexes fit,
We die and rise the same, and prove
Mysterious by this love.

We can die by it, if not live by love,
And if unfit for tombs and hearse
Our legend be, it will be fit for verse; 30
And if no piece of Chronicle we prove,
We'll build in sonnets pretty rooms;
As well a well-wrought urn becomes
The greatest ashes, as half-acre tombs,
And by these hymns, all shall approve
Us *Canoniz'd* for Love:

And thus invoke us; You whom reverend love
Made one another's hermitage;
You, to whom love was peace, that now is rage;
Who did the whole world's soul contract, and drove 40
Into the glasses of your eyes
(So made such mirrors and such spies

That they did all to you epitomize,)
Countries, Towns, Courts: Beg from above
A pattern of your love!

A VALEDICTION: FORBIDDING MOURNING

JOHN DONNE

As virtuous men pass mildly away,
And whisper to their souls to go,
Whilst some of their sad friends do say,
The breath goes now, and some say, No;

So let us melt, and make no noise,
No tear-floods, nor sigh-tempests move;
'Twere profanation of our joys
To tell the laity our love.

Moving of th' earth brings harms and fears,
Men reckon what it did and meant;
But trepidation of the spheres,
Though greater far, is innocent.

Dull sublunary lovers' love,
Whose soul is sense, cannot admit
Absence, because it doth remove
Those things which elemented it.

But we by a love so much refined
That ourselves know not what it is,
Inter-assurèd of the mind,
Care less eyes, lips, hands to miss.

Our two souls therefore, which are one,
Though I must go, endure not yet
A breach, but an expansion,
Like gold to airy thinness beat.

If they be two, they are two so
As stiff twin compasses are two;

Thy soul, the fixed foot, makes no show
To move, but doth if the' other do.

And though it in the center sit,
Yet when the other far doth roam,
It leans, and hearkens after it,
And grows erect as that comes home.

Such wilt thou be to me who must,
Like th' other foot, obliquely run,
Thy firmness makes my circle just,
And makes me end where I begun.

❡ THE DREAM

JOHN DONNE

Dear love, for nothing less than thee
Would I have broke this happy dream;
It was a theme
For reason, much too strong for fantasy.
Therefore thou waked'st me wisely; yet
My dream thou brok'st not, but continued'st it.
Thou art so true that thoughts of thee suffice
To make dreams truths and fables histories;
Enter these arms, for since thou thought'st it best
Not to dream all my dream, let's act the rest.

As lightning, or a taper's light,
Thine eyes, and not thy noise, waked me;
Yet I thought thee—
For thou lov'st truth—an angel, at first sight;
But when I saw thou saw'st my heart,
And knew'st my thoughts beyond an angel's art,
When thou knew'st what I dreamt, when thou knew'st when
Excess of joy would wake me, and cam'st then,
I must confess it could not choose but be
Profane to think thee anything but thee.

Coming and staying show'd thee thee,
But rising makes me doubt that now
  Thou art not thou.
That Love is weak where Fear's as strong as he;
'Tis not all spirit pure and brave
If mixture it of Fear, Shame, Honour have.
Perchance as torches, which must ready be,
Men light and put out, so thou deal'st with me.
Thou cam'st to kindle, go'st to come; then I
Will dream that hope again, but else would die.

❨ THE ECSTASY

JOHN DONNE

Where, like a pillow on a bed,
  A pregnant bank swelled up to rest
The violet's reclining head,
  Sat we two, one another's best.
Our hands were firmly cèmented
  With a fast balm, which thence did spring;
Our eye-beams twisted, and did thread
  Our eyes upon one double string;
So to'entergraft our hands, as yet
  Was all the means to make us one, 10
And pictures in our eyes to get
  Was all our propagation.
As 'twixt two equal armies fate
  Suspends uncertain victory,
Our souls, which to advance their state
  Were gone out, hung 'twixt her and me.
And whilst our souls negotiate there,
  We like sepulchral statues lay;
All day, the same our postures were,
  And we said nothing, all the day. 20
If any, so by love refined
  That he soul's language understood,
And by good love were grown all mind,
  Within convenient distance stood,

He, though he knew not which soul spake,
  Because both meant, both spake the same,
Might thence a new concoction take
  And part far purer than he came.
This ecstasy doth unperplex,
  We said, and tell us what we love: 30
We see by this it was not sex,
  We see we saw not what did move;
But as all several souls contain
  Mixture of things, they know not what,
Love these mixed souls doth mix again
  And makes both one, each this and that.
A single violet transplant,
  The strength, the color, and the size,
All which before was poor and scant,
  Redoubles still, and multiplies. 40
When love with one another so
  Interinanimates two souls,
That abler soul, which thence doth flow,
  Defects of loneliness controls.
We then, who are this new soul, know
  Of what we are composed, and made,
For th' atomies of which we grow
  Are souls, whom no change can invade.
But O alas! so long, so far,
  Our bodies why do we forbear? 50
They are ours, though they are not we; we are
  Th' intelligences, they the spheres.
We owe them thanks, because they thus
  Did us, to us, at first convey,
Yielded their forces, sense, to us,
  Nor are dross to us, but allay.
On man heaven's influence works not so,
  But that it first imprints the air;
So soul into the soul may flow,
  Though it to body first repair. 60
As our blood labours to beget
  Spirits, as like souls as it can;
Because such fingers need to knit

That subtle knot, which makes us man;
So must pure lovers' souls descend
T'affections, and to faculties,
Which sense may reach and apprehend,
Else a great prince in prison lies.
To our bodies turn we then, that so
Weak men on love reveal'd may look; 70
Love's mysteries in souls do grow,
But yet the body is his book.
And if some lover, such as we,
Have heard this dialogue of one,
Let him still mark us, he shall see
Small change when we're to bodies gone.

IF POISONOUS MINERALS

JOHN DONNE

If poisonous minerals, and if that tree
Whose fruit threw death on else immortal us,
If lecherous goats, if serpents envious
Cannot be damned, Alas! why should I be?
Why should intent or reason, born in me,
Make sins, else equal, in me more heinous?
And mercy being easy, and glorious
To God, in his stern wrath why threatens he?
But who am I, that dare dispute with thee,
O God? O! of thine only worthy blood,
And my tears, make a heavenly Lethean flood,
And drown in it my sin's black memory;
That thou remember them, some claim as debt,
I think it mercy, if thou wilt forget.

DEATH BE NOT PROUD

JOHN DONNE

Death, be not proud, though some have callèd thee
Mighty and dreadful, for thou art not so;

For, those whom thou think'st thou dost overthrow,
Die not, poor Death, nor yet canst thou kill me.
From rest and sleep, which but thy pictures be,
Much pleasure; then from thee much more must flow;
And soonest our best men with thee do go,
Rest of their bones, and soul's delivery.
Thou art slave to Fate, Chance, kings, and desperate men,
And dost with poison, war, and sickness dwell,
And poppy or charms can make us sleep as well
And better than thy stroke. Why swell'st thou then?
One short sleep past, we wake eternally,
And death shall be no more. Death, thou shalt die!

❨ BATTER MY HEART, THREE PERSONED GOD

JOHN DONNE

Batter my heart, three personed God; for you
As yet but knock, breathe, shine, and seek to mend;
That I may rise and stand, o'erthrow me and bend
Your force to break, blow, burn and make me new.
I, like an usurped town, to another due,
Labour to admit you, but Oh, to no end;
Reason, your viceroy in me, me should defend,
But is captived and proves weak or untrue.
Yet dearly I love you and would be loved fain,
But am betrothed unto your enemy:
Divorce me, untie or break that knot again,
Take me to you, imprison me, for I
Except you enthrall me, never shall be free,
Nor ever chaste, except you ravish me.

❨ A HYMN TO GOD THE FATHER

JOHN DONNE

Wilt thou forgive that sin where I begun,
  Which was my sin, though it were done before?
Wilt thou forgive those sinnes through which I run,

And do run still; though still I do deplore?
When thou hast done, thou hast not done,
For I have more.

Wilt thou forgive that sin which I have won
Others to sin, and made my sin their door?
Wilt thou forgive that sin which I did shun
A year or two; but wallowed in a score?
When thou hast done, thou hast not done,
For I have more.

I have a sin of fear, that, when I have spun
My last thread, I shall perish on the shore;
Swear by thyself that at my death thy Son
Shall shine as he shines now, and heretofore;
And, having done that, thou hast done,
I fear no more.

HOLD BACK THY HOURS, DARK NIGHT

JOHN FLETCHER

Hold back thy hours, dark Night, till we have done;
The Day will come too soon.
Young maids will curse thee, if you steal'st away
And leav'st their losses open to the day.
Stay, stay, and hide
The blushes of the bride.

Stay, gentle Night, and with thy darkness cover
The kisses of her lover.
Stay, and confound her tears and her shrill cryings,
Her weak denials, vows, and often-dyings;
Stay, and hide all:
But help not, though she call.

A DIRGE

JOHN WEBSTER

Call for the robin redbreast and the wren,
Since o'er shady groves they hover,
And with leaves and flowers do cover
The friendless bodies of unburied men.
Call unto his funeral dole
The ant, the field-mouse, and the mole,
To rear him hillocks that shall keep him warm,
And, when gay tombs are robbed, sustain no harm;
But keep the wolf far thence, that's foe to men,
For with his nails he'll dig them up again.

CORINNA'S GOING A-MAYING

ROBERT HERRICK

Get up, get up for shame, the blooming morn
Upon her wings presents the god unshorn.
  See how Aurora throws her fair
  Fresh-quilted colors through the air:
  Get up, sweet slug-a-bed, and see
  The dew bespangling herb and tree.
Each flower has wept and bowèd toward the east
Above an hour since: yet you not dressed;
  Nay! not so much as out of bed?
  When all the birds have matins said
  And sung their thankful hymns, 'tis sin,
  Nay, profanation to keep in,
Whenas a thousand virgins on this day
Spring, sooner than the lark, to fetch in May.

Rise and put on your foliage, and be seen
To come forth like the springtime, fresh and green,
  And sweet as Flora. Take no care
  For jewels for your gown or hair;
  Fear not, the leaves will strew
  Gems in abundance upon you; 20

Besides, the childhood of the day has kept,
Against you come, some orient pearls unwept;
  Come and receive them while the light
  Hangs on the dew-locks of the night,
  And Titan on the eastern hill
  Retires himself, or else stands still
Till you come forth. Wash, dress, be brief in praying:
Few beads are best when once we go a-Maying.

Come, my Corinna, come; and coming, mark
How each field turns a street, each street a park 30
  Made green and trimmed with trees; see how
  Devotion gives each house a bough
  Or branch; each porch, each door, ere this,
  An ark, a tabernacle is,
Made up of white-thorn neatly interwove,
As if here were those cooler shades of love.
  Can such delights be in the street
  And open fields, and we not see't?
  Come, we'll abroad, and let's obey
  The proclamation made for May, 40
And sin no more, as we have done, by staying;
But, my Corinna, come, let's go a-Maying.

There's not a budding boy or girl this day
But is got up, and gone to bring in May.
  A deal of youth, ere this, is come
  Back, and with white-thorn laden, home.
  Some have dispatched their cakes and cream
  Before that we have left to dream:
And some have wept, and wooed, and plighted troth,
And chose their priest, ere we can cast off sloth: 50
  Many a green-gown has been given;
  Many a kiss, both odd and even:
  Many a glance too has been sent
  From out the eye, love's firmament;
Many a jest told of the keys betraying
This night, and locks picked, yet we're not a-Maying.

Come, let us go while we are in our prime;
And take the harmless folly of the time.
We shall grow old apace, and die
Before we know our liberty. 60
Our life is short, and our days run
As fast away as does the sun;
And, as a vapor or a drop of rain,
Once lost, can ne'er be found again,
So when or you or I are made
A fable, song, or fleeting shade,
All love, all liking, all delight
Lies drowned with us in endless night.
Then while time serves, and we are but decaying,
Come, my Corinna, come let's go a-Maying.

¶ TO ELECTRA

ROBERT HERRICK

I dare not ask a kiss;
I dare not beg a smile;
Lest having that or this,
I might grow proud the while.

No, no, the utmost share
Of my desire shall be
Only to kiss that air
That lately kissèd thee.

¶ AN ODE FOR BEN JONSON

ROBERT HERRICK

Ah, Ben!
Say how or when
Shall we, thy guests,
Meet at those lyric feasts
Made at the Sun,

The Dog, the Triple Tun?
Where we such clusters had
As made us nobly wild, not mad;
And yet each verse of thine
Out-did the meat, out-did the frolic wine.

My Ben!
Or come again,
Or send to us
Thy wit's great overplus;
But teach us yet
Wisely to husband it,
Lest we that talent spend;
And, having once brought to an end
That precious stock, the store
Of such a wit the world should have no more.

THE NIGHT-PIECE: TO JULIA

ROBERT HERRICK

Her eyes the glow worm lend thee;
The shooting stars attend thee;
And the elves also,
Whose little eyes glow,
Like the sparks of fire, befriend thee.

No will-o'-the-wisp mislight thee;
Nor snake, or slow worm bite thee.
But on, on thy way,
Not making a stay,
Since ghost there's none to affright thee.

Let not the dark thee cumber;
What though the moon does slumber?
The stars of the night
Will lend thee their light,
Like tapers clear without number.

Then, Julia, let me woo thee,
Thus, thus to come unto me.
  And when I shall meet
  Thy silvery feet,
My soul I'll pour into thee.

UPON JULIA'S CLOTHES

ROBERT HERRICK

Whenas in silks my Julia goes
Then, then (methinks) how sweetly flows
That liquefaction of her clothes.

Next, when I cast mine eyes and see
That brave vibration each way free;
O how that glittering taketh me!

DELIGHT IN DISORDER

ROBERT HERRICK

A sweet disorder in the dress
Kindles in clothes a wantonness:
A lawn about the shoulders thrown
Into a fine distraction,
An erring lace, which here and there
Enthralls the crimson stomacher,
A cuff neglectful, and thereby
Ribbands to flow confusedly,
A winning wave (deserving note)
In the tempestuous petticoat,
A careless shoe-string, in whose tie
I see a wild civility,
Do more bewitch me, than when art
Is too precise in every part.

TO DIANEME

ROBERT HERRICK

Sweet, be not proud of those two eyes,
Which, star-like, sparkle in their skies;
Nor be you proud that you can see
Al. hearts your captives, yours yet free;
Be you not proud of that rich hair,
Which wantons with the love-sick air:
Whenas that ruby which you wear,
Sunk from the tip of your soft ear,
Will last to be a precious stone,
When all your world of beauty's gone.

THE COLLAR

GEORGE HERBERT

I struck the board, and cried, "No more;
I will abroad."
What, shall I ever sigh and pine?
My lines and life are free; free as the road,
Loose as the wind, as large as store.
Shall I be still in suit?
Have I no harvest but a thorn
To let me blood, and not restore
What I have lost with cordial fruit?
Sure there was wine 10
Before my sighs did dry it; there was corn
Before my tears did drown it;
Is the year only lost to me?
Have I no bays to crown it,
No flowers, no garlands gay? all blasted,
All wasted?
Not so, my heart; but there is fruit,
And thou hast hands.
Recover all thy sigh-blown age
On double pleasures; leave thy cold dispute 20

Of what is fit and not; forsake thy cage,
Thy rope of sands
Which petty thoughts have made, and made to thee
Good cable, to enforce and draw,
And be thy law,
While thou didst wink and wouldst not see.
Away! take heed;
I will abroad.
Call in thy death's-head there, tie up thy fears;
He that forbears 30
To suit and serve his need
Deserves his load.
But as I raved and grew more fierce and wild
At every word,
Methought I heard one calling, "Child";
And I replied, "My Lord."

THE PULLEY

GEORGE HERBERT

When God at first made man,
Having a glass of blessings standing by,
"Let us," said He, "pour on him all we can;
Let the world's riches, which dispersèd lie,
Contract into a span."

So strength first made a way,
Then beauty flowed, then wisdom, honor, pleasure;
When almost all was out, God made a stay,
Perceiving that, alone of all His treasure,
Rest in the bottom lay.

"For if I should," said He,
"Bestow this jewel also on My creature,
He would adore My gifts instead of Me,
And rest in Nature, not the God of Nature;
So both should losers be.

"Yet let him keep the rest,
But keep them with repining restlessness;
Let him be rich and weary, that at least
If goodness lead him not, yet weariness
May toss him to My breast."

LIFE

GEORGE HERBERT

I made a posie, while the day ran by:
Here will I smell my remnant out, and tie
My life within this band.
But time did beckon to the flowers, and they
By noon most cunningly did steal away
And wither'd in my hand.

My hand was next to them, and then my heart:
I took, without more thinking, in good part
Time's gentle admonition:
Who did so sweetly death's sad taste convey,
Making my mind to smell my fatal day,
Yet sug'ring the suspicion.

Farewell, dear flowers, sweetly your time ye spent,
Fit, while ye liv'd, for smell or ornament,
And after death for cures.
I follow straight without complaints or grief,
Since, if my scent be good, I care not if
It be as short as yours.

LOVE

GEORGE HERBERT

Love bade me welcome; yet my soul drew back,
Guilty of dust and sin.
But quick-eyed Love, observing me grow slack
From my first entrance in,

Drew nearer to me, sweetly questioning
    If I lacked anything.

"A guest," I answered, "worth to be here."
    Love said, "You shall be he."
"I, the unkind, ungrateful? Ah, my dear,
    I cannot look on Thee."
Love took my hand, and smiling, did reply,
    "Who made the eyes but I?"

"Truth, Lord, but I have marred them: let my shame
    Go where it doth deserve."
"And know you not," says Love, "who bore the blame?"
    "My dear, then I will serve."
"You must sit down," says Love, "and taste my meat."
    So I did sit and eat.

❡ CHURCH MONUMENTS

GEORGE HERBERT

While that my soul repairs to her devotion,
Here I intomb my flesh, that it betimes
May take acquaintance of this heap of dust;
To which the blast of death's incessant motion,
Fed with the exhalation of our crimes,
Drives all at last. Therefore I gladly trust

My body to this school, that it may learn
To spell his elements, and find his birth
Written in dusty heraldry and lines;
Which dissolution sure doth best discern,
Comparing dust with dust, and earth with earth.
These laugh at jet, and marble put for signs,

To sever the good fellowship of dust,
And spoil the meeting. What shall point out them,
When they shall bow, and kneel, and fall down flat
To kiss those heaps, which now they have in trust?

Dear flesh, while I do pray, learn here thy stem
And true descent; that when thou shalt grow fat,

And wanton in thy cravings, thou mayst know,
That flesh is but the glass, which holds the dust
That measures all our time; which also shall
Be crumbled into dust. Mark, here below,
How tame those ashes are, how free from lust,
That thou mayst fit thyself against thy fall.

SONG

THOMAS CAREW

Ask me no more where Jove bestows,
When June is past, the fading rose;
For in your beauty's orient deep
These flowers, as in their causes, sleep.

Ask me no more whither doth stray
The golden atoms of the day;
For in pure love heaven did prepare
Those powders to enrich your hair.

Ask me no more whither doth haste
The nightingale when May is past;
For in your sweet dividing[1] throat
She winters, and keeps warm her note.

Ask me no more where those stars light
That downwards fall in dead of night;
For in your eyes they sit, and there
Fixèd become as in their sphere.

Ask me no more if east or west
The phoenix builds her spicy nest;
For unto you at last she flies,
And in your fragrant bosom dies.

[1] dividing—*singing*

PERSUASIONS TO JOY: A SONG

THOMAS CAREW

If the quick spirits in your eye
Now languish and anon must die;
If every sweet and every grace
Must fly from that forsaken face;
  Then, Celia, let us reap our joys
  Ere Time such goodly fruit destroys.

Or if that golden fleece must grow
For ever free from agèd snow;
If those bright suns must know no shade,
Nor your fresh beauties ever fade;
  Then fear not, Celia, to bestow
  What, still being gather'd, still must grow.

Thus either Time his sickle brings
In vain, or else in vain his wings.

DEATH THE LEVELLER

JAMES SHIRLEY

The glories of our blood and state
  Are shadows, not substantial things;
There is no armour against Fate;
  Death lays his icy hand on kings:
      Sceptre and crown
      Must tumble down,
And in the dust be equal made
With the poor crookèd scythe and spade.

Some men with swords may reap the field,
  And plant fresh laurels where they kill;
But their strong nerves at last must yield;
  They tame but one another still:
      Early or late
      They stoop to fate,

And must give up their murmuring breath
When they, pale captives, creep to death.

The garlands wither on your brow;
Then boast no more your mighty deeds!
Upon Death's purple altar now
See where the victor-victim bleeds.
Your heads must come
To the cold tomb:
Only the actions of the just
Smell sweet and blossom in their dust.

GO, LOVELY ROSE

EDMUND WALLER

Go, lovely Rose—
Tell her that wastes her time and me
That now she knows,
When I resemble her to thee,
How sweet and fair she seems to be.

Tell her that's young,
And shuns to have her graces spied,
That hadst thou sprung
In deserts where no men abide,
Thou must have uncommended died.

Small is the worth
Of beauty from the light retired:
Bid her come forth,
Suffer herself to be desired,
And not blush so to be admired.

Then die—that she
The common fate of all things rare
May read in thee:
How small a part of time they share
That are so wondrous sweet and fair.

❡ HOW SOON HATH TIME

JOHN MILTON

How soon hath Time the subtle thief of youth,
Stoln on his wing my three and twentieth year!
My hasting days fly on with full career,
But my late spring no bud or blossom shew'th.
Perhaps my semblance might deceive the truth,
That I to manhood am arriv'd so near,
And inward ripeness doth much less appear,
That some more timely-happy spirits indu'th.
Yet be it less or more, or soon or slow,
It shall be still in strictest measure ev'n,
To that same lot, however mean, or high,
Toward which Time leads me, and the will of Heav'n;
All is, if I have grace to use it so,
As ever in my great task Master's eye.

❡ ON THE LATE MASSACRE IN PIEDMONT

JOHN MILTON

Avenge O Lord thy slaughter'd Saints, whose bones
Lie scatter'd on the Alpine mountains cold,
Ev'n them who kept thy truth so pure of old
When all our Fathers worship't Stocks and Stones,
Forget not: in thy book record their groans
Who were thy Sheep and in their ancient Fold
Slain by the bloody *Piedmontese* that roll'd
Mother with Infant down the Rocks. Their moans
The Vales redoubl'd to the Hills, and they
To Heav'n. Their martyr'd blood and ashes sow
O'er all th' *Italian* fields where still doth sway
The triple Tyrant: that from these may grow
A hundred-fold, who having learnt thy way
Early may fly the *Babylonian* woe.

TO CYRIACK SKINNER

JOHN MILTON

Cyriack, this three years' day these eyes, though clear
To outward view, of blemish or of spot,
Bereft of light, their seeing have forgot;
Nor to their idle orbs doth sight appear
Of sun or moon or star throughout the year,
Or man or woman. Yet I argue not
Against Heaven's hand or will, nor bate a jot
Of heart or hope, but still bear up and steer
Right onward. What supports me, dost thou ask?
The conscience, friend, to have lost them overplied
In liberty's defence, my noble task,
Of which all Europe talks from side to side.
This thought might lead me through the world's vain mask
Content, though blind, had I no better guide.

ON HIS BLINDNESS

JOHN MILTON

When I consider how my light is spent
Ere half my days in this dark world and wide,
And that one talent which is death to hide
Lodged with me useless, though my soul more bent
To serve therewith my Maker, and present
My true account, lest he returning chide,
"Doth God exact day-labor, light denied?"
I fondly ask. But Patience, to prevent
That murmur, soon replies, "God doth not need
Either man's work or his own gifts. Who best
Bear his mild yoke, they serve him best. His state
Is kingly: thousands at his bidding speed,
And post o'er land and ocean without rest;
They also serve who only stand and wait."

LYCIDAS

JOHN MILTON

Yet once more, O ye laurels, and once more
Ye myrtles brown, with ivy never-sear,
I come to pluck your berries harsh and crude,
And with forc'd fingers rude,
Shatter your leaves before the mellowing year.
Bitter constraint and sad occasion dear
Compels me to disturb your season due:
For Lycidas is dead, dead ere his prime,
Young Lycidas, and hath not left his peer.
Who would not sing for Lycidas? he knew 10
Himself to sing, and build the lofty rhyme.
He must not float upon his watery bier
Unwept, and welter to the parching wind,
Without the meed of some melodious tear.
  Begin then, Sisters of the sacred well
That from beneath the seat of Jove doth spring;
Begin, and somewhat loudly sweep the string;
Hence with denial vain and coy excuse:
So may some gentle Muse
With lucky words favor *my* destined urn; 20
And as he passes, turn
And bid fair peace be to my sable shroud.
  For we were nursed upon the self-same hill,
Fed the same flock by fountain, shade, and rill.
Together both, ere the high lawns appeared
Under the opening eye-lids of the Morn,
We drove a-field, and both together heard
What time the gray-fly winds her sultry horn,
Battening our flocks with the fresh dews of night;
Oft till the star, that rose at evening bright, 30
Toward heaven's descent had sloped his westering wheel.
Meanwhile the rural ditties were not mute;
Tempered to the oaten flute,
Rough Satyrs danced, and Fauns with cloven heel
From the glad sound would not be absent long;

And old Damoetas loved to hear our song.
  But, O! the heavy change, now thou art gone,
Now thou art gone, and never must return!
Thee, Shepherd, thee the woods and desert caves,
With wild thyme and the gadding vine o'ergrown, 40
And all their echoes, mourn:
The willows and the hazel copses green
Shall now no more be seen
Fanning their joyous leaves to thy soft lays.
As killing as the canker to the rose,
Or taint-worm to the weanling herds that graze,
Or frost to flowers, that their gay wardrobe wear
When first the white-thorn blows;
Such, Lycidas, thy loss to shepherd's ear.
  Where were ye, Nymphs, when the remorseless deep 50
Closed o'er the head of your loved Lycidas?
For neither were ye playing on the steep
Where your old bards, the famous Druids, lie,
Nor on the shaggy top of Mona high,
Nor yet where Deva spreads her wizard stream.
Ay me! I fondly dream
"Had ye been there,"—for what could that have done?
What could the Muse herself that Orpheus bore,
The Muse herself, for her enchanting son,
Whom universal nature did lament, 60
When by the rout that made the hideous roar
His gory visage down the stream was sent,
Down the swift Hebrus to the Lesbian shore?
  Alas! what boots it with uncessant care
To tend the homely, slighted, shepherd's trade
And strictly meditate the thankless Muse?
Were it not better done, as others use,
To sport with Amaryllis in the shade,
Or with the tangles of Neaera's hair?
Fame is the spur that the clear spirit doth raise 70
(That last infirmity of noble mind)
To scorn delights, and live laborious days;
But the fair guerdon when we hope to find,
And think to burst out into sudden blaze,

Comes the blind Fury with the abhorred shears
And slits the thin-spun life. "But not the praise,"
Phoebus replied, and touched my trembling ears:
"Fame is no plant that grows on mortal soil,
Nor in the glistering foil
Set off to the world, nor in broad rumor lies: 80
But lives and spreads aloft by those pure eyes
And perfect witness of all-judging Jove;
As he pronounces lastly on each deed,
Of so much fame in heaven expect thy meed."
  O fountain Arethuse, and thou honored flood,
Smooth-sliding Mincius, crowned with vocal reeds,
That strain I heard was of a higher mood.
But now my oat proceeds,
And listens to the herald of the sea
That came in Neptune's plea. 90
He asked the waves, and asked the felon winds,
What hard mishap hath doomed this gentle swain?
And questioned every gust of rugged wings
That blows from off each beakèd promontory.
They knew not of his story;
And sage Hippotades their answer brings,
That not a blast was from his dungeon strayed:
The air was calm, and on the level brine
Sleek Panope with all her sisters played.
It was that fatal and perfidious bark, 100
Built in the eclipse, and rigged with curses dark,
That sunk so low that sacred head of thine.
  Next, Camus, reverend Sire, went footing slow,
His mantle hairy, and his bonnet sedge,
Inwrought with figures dim, and on the edge
Like to that sanguine flower inscribed with woe.
"Ah! who hath reft," quoth he, "my dearest pledge?"
Last came, and last did go,
The Pilot of the Galilean Lake;
Two massy keys he bore of metals twain 110
(The golden opes, the iron shuts amain).
He shook his mitred locks, and stern bespake:—
"How well could I have spared for thee, young swain,

Enow of such as, for their bellies' sake,
Creep, and intrude, and climb into the fold!
Of other care they little reckoning make
Than how to scramble at the shearers' feast,
And shove away the worthy bidden guest.
Blind mouths! that scarce themselves know how to hold
A sheephook, or have learnt aught else the least 120
That to the faithful Herdman's art belongs!
What recks it them? What need they? They are sped;
And, when they list, their lean and flashy songs
Grate on their scrannel pipes of wretched straw;
The hungry sheep look up, and are not fed,
But, swoln with wind and the rank mist they draw,
Rot inwardly, and foul contagion spread;
Besides what the grim Wolf with privy paw
Daily devours apace, and nothing said.
But that two-handed engine at the door 130
Stands ready to smite once, and smite no more."
  Return, Alpheus; the dread voice is past
That shrunk thy streams; return, Sicilian Muse,
And call the vales, and bid them hither cast
Their bells and flowerets of a thousand hues.
Ye valleys low, where the mild whispers use
Of shades, and wanton winds, and gushing brooks,
On whose fresh lap the swart star sparely looks,
Throw hither all your quaint enamelled eyes,
That on the green turf sucked the honeyed showers, 140
And purple all the ground with vernal flowers.
Bring the rathe primrose that forsaken dies,
The tufted crow-toe, and pale jessamine,
The white pink, and the pansy freaked with jet,
The glowing violet,
The musk-rose, and the well-attired woodbine,
With cowslips wan that hang the pensive head,
And every flower that sad embroidery wears;
Bid amaranthus all his beauty shed,
And daffodillies fill their cups with tears, 150
To strew the laureate hearse where Lycid lies.
For so, to interpose a little ease,

Let our frail thoughts dally with false surmise:
Ay me! whilst thee the shores and sounding seas
Wash far away, where'er thy bones are hurled;
Whether beyond the stormy Hebrides,
Where thou perhaps under the whelming tide
Visit'st the bottom of the monstrous world;
Or whether thou, to our moist vows denied,
Sleep'st by the fable of Bellerus old, 160
Where the great Vision of the guarded mount
Looks toward Namancos and Bayona's hold.
Look homeward, Angel, now, and melt with ruth;
And, O ye dolphins, waft the hapless youth.
Weep no more, woeful shepherds, weep no more,
For Lycidas, your sorrow, is not dead,
Sunk though he be beneath the watery floor;
So sinks the day-star in the ocean bed,
And yet anon repairs his drooping head,
And tricks his beams, and with new-spangled ore 170
Flames in the forehead of the morning sky:
So Lycidas sunk low, but mounted high
Through the dear might of Him that walked the waves;
Where, other groves and other streams along,
With nectar pure his oozy locks he laves,
And hears the unexpressive nuptial song
In the blest kingdoms meek of joy and love.
There entertain him all the saints above
In solemn troops, and sweet societies,
That sing, and singing in their glory move, 180
And wipe the tears for ever from his eyes.
Now, Lycidas, the shepherds weep no more;
Henceforth thou art the Genius of the shore
In thy large recompense, and shalt be good
To all that wander in that perilous flood.
Thus sang the uncouth swain to the oaks and rills,
While the still morn went out with sandals gray;
He touched the tender tops of various quills,
With eager thought warbling his Doric lay:
And now the sun had stretched out all the hills, 190
And now was dropt into the western bay.

At last he rose, and twitched his mantle blue:
Tomorrow to fresh woods, and pastures new.

LIGHT

JOHN MILTON

Hail holy light, offspring of Heav'n first-born,
Or of th' Eternal Coeternal beam
May I express thee unblam'd? since God is light,
And never but in unapproachèd light
Dwelt from Eternity, dwelt then in thee,
Bright effluence of bright essence increate.
Or hearest thou rather pure Ethereal stream,
Whose Fountain who shall tell? before the Sun,
Before the Heavens thou wert, and at the voice
Of God, as with a Mantle didst invest 10
The rising world of water dark and deep,
Won from the void and formless infinite.
Thee I re-visit now with bolder wing,
Escaped the *Stygian Pool,* thought long detained
In that obscure sojourn, while in my flight
Through utter and through middle darkness borne
With other notes then to th' *Orphean* Lyre
I sung of *Chaos* and *Eternal Night,*
Taught by the heavenly Muse to venture down
The dark descent, and up to reascend, 20
Though hard and rare: thee I revisit safe,
And feel thy sovereign vital Lamp; but thou
Revisitest not these eyes, that roll in vain
To find thy piercing ray, and find no dawn;
So thick a drop serene hath quenched their Orbs,
Or dim suffusion veiled. Yet not the more
Cease I to wander where the Muses haunt
Clear Spring, or shady Grove, or Sunny Hill,
Smit with the love of sacred song; but chief
Thee *Zion* and the flowery Brooks beneath 30
That wash thy hallowed feet, and warbling flow,
Nightly I visit: nor sometimes forget

Those other two equalled with me in Fate,
So were I equalled with them in renown,
Blind *Thamyris* and blind *Maeonides,*
And *Tiresias* and *Phineus* Prophets old.
Then feed on thoughts, that voluntary move
Harmonious numbers; as the wakeful Bird
Sings darkling, and in shadiest Covert hid
Tunes her nocturnal Note. Thus with the Year 40
Seasons return, but not to me returns
Day, or the sweet approach of Even or Morn,
Or sight of vernal bloom, or Summer's Rose,
Or flocks, or herds, or human face divine;
But cloud instead, and ever-during dark
Surrounds me, from the cheerful ways of men
Cut off, and for the Book of knowledge fair
Presented, with a Universal blank
Of Nature's works to me expung'd and raised,
And wisdom at one entrance quite shut out. 50
So much the rather thou Celestial light
Shine inward, and the mind through all her powers
Irradiate, there plant eyes, all mist from thence
Purge and disperse, that I may see and tell
Of things invisible to mortal sight.

From *Paradise Lost*

WHY SO PALE AND WAN?

SIR JOHN SUCKLING

Why so pale and wan, fond lover?
  Prithee, why so pale?
Will, when looking well can't move her,
  Looking ill prevail?
  Prithee, why so pale?

Why so dull and mute, young sinner?
  Prithee, why so mute?
Will, when speaking well can't win her,

Saying nothing do't?
Prithee, why so mute?

Quit, quit for shame, this will not move,
This cannot take her;
If of herself she will not love,
Nothing can make her.
The devil take her.

SONG

SIR JOHN SUCKLING

No, no, fair heretic, it needs must be
But an ill love in me
And worse for thee;
For were it in my power
To love thee now this hour
More than I did the last,
I would then so fall
I might not love at all.
Love that can flow, and can admit increase,
Admits as well an ebb, and may grow less.

True love is still the same. The torrid zones,
And those more frigid ones,
It must not know:
For love grown cold or hot
Is lust, or friendship, not
The thing we have.
For that's a flame would die
Held down, or up too high.
Then think I love more than I can express,
And would love more could I but love thee less.

(UPON THE BODY OF OUR BLESSED LORD, NAKED AND BLOODY

RICHARD CRASHAW

They have left thee naked, Lord; O that they had!
This garment too I would they had denied.

Thee with thyself they have too richly clad,
Opening the purple wardrobe in thy side.

O never could there be garment too good
For thee to wear, but this, of thine own blood.

(from THE FLAMING HEART UPON THE BOOK AND PICTURE OF THE SERAPHICAL SAINT TERESA
(as she is usually expressed with a seraphine beside her)

RICHARD CRASHAW

Live here, great heart, and love and die and kill,
And bleed and wound, and yield and conquer still.
Let this immortal life, where'er it comes,
Walk in a crowd of loves and martyrdoms.
Let mystic deaths wait on 't, and wise souls be
The love-slain witnesses of this life of thee.
O sweet incendiary! show here thy art,
Upon this carcass of a hard, cold heart,
Let all thy scatter'd shafts of light, that play
Among the leaves of thy large books of day,
Combin'd against this breast, at once break in
And take away from me my self and sin;
This gracious robbery shall thy bounty be,
And my best fortunes such fair spoils of me.
O thou undaunted daughter of desires!
By all thy dower of lights and fires;
By all the eagle in thee, all the dove;
By all thy lives and deaths of love:

By thy large draugths of intellectual day,
And by thy thirsts of love more large than they;
By all thy brim-fill'd bowls of fierce desire,
By thy last morning's draught of liquid fire;
By the full kingdom of that final kiss
That seiz'd thy parting soul, and sealed thee his;
By all the heav'ns thou hast in him,
Fair sister of the seraphim!
By all of him we have in thee;
Leave nothing of myself in me.
Let me so read thy life, that I
Unto all life of mine may die.

THE GARDEN

ANDREW MARVELL

How vainly men themselves amaze
To win the palm, the oak, or bays,
And their incessant labors see
Crown'd from some single herb or tree,
Whose short and narrowed vergèd shade
Does prudently their toils upbraid;
While all flow'rs and all trees do close
To weave the garlands of repose.

Fair Quiet, have I found thee here,
And Innocence, thy sister dear! 10
Mistaken long, I sought you then
In busy companies of men.
Your sacred plants, if here below,
Only among the plants will grow.
Society is all but rude,
To this delicious solitude.

No white nor red was ever seen
So am'rous as this lovely green.
Fond lovers, cruel as their flame,
Cut in these trees their mistress' name; 20

Little, Alas, they know, or heed,
How far these beauties hers exceed!
Fair trees, where s'eer your barks I wound
No name shall but your own be found.

When we have run our passion's heat,
Love hither makes his best retreat.
The gods that mortal beauty chase,
Still in a tree did end their race:
Apollo hunted Daphne so,
Only that she might laurel grow; 30
And Pan did after Syrinx speed,
Not as a nymph, but for a reed.

What wondrous life is this I lead!
Ripe apples drop about my head;
The luscious clusters of the vine
Upon my mouth do crush their wine;
The nectarine, and curious peach,
Into my hands themselves do reach;
Stumbling on melons, as I pass,
Ensnared with flowers, I fall on grass. 40

Meanwhile the mind, from pleasure less,
Withdraws into its happiness;
The mind, that ocean where each kind
Does straight its own resemblance find,
Yet it creates, transcending these,
Far other worlds and other seas,
Annihilating all that's made
To a green thought in a green shade.

Here at the fountain's sliding foot,
Or at some fruit tree's mossy root, 50
Casting the body's vest aside,
My soul into the boughs does glide;
There, like a bird, it sits and sings,
Then whets and combs its silver wings,

And till prepared for longer flight,
Waves in its plumes the various light.

Such was that happy garden-state,
While man there walked without a mate;
After a place so pure and sweet,
What other help could yet be meet! 60
But 'twas beyond a mortal's share
To wander solitary there:
Two paradises 'twere, in one,
To live in paradise alone.

How well the skilful gardner drew
Of flowers and herbs this dial new,
Where, from above, the milder sun
Does through a fragrant zodiac run;
And as it works, th' industrious bee
Computes its time as well as we. 70
How could such sweet and wholesome hours
Be reckoned but with herbs and flowers!

even tho a lyric poem — DRAMATIC — 2 characters PERSUADE
TONE - facetious & whimsical no maintain this tone throughout poem

⁋ TO HIS COY MISTRESS

ANDREW MARVELL

TONE - change flesh, body, pleasure
Enjoy of this moment

hyperbole
farfetched imagery not persuasive

Had we but world enough, and time,
This coyness, lady, were no crime.
We would sit down, and think which way
To walk, and pass our long love's day.
Thou by the Indian Ganges' side
Should'st rubies find: I by the tide
Of Humber would complain. I would
Love you ten years before the Flood,
And you should, if you please, refuse
Till the conversion of the Jews. 10
My vegetable love should grow
Vaster than empires, and more slow.
An hundred years should go to praise
Thine eyes, and on thy forehead gaze:

not Christian reject immortality of soul glorifies body

POEM - NOT NECESSARILY MARVELL'S philosophy
think of her mainly as bed partner
no mention - rational part — weaken poem
sees life in phys. pleasures carpe diem

Two hundred to adore each breast:
But thirty thousand to the rest;
An age at least to every part,
And the last age should show your heart.
For, lady, you deserve this state,
Nor would I love at lower rate. 20
But at my back I always hear
Time's wingèd chariot hurrying near;
And yonder all before us lie
Deserts of vast eternity.
Thy beauty shall no more be found,
Nor in thy marble vault shall sound
My echoing song; then worms shall try
That long preserved virginity,
And your quaint honor turn to dust,
And into ashes all my lust. 30
The grave's a fine and private place,
But none, I think, do there embrace.
Now therefore, while the youthful hue
Sits on thy skin like morning dew,
And while thy willing soul transpires
At every pore with instant fires,
Now let us sport us while we may;
And now, like am'rous birds of prey,
Rather at once our time devour,
Than languish in his slow-chapped power. 40
Let us roll all our strength, and all
Our sweetness, up into one ball;
And tear our pleasures with rough strife
Thorough the iron gates of life.
Thus, though we cannot make our sun
Stand still, yet we will make him run.

BERMUDAS

ANDREW MARVELL

Where the remote Bermudas ride
In th' ocean's bosom unespy'd,

From a small boat that rowed along,
The list'ning winds receiv'd this song:

"What should we do but sing His praise,
That led us through the watery maze,
Unto an isle so long unknown,
And yet far kinder than our own?
Where He the huge sea-monsters wracks,
That lift the deep upon their backs. 10
He lands us on a grassy stage,
Safe from the storms, and prelate's rage.
He gave us this eternal spring,
Which here enamels everything,
And sends the fowls to us in care,
On daily visits through the air.
He hangs in shades the orange bright,
Like golden lamps in a green night,
And does in the pomegranates close
Jewels more rich than Ormus shows. 20
He makes the figs our mouths to meet,
And throws the melons at our feet.
But apples plants of such a price,
No tree could ever bear them twice.
With cedars, chosen by His hand,
From Lebanon, he stores the land,
And makes the hollow seas, that roar
Proclaim the ambergris on shore.
He cast (of which we rather boast)
The Gospel's pearl upon our coast 30
And in these rocks for us did frame
A temple, where to sound His name.
Oh let our voice His praise exalt,
Till it arrive at Heaven's vault,
Which thence (perhaps) rebounding, may
Echo beyond the Mexique Bay."

Thus sung they, in the English boat,
An holy and a cheerful note;

And all the way, to guide their chime,
With falling oars they kept the time. 40

⁋ THE RETREAT

HENRY VAUGHAN

Happy those early days, when I
Shin'd in my angel-infancy!
Before I understood this place
Appointed for my second race,
Or taught my soul to fancy aught
But a white, celestial thought;
When yet I had not walkt above
A mile or two from my first love,
And looking back (at that short space)
Could see a glimpse of His bright face;
When on some gilded cloud, or flower,
My gazing soul would dwell an hour,
And in those weaker glories spy
Some shadows of eternity;
Before I taught my tongue to wound
My conscious with a sinful sound,
Or had the black art to dispense
A sev'ral sin to ev'ry sense,
But felt through all this fleshly dress
Bright shoots of everlastingness.
O how I long to travel back,
And tread again that ancient track!
That I might once more reach that plain,
Where first I left my glorious train,
From whence th' enlightened spirit sees
That shady City of Palm Trees;
But, ah! my soul with too much stay
Is drunk, and staggers in the way:
Some men a forward motion love,
But I by backward steps would move,
And when this dust falls to the urn,
In that state I came return.

THE NIGHT

HENRY VAUGHAN

John iii. 2

Through that pure virgin-shrine,
That sacred veil drawn o'er thy glorious noon,
That men might look and live, as glow-worms shine,
And face the moon,
Wise Nicodemus saw such light
As made him know his God by night.

Most blest believer he!
Who in that land of darkness and blind eyes
Thy long-expected healing wings could see
When thou didst rise, 10
And what can never more be done,
Did at midnight speak with the Sun!

Oh, who will tell me where
He found thee at that dead and silent hour!
What hallowed solitary ground did bear
So rare a flower,
Within whose sacred leaves did lie
The fullness of the deity.

No mercy-seat of gold,
No dead and dusty cherub, nor carved stone, 20
But his own living works did my Lord hold
And lodge alone,
Where trees and herbs did watch and peep
And wonder, while the Jews did sleep.

Dear night! this world's defeat;
The stop to busy fools; care's check and curb;
The day of spirits; my soul's calm retreat
Which none disturb;
Christ's progress, and his prayer time;
The hours to which high heaven doth chime; 30

God's silent, searching flight;
When my Lord's head is filled with dew, and all
His locks are wet with the clear drops of night;
His still, soft call;
His knocking time; the soul's dumb watch,
When spirits their fair kindred catch.

Were all my loud, evil days
Calm and unhaunted as is thy dark tent,
Whose peace but by some angel's wing or voice
Is seldom rent, 40
Then I in heaven all the long year
Would keep, and never wander here.

But living where the sun
Doth all things wake, and where all mix and tire
Themselves and others, I consent and run
To ev'ry mire,
And by this world's ill-guiding light,
Err more than I can do by night.

There is in God (some say)
A deep, but dazzling darkness; as men here 50
Say it is late and dusky, because they
See not all clear.
O for that night! where I in him
Might live invisible and dim.

¶ TO THE MEMORY OF MR. OLDHAM

JOHN DRYDEN

Farewell, too little and too lately known,
Whom I began to think and call my own:
For sure our souls were near allied, and thine
Cast in the same poetic mold with mine.
One common note on either lyre did strike,

And knaves and fools we both abhorred alike.
To the same goal did both our studies drive:
The last set out the soonest did arrive.
Thus Nisus fell upon the slippery place,
Whilst his young friend performed and won the race.
O early ripe! to thy abundant store
What could advancing age have added more?
It might (what nature never gives the young)
Have taught the numbers of thy native tongue.
But satire needs not those, and wit will shine
Through the harsh cadence of a rugged line.
A noble error, and but seldom made,
When poets are by too much force betray'd.
Thy generous fruits, though gathered ere their prime,
Still showed a quickness; and maturing time
But mellows what we write to the dull sweets of rhyme.
Once more, hail, and farewell! farewell, thou young,
But ah! too short, Marcellus of our tongue!
Thy brows with ivy and with laurels bound;
But Fate and gloomy night encompass thee around.

A SONG FOR ST. CECILIA'S DAY

JOHN DRYDEN

I

From harmony, from heav'nly harmony,
  This universal frame began:
  When Nature underneath a heap
    Of jarring atoms lay,
  And could not heave her head,
The tuneful voice was heard from high:
  "Arise, ye more than dead."
Then cold, and hot, and moist, and dry,
In order to their stations leap,
    And Music's pow'r obey. 10
From harmony, from heav'nly harmony,
  This universal frame began:

From harmony to harmony
Through all the compass of the notes it ran
The diapason closing full in Man.

2

What passion cannot Music raise and quell!
When Jubal struck the corded shell,
His list'ning brethren stood around,
And, wond'ring, on their faces fell
To worship that celestial sound. 20
Less than a god they thought there could not dwell
Within the hollow of that shell
That spoke so sweetly and so well.
What passion cannot Music raise and quell!

3

The Trumpet's loud clangour
Excites us to arms,
With shrill notes of anger,
And mortal alarms.
The double double double beat
Of the thund'ring Drum 30
Cries: "Hark! the foes come;
Charge, charge, 'tis too late to retreat."

4

The soft complaining Flute
In dying notes discovers
The woes of hopeless lovers,
Whose dirge is whisper'd by the warbling Lute.

5

Sharp Violins proclaim
Their jealous pangs, and desperation,
Fury, frantic indignation,

Depth of pains, and height of passion, 40
For the fair, disdainful dame.

6

But oh! what art can teach,
What human voice can reach,
The sacred Organ's praise?
Notes inspiring holy love,
Notes that wing their heav'nly ways
To mend the choirs above.

7

Orpheus could lead the savage race;
And trees unrooted left their place,
Sequacious of the lyre; 50
But bright Cecilia rais'd the wonder high'r:
When to her Organ vocal breath was giv'n,
An angel heard, and straight appear'd,
Mistaking earth for heav'n.

GRAND CHORUS

As from the pow'r of sacred lays
The spheres began to move,
And sung the great Creator's praise
To all the blest above;
So, when the last and dreadful hour
This crumbling pageant shall devour, 60
The Trumpet shall be heard on high,
The dead shall live, the living die,
And Music shall untune the sky.

PROLOGUE TO "THE TEMPEST"

JOHN DRYDEN

As when a tree's cut down, the secret root
Lives under ground, and thence new branches shoot

So from old Shakspeare's honour'd dust, this day
Springs up and buds a new-reviving play:
Shakspeare, who (taught by none) did first impart
To Fletcher wit—to labouring Jonson art.
He, monarch-like, gave those, his subjects, law;
And is that nature which they paint and draw.
Fletcher reach'd that which on his heights did grow,
While Jonson crept, and gather'd all below. 10
This did his love, and this his mirth, digest:
One imitates him most, the other best.
If they have since outwrit all other men,
'T is with the drops which fell from Shakspeare's pen.
The storm, which vanish'd on the neighbouring shore
Was taught by Shakspeare's Tempest first to roar.
That innocence and beauty, which did smile
In Fletcher, grew on this enchanted isle.
But Shakspeare's magic could not copied be;
Within that circle none durst walk but he. 20
I must confess 't was bold, nor would you now
That liberty to vulgar wits allow,
Which works by magic supernatural things:
But Shakspeare's power is sacred as a king's.
Those legends from old priesthood were received,
And he then writ as people then believed.
But if for Shakspeare we your grace implore,
We for our theatre shall want it more:
Who, by our dearth of youths, are forced to employ
One of our women to present a boy; 30
And that's a transformation, you will say,
Exceeding all the magic in the play.
Let none expect, in the last act, to find
Her sex transform'd from man to woman-kind.
Whate'er she was before the play began,
All you shall see of her is perfect man.
Or, if your fancy will be farther led
To find her woman—it must be a-bed.

THE TREE

ANNE, COUNTESS OF WINCHILSEA

Fair tree! for thy delightful shade
'Tis just that some return be made;
Sure, some return is due from me
To thy cool shadows and to thee.
When thou to birds dost shelter give,
Thou music dost from them receive;
If travellers beneath thee stay,
Till storms have worn themselves away,
That time in praising thee they spend,
And thy protecting pow'r commend;
The shepherd, here from scorching freed,
Tunes to thy dancing leaves his reed;
Whilst his lov'd nymph, in thanks, bestows
Her flow'ry chaplets on thy boughs.
Shall I then only silent be,
And no return be made by me?
No: let this wish upon thee wait,
And still to flourish be thy fate;
To future ages may'st thou stand,
Untouch'd by the rash workman's hand,
Till that large stock of sap is spent
Which gives thy summer's ornament;
Til the fierce winds that vainly strive
To shock thy greatness whilst alive,
Shall on thy lifeless hour attend,
Prevent the axe, and grace thy end:
Their scatter'd strength together call,
And to the clouds proclaim thy fall,
Who then their ev'ning dews may spare,
When thou no longer art their care,
But shalt, like ancient heroes, burn,
And some bright hearth be made thy urn.

THE PROGRESS OF BEAUTY

JONATHAN SWIFT

When first Diana leaves her Bed,
Vapors and Steams her Looks disgrace;
A frouzy dirty colour'd red
Sits on her cloudy wrinckled Face.

But by degrees when mounted high
Her artificiall Face appears
Down from her Window in the Sky;
Her spots are gone, her Visage clears.

'Twixt earthly Femals and the Moon
All Parallells exactly run; 10
If Celia should appear too soon
Alas, the Nymph would be undone.

To see her from her Pillow rise
All reeking in a cloudy Steam,
Crackt Lips, foul Teeth, and gummy Eyes,
Poor Strephon, how would he blaspheme!

The Soot or Powder which was wont
To make her Hair look black as Jet,
Falls from her Tresses on her Front,
A mingled Mass of Dirt and Sweat. 20

Three Colours, Black, and Red, and White,
So gracefull in their proper Place,
Remove them to a diff'rent Light
They form a frightfull hideous Face;

For instance: when the Lilly slipps
Into the Precincts of the Rose,
And takes Possession of the Lips,
Leaving the Purple to the Nose.

So Celia went entire to bed,
All her Complexions safe and sound; 30
But when she rose, the black and red,
Though still in Sight, had chang'd their Ground.

The Black, which would not be confin'd,
A more inferior Station seeks,
Leaving the fiery red behind,
And mingles in her muddy Cheeks.

The Paint by Perspiration cracks,
And falls in Rivulets of Sweat,
On either Side you see the Tracks,
While at her Chin the Conflu'ents met. 40

A Skillful Houswife thus her Thumb
With Spittle while she spins, anoints,
And thus the brown Meanders come
In trickling Streams betwixt her Joynts.

But Celia can with ease reduce
By help of Pencil, Paint and Brush
Each Colour to it's Place and Use,
And teach her Cheeks again to blush.

She knows her Early self no more,
But fill'd with Admiration, stands, 50
As Other Painters oft adore
The Workmanship of their own Hands.

Thus after four important Hours
Celia's the Wonder of her Sex;
Say, which among the Heav'nly Pow'rs
Could cause such wonderfull Effects.

Venus, indulgent of her Kind,
Gave Women all their Hearts could wish
When first she taught them where to find
White Lead, and Lusitanian Dish. 60

Love with White lead cements his Wings,
White lead was sent us to repair
Two brightest, brittlest earthly Things,
A Lady's Face, and China ware.

She ventures now to lift the Sash,
The Window is her proper Sphear;
Ah Lovely Nymph, be not too rash,
Nor let the Beaux approach too near.

Take Pattern by your Sister Star,
Delude at once and Bless our Sight; 70
When you are seen, be seen from far,
And chiefly chuse to shine by Night.

In the Pell-mell when passing by,
Keep up the Glasses of your Chair;
Then each transported Fop will cry,
G—d d—m me, Jack, she's wondrous fair!

But Art no longer can prevayl
When the Materialls all are gone;
The best Mechanick Hand must fayl
Where Nothing's left to work upon. 80

Matter, as wise Logicians say,
Cannot without a Form subsist;
And Form, say I, as well as They,
Must fayl if Matter brings no Grist.

And this is fair Diana's Case:
For all Astrologers maintain
Each Night a Bit drops off her Face
When Mortals say she's in her Wain.

While Partridge wisely shews the Cause
Efficient of the Moon's Decay, 90
That Cancer with his pois'nous Claws
Attacks her in the milky Way;

But Gadbury in Art profound
From her pale Cheeks pretends to show
That Swain Endymion is not sound,
Or else that Mercury's her Foe.

But let the Cause be what it will,
In half a Month she looks so thin
That Flamstead can with all his Skill
See but her Forehead and her Chin. 100

Yet as she wasts, she grows discreet,
Till Midnight never shows her Head;
So rotting Celia stroles the Street
When sober Folks are all a-bed.

For sure if this be Luna's Fate,
Poor Celia, but of mortall Race,
In vain expects a longer Date
To the Materialls of Her Face.

When Mercury her Tresses mows,
To think of Oyl and Soot is vain, 110
No Painting can restore a Nose,
Nor will her Teeth return again.

Two Balls of Glass may serve for Eyes,
White Lead can plaister up a Cleft;
But these, alas, are poor Supplyes
If neither Cheeks, nor Lips, be left.

Ye Pow'rs who over Love preside,
Since mortal Beautys drop so soon,
If you would have us well supply'd,
Send us new Nymphs with each new Moon. 120

❡ THE UNIVERSAL PRAYER

Deo Opt. Max.

ALEXANDER POPE

Father of All! in every Age,
  In every Clime adored,
By Saint, by Savage, and by Sage,
  Jehovah, Jove, or Lord!

Thou Great First Cause, least understood:
  Who all my Sense confined
To know but this, that Thou art Good,
  And that myself am blind;

Yet gave me, in this dark Estate,
  To see the Good from Ill; 10
And binding Nature fast in Fate,
  Left free the Human Will.

What Conscience dictates to be done,
  Or warns me not to do,
This, teach me more than Hell to shun,
  That, more than Heaven pursue.

What Blessings thy free Bounty gives,
  Let me not cast away;
For God is payed when Man receives;
  To enjoy is to obey. 20

Yet not to Earth's contracted Span
  Thy Goodness led me bound,
Or think Thee Lord alone of Man,
  When thousand Worlds are round:

Let not this weak, unknowing hand
  Presume thy bolts to throw,
And deal damnation round the land,
  On each I judge thy Foe.

If I am right, thy grace impart,
  Still in the right to stay; 30
If I am wrong, oh teach my heart
  To find that better way.

Save me alike from Foolish Pride
  Or impious Discontent,
At aught thy Wisdom has denied,
  Or aught thy Goodness lent.

Teach me to feel another's Woe,
  To hide the Fault I see;
That Mercy I to others show,
  That Mercy show to me. 40

Mean though I am, not wholly so,
  Since quickened by thy Breath;
Oh lead me wheresoe'er I go,
  Through this day's Life or Death.

This day, be Bread and Peace my Lot:
  All else beneath the Sun,
Thou know'st if best bestowed or not;
  And let Thy Will be done.

To thee, whose Temple is all Space,
  Whose Altar Earth, Sea, Skies, 50
One Chorus let all Being raise,
  All Nature's Incense rise!

conclusion to THE DUNCAID

ALEXANDER POPE

6

  In vain, in vain—the all-composing hour
Resistless falls: the Muse obeys the power.
She comes! she comes! the sable throne behold
Of Night primeval and of Chaos old!
Before her, Fancy's gilded clouds decay,

And all its varying rainbows die away.
Wit shoots in vain its momentary fires,
The meteor drops, and in a flash expires.
As one by one, at dread Medea's strain,
The sickening stars fade off th' ethereal plain;
As Argus' eyes, by Hermes' wand oppressed,
Closed one by one to everlasting rest:
Thus at her felt approach, and secret might,
Art after art goes out, and all is night.
See skulking Truth to her old cavern fled,
Mountains of casuistry heaped o'er her head!
Philosophy, that leaned on Heaven before,
Shrinks to her second cause, and is no more.
Physic of Metaphysic begs defence,
And Metaphysic calls for aid on Sense!
See Mystery to Mathematics fly!
In vain! they gaze, turn giddy, rave, and die.
Religion blushing veils her sacred fires,
And unawares Morality expires.
Nor public flame, nor private, dares to shine;
Nor human spark is left, nor glimpse divine!
Lo! thy dread empire, Chaos! is restored;
Light dies before thy uncreating word:
Thy hand, great Anarch! lets the curtain fall;
And universal darkness buries all.

¶ THE RAPE OF THE LOCK

ALEXANDER POPE

CANTO I

What dire offence from amorous causes springs,
What mighty contests rise from trivial things,
I sing—This verse to Caryl, Muse! is due:
This, even Belinda may vouchsafe to view:
Slight is the subject, but not so the praise,
If She inspire, and He approve my lays.

Say what strange motive, Goddess! could compel
A well-bred Lord to assault a gentle Belle?
O say what stranger cause, yet unexplored,
Could make a gentle Belle reject a Lord? 10
In tasks so bold, can little men engage,
And in soft bosoms dwells such mighty Rage?
Sol through white curtains shot a timorous ray,
And oped those eyes that must eclipse the day:
Now lap-dogs give themselves the rousing shake,
And sleepless lovers, just at twelve, awake:
Thrice rung the bell, the slipper knocked the ground,
And the pressed watch returned a silver sound.
Belinda still her downy pillow prest,
Her guardian Sylph prolonged the balmy rest: 20
'Twas He had summoned to her silent bed
The morning-dream that hovered o'er her head;
A Youth more glittering than a Birth-night Beau,
(That even in slumber caused her cheek to glow)
Seemed to her ear his winning lips to lay,
And thus in whispers said, or seemed to say:
"Fairest of mortals, thou distinguished care
Of thousand bright Inhabitants of Air!
If e'er one vision touched thy infant thought,
Of all the Nurse and all the Priest have taught; 30
Of airy Elves by moonlight shadows seen,
The silver token, and the circled green,
Or virgins visited by Angel-powers,
With golden crowns and wreaths of heavenly flowers;
Hear and believe! thy own importance know,
Nor bound thy narrow views to things below.
Some secret truths, from learnèd pride concealed,
To Maids alone and Children are revealed:
What though no credit doubting Wits may give?
The Fair and Innocent shall still believe. 40
Know, then, unnumbered Spirits round thee fly,
The light Militia of the lower sky:
These, though unseen, are ever on the wing,
Hang o'er the Box, and hover round the Ring.
Think what an equipage thou hast in Air,

And view with scorn two Pages and a Chair.
As now your own, our beings were of old,
And once inclosed in Woman's beauteous mould;
Thence, by a soft transition, we repair
From earthly Vehicles to these of air. 50
Think not, when Woman's transient breath is fled,
That all her vanities at once are dead;
Succeeding vanities she still regards,
And though she plays no more, o'erlooks the cards.
Her joy in gilded Chariots, when alive,
And love of Ombre, after death survive.
For when the Fair in all their pride expire,
To their first Elements their Souls retire:
The Sprites of fiery Termagants in Flame
Mount up, and take a Salamander's name. 60
Soft yielding minds to Water glide away,
And sip, with Nymphs, their elemental Tea.
The graver Prude sinks downward to a Gnome,
In search of mischief still on Earth to roam.
The light Coquettes in Sylphs aloft repair,
And sport and flutter in the fields of Air.
Know further yet; whoever fair and chaste
Rejects mankind, is by some Sylph embraced:
For Spirits, freed from mortal laws, with ease
Assume what sexes and what shapes they please. 70
What guards the purity of melting Maids,
In courtly balls, and midnight masquerades,
Safe from the treach'rous friend, the daring spark,
The glance by day, the whisper in the dark,
When kind occasion prompts their warm desires,
When music softens, and when dancing fires?
'Tis but their Sylph, the wise Celestials know,
Though Honor is the word with Men below.
Some nymphs there are, too conscious of their face,
For life predestined to the Gnomes' embrace. 80
These swell their prospects and exalt their pride,
When offers are disdained, and love denied:
Then gay Ideas crowd the vacant brain,
While Peers, and Dukes, and all their sweeping train,

And Garters, Stars, and Coronets appear,
And in soft sounds, Your Grace salutes their ear.
'Tis these that early taint the female soul,
Instruct the eyes of young Coquettes to roll,
Teach Infant-cheeks a bidden blush to know,
And little hearts to flutter at a Beau. 90
  Oft, when the world imagine women stray,
The Sylphs through mystic mazes guide their way,
Through all the giddy circle they pursue,
And old impertinence expel by new.
What tender maid but must a victim fall
To one man's treat, but for another's ball?
When Florio speaks what virgin could withstand,
If gentle Damon did not squeeze her hand?
With varying vanities, from every part,
They shift the moving Toyshop of their heart; 100
Where wigs with wigs, with sword-knots sword-knots strive,
Beaux banish beaux, and coaches coaches drive.
This erring mortals Levity may call;
Oh blind to truth! the Sylphs contrive it all.
  Of these am I, who they protection claim,
A watchful sprite, and Ariel is my name.
Late, as I ranged the crystal wilds of air,
In the clear Mirror of thy ruling Star
I saw, alas! some dread event impend,
Ere to the main this morning sun descend, 110
But heaven reveals not what, or how, or where:
Warned by the Sylph, oh pious maid, beware!
This to disclose is all thy guardian can:
Beware of all, but most beware of Man!
  He said; when Shock, who thought she slept too long,
Leaped up, and waked his mistress with his tongue.
'Twas then, Belinda, if report say true,
Thy eyes first opened on a Billet-doux;
Wounds, Charms, and Ardors were no sooner read,
But all the Vision vanished from thy head. 120
  And now, unveiled, the Toilet stands displayed,
Each silver Vase in mystic order laid.
First, robed in white, the Nymph intent adores,

With head uncovered, the Cosmetic powers.
A heav'nly image in the glass appears,
To that she bends, to that her eyes she rears;
Th' inferior Priestess, at her altar's side,
Trembling begins the sacred rites of Pride.
Unnumbered treasures ope at once, and here
The various off'rings of the world appear; 130
From each she nicely culls with curious toil,
And decks the Goddess with the glitt'ring spoil.
This casket India's glowing gems unlocks,
And all Arabia breathes from yonder box.
The Tortoise here and Elephant unite,
Transformed to combs, the speckled, and the white.
Here files of pins extend their shining rows,
Puffs, Powders, Patches, Bibles, Billet-doux.
Now awful Beauty puts on all its arms;
The fair each moment rises in her charms, 140
Repairs her smiles, awakens every grace,
And calls forth all the wonders of her face;
Sees by degrees a purer blush arise,
And keener lightnings quicken in her eyes.
The busy Sylphs surround their darling care,
These set the head, and those divide the hair,
Some fold the sleeve, whilst others plait the gown;
And Betty's praised for labors not her own.

CANTO II

Not with more glories, in th' ethereal plain,
The Sun first rises o'er the purpled main,
Than, issuing forth, the rival of his beams
Launched on the bosom of the silver Thames.
Fair Nymphs, and well-drest Youths around her shone,
But every eye was fixed on her alone.
On her white breast a sparkling Cross she wore,
Which Jews might kiss, and Infidels adore.
Her lively looks a sprightly mind disclose,
Quick as her eyes, and as unfixed as those: 10

Favors to none, to all she smiles extends;
Oft she rejects, but never once offends.
Bright as the sun, her eyes the gazers strike,
And, like the sun, they shine on all alike.
Yet graceful ease, and sweetness void of pride,
Might hide her faults, if Belles had faults to hide:
If to her share some female errors fall,
Look on her face, and you'll forget 'em all.
  This Nymph, to the destruction of mankind,
Nourished two Locks, which graceful hung behind 20
In equal curls, and well conspired to deck
With shining ringlets the smooth iv'ry neck.
Love in these labyrinths his slaves detains,
And mighty hearts are held in slender chains.
With hairy springs we the birds betray,
Slight lines of hair surprise the finny prey,
Fair tresses man's imperial race ensnare,
And beauty draws us with a single hair.
  Th' advent'rous Baron the bright locks admired;
He saw, he wished, and to the prize aspired. 30
Resolved to win, he meditates the way,
By force to ravish, or by fraud betray;
For when success a Lover's toil attends,
Few ask, if fraud or force attained his ends.
  For this, ere Phœbus rose, he had implored
Propitious heaven, and every power adored,
But chiefly Love—to Love an Altar built,
Of twelve vast French Romances, neatly gilt.
There lay three garters, half a pair of gloves;
And all the trophies of his former loves; 40
With tender Billet-doux he lights the pyre,
And breathes three am'rous sighs to raise the fire.
Then prostrate falls, and begs with ardent eyes
Soon to obtain, and long possess the prize:
The powers gave ear, and granted half his prayer,
The rest, the winds dispersed in empty air.
  But now secure the painted vessel glides,
The sun-beams trembling on the floating tides:
While melting music steals upon the sky,

And softened sounds along the waters die; 50
Smooth flow the waves, the Zephyrs gently play,
Belinda smiled, and all the world was gay.
All but the Sylph—with careful thoughts opprest,
Th' impending woe sat heavy on his breast.
He summons strait his Denizens of air;
The lucid squadrons round the sails repair:
Soft o'er the shrouds aërial whispers breathe,
That seemed but Zephyrs to the train beneath.
Some to the sun their insect-wings unfold,
Waft on the breeze, or sink in clouds of gold; 60
Transparent forms, too fine for mortal sight,
Their fluid bodies half dissolved in light,
Loose to the wind their airy garments flew,
Thin glitt'ring textures of the filmy dew,
Dipt in the richest tincture of the skies,
Where light disports in ever-mingling dyes,
While every beam new transient colors flings,
Colors that change whene'er they wave their wings.
Amid the circle, on the gilded mast,
Superior by the head, was Ariel placed; 70
His purple pinions opening to the sun,
He raised his azure wand, and thus begun.
 Ye Sylphs and Sylphids, to your chief give ear!
Fays, Fairies, Genii, Elves, and Dæmons, hear!
Ye know the spheres and various tasks assigned
By laws eternal to th' aërial kind.
Some in the fields of purest Æther play,
And bask and whiten in the blaze of day.
Some guide the course of wand'ring orbs on high,
Or roll the planets through the boundless sky. 80
Some less refined, beneath the moon's pale light
Pursue the stars that shoot athwart the night,
Or suck the mists in grosser air below,
Or dip their pinions in the painted bow,
Or brew fierce tempests on the wintry main,
Or o'er the glebe distil the kindly rain.
Others on earth o'er human race preside,
Watch all their ways, and all their actions guide:

Of these the chief the care of Nations own,
And guard with Arms divine the British Throne. 90
  Our humbler province is to tend the Fair,
Not a less pleasing, though less glorious care;
To save the powder from too rude a gale,
Nor let th' imprisoned essences exhale;
To draw fresh colors from the vernal flowers;
To steal from rainbows e'er they drop in showers
A brighter wash; to curl their waving hairs,
Assist their blushes, and inspire their airs;
Nay oft, in dreams, invention we bestow,
To change a Flounce, or add a Furbelow. 100
  This day, black Omens threat the brightest Fair,
That e'er deserved a watchful spirit's care;
Some dire disaster, or by force, or slight;
But what, or where, the fates have wrapt in night.
Whether the nymph shall break Diana's law,
Or some frail China jar receive a flaw;
Or stain her honor or her new brocade;
Forget her prayers, or miss a masquerade;
Or lose her heart, or necklace, at a ball;
Or whether Heaven has doomed that Shock must fall. 110
Haste, then, ye spirits! to your charge repair:
The flutt'ring fan be Zephyretta's care;
The drops to thee, Brillante, we consign;
And, Momentilla, let the watch be thine;
Do thou, Crispissa, tend her fav'rite Lock;
Ariel himself shall be the guard of Shock.
  To fifty chosen Sylphs, of special note,
We trust th' important charge, the Petticoat:
Oft have we known that seven-fold fence to fail,
Though stiff with hoops, and armed with ribs of whale; 120
Form a strong line about the silver bound,
And guard the wide circumference around.
  Whatever spirit, careless of his charge,
His post neglects, or leaves the fair at large,
Shall feel sharp vengeance soon o'ertake his sins,
Be stopped in vials, or transfixed with pins;
Or plunged in lakes of bitter washes lie,

Or wedged whole ages in a bodkin's eye:
Gums and Pomatums shall his flight restrain,
While clogged he beats his silken wings in vain; 130
Or Alum styptics with contracting power
Shrink his thin essence like a riveled flower:
Or, as Ixion fixed, the wretch shall feel
The giddy motion of the whirling Mill,
In fumes of burning Chocolate shall glow,
And tremble at the sea that froths below!
  He spoke; the spirits from the sails descend;
Some, orb in orb, around the nymph extend;
Some thrid the mazy ringlets of her hair;
Some hang upon the pendants of her ear: 140
With beating hearts the dire event they wait,
Anxious, and trembling for the birth of Fate.

CANTO III

Close by those meads, forever crowned with flowers,
Where Thames with pride surveys his rising towers,
There stands a structure of majestic frame,
Which from the neighb'ring Hampton takes its name.
Here Britain's statesmen oft the fall foredoom
Of foreign Tyrants and of Nymphs at home;
Here thou, great ANNA! whom three realms obey,
Dost sometimes counsel take—and sometimes Tea.
  Hither the heroes and the nymphs resort,
To taste awhile the pleasures of a Court; 10
In various talk th' instructive hours they past,
Who gave the ball, or paid the visit last;
One speaks the glory of the British Queen,
And one describes a charming Indian screen;
A third interprets motions, looks, and eyes;
At every word a reputation dies.
Snuff, or the fan, supply each pause of chat,
With singing, laughing, ogling, *and all that.*
  Meanwhile, declining from the noon of day,
The sun obliquely shoots his burning ray; 20

The hungry Judges soon the sentence sign,
And wretches hang that jury-men may dine;
The merchant from th' Exchange returns in peace,
And the long labors of the Toilet cease.
Belinda now, whom thirst of fame invites,
Burns to encounter two advent'rous Knights,
At Ombre singly to decide their doom;
And swells her breast with conquests yet to come.
Straight the three bands prepare in arms to join,
Each band the number of the sacred nine. 30
Soon as she spreads her hand, th' aërial guard
Descend, and sit on each important card:
First Ariel perched upon a Matadore,
Then each, according to the rank they bore;
For Sylphs, yet mindful of their ancient race,
Are, as when women, wondrous fond of place.
  Behold, four Kings in majesty revered,
With hoary whiskers and a forky beard;
And four fair Queens whose hands sustain a flower,
Th' expressive emblem of their softer power; 40
Four Knaves in garbs succinct, a trusty band,
Caps on their heads, and halberts in their hand;
And particolored troops, a shining train,
Draw forth to combat on the velvet plain.
  The skilful Nymph reviews her force with care:
Let Spades be trumps! she said, and trumps they were.
  Now move to war her sable Matadores,
In show like leaders of the swarthy Moors.
Spadillio first, unconquerable Lord!
Led off two captive trumps, and swept the board. 50
As many more Manillio forced to yield,
And marched a victor from the verdant field.
Him Basto followed, but his fate more hard
Gained but one trump and one Plebeian card.
With his broad sabre next, a chief in years,
The hoary Majesty of Spades appears,
Puts forth one manly leg, to sight revealed,
The rest, his many-colored robe concealed.
The rebel Knave, who dares his prince engage,

Proves the just victim of his royal rage. 60
Even mighty Pam, that Kings and Queens o'erthrew
And mowed down armies in the fights of Lu,
Sad chance of war! now destitute of aid,
Falls undistinguished by the victor spade!
  Thus far both armies to Belinda yield;
Now to the Baron fate inclines the field.
His warlike Amazon her host invades,
Th' imperial consort of the crown of Spades.
The Club's black Tyrant first her victim died,
Spite of his haughty mien, and barb'rous pride: 70
What boots the regal circle on his head,
His giant limbs, in state unwieldy spread;
That long behind he trails his pompous robe,
And, of all monarchs, only grasps the globe?
  The Baron now his Diamonds pours apace;
Th' embroidered King who shows but half his face,
And his refulgent Queen, with powers combined
Of broken troops an easy conquest find.
Clubs, Diamonds, Hearts, in wild disorder seen,
With throngs promiscuous strow the level green. 80
Thus when dispersed a routed army runs,
Of Asia's troops, and Afric's sable sons,
With like confusion different nations fly,
Of various habit, and of various dye,
The pierced battalions dis-united fall,
In heaps on heaps; one fate o'erwhelms them all.
  The Knave of Diamonds tries his wily arts,
And wins (oh shameful chance!) the Queen of Hearts.
At this, the blood the virgin's cheek forsook,
A livid paleness spreads o'er all her look; 90
She sees, and trembles at th' approaching ill,
Just in the jaws of ruin, and Codille.
And now (as oft in some distempered State)
On one nice Trick depends the general fate.
An Ace of Hearts steps forth: The King unseen
Lurked in her hand, and mourned his captive Queen:
He springs to Vengeance with an eager pace,
And falls like thunder on the prostrate Ace.

The nymph exulting fills with shouts the sky;
The walls, the woods, and long canals reply. 100
  Oh thoughtless mortals! ever blind to fate,
Too soon dejected, and too soon elate.
Sudden, these honors shall be snatched away,
And cursed for ever this victorious day.
  For lo! the board with cups and spoons is crowned,
The berries crackle, and the mill turns round;
On shining Altars of Japan they raise
The silver lamp; the fiery spirits blaze:
From silver spouts the grateful liquors glide,
While China's earth receives the smoking tide: 110
At once they gratify their scent and taste,
And frequent cups prolong the rich repast.
Straight hover round the Fair her airy band;
Some, as she sipped, the fuming liquor fanned,
Some o'er her lap their careful plumes displayed,
Trembling, and conscious of the rich brocade.
Coffee (which makes the politician wise,
And see through all things with his half-shut eyes)
Sent up in vapors to the Baron's brain
New Stratagems, the radiant Lock to gain. 120
Ah cease, rash youth! desist ere 'tis too late,
Fear the just Gods, and think of Scylla's Fate!
Changed to a bird, and sent to flit in air,
She dearly pays for Nisus' injured hair!
  But when to mischief mortals bend their will,
How soon they find fit instruments of ill!
Just then, Clarissa drew with tempting grace
A two-edged weapon from her shining case:
So Ladies in Romance assist their Knight,
Present the spear, and arm him for the fight. 130
He takes the gift with rev'rence, and extends
The little engine on his fingers' ends;
This just behind Belinda's neck he spread,
As o'er the fragrant steams she bends her head.
Swift to the Lock a thousand Sprites repair,
A thousand wings, by turns, blow back the hair;
And thrice they twitched the diamond in her ear;

Thrice she looked back, and thrice the foe drew near.
Just in that instant, anxious Ariel sought
The close recesses of the Virgin's thought; 40
As on the nosegay in her breast reclined,
He watched th' Ideas rising in her mind,
Sudden he viewed, in spite of all her art,
An earthly Lover lurking at her heart.
Amazed, confused, he found his power expired,
Resigned to fate, and with a sigh retired.
The Peer now spreads the glitt'ring Forfex wide,
T' inclose the Lock; now joins it, to divide.
Even then, before the fatal engine closed,
A wretched Sylph too fondly interposed; 150
Fate urged the shears, and cut the Sylph in twain,
(But airy substance soon unites again)
The meeting points the sacred hair dissever
From the fair head, forever, and forever!
Then flashed the living lightning from her eyes,
And screams of horror rend th' affrighted skies.
Not louder shrieks to pitying heaven are cast,
When husbands, or when lap-dogs breathe their last;
Or when rich China vessels fall'n from high,
In glitt'ring dust and painted fragments lie! 160
Let wreaths of triumph now my temples twine,
(The victor cried) the glorious Prize is mine!
While fish in streams, or birds delight in air,
Or in a coach and six the British Fair,
As long as *Atalantis* shall be read,
Or the small pillow grace a Lady's bed,
While visits shall be paid on solemn days,
When num'rous wax-lights in bright order blaze,
While nymphs take treats, or assignations give,
So long my honor, name, and praise shall live! 170
What Time would spare, from Steel receives its date,
And monuments, like men, submit to fate!
Steel could the labor of the Gods destroy,
And strike to dust th' imperial towers of Troy;
Steel could the works of mortal pride confound,
And hew triumphal arches to the ground.

What wonder then, fair nymph! thy hairs should feel,
The conq'ring force of unresisted steel?

CANTO IV

But anxious cares the pensive nymph oppressed,
And secret passions labored in her breast.
Not youthful kings in battle seized alive,
Not scornful virgins who their charms survive,
Not ardent lovers robbed of all their bliss,
Not ancient ladies when refused a kiss,
Not tyrants fierce that unrepenting die,
Not Cynthia when her manteau's pinned awry,
E'er felt such rage, resentment, and despair,
As thou, sad Virgin! for thy ravished Hair. 10
For, that sad moment, when the Sylphs withdrew
And Ariel weeping from Belinda flew,
Umbriel, a dusky, melancholy sprite,
As ever sullied the fair face of light,
Down to the central earth, his proper scene,
Repaired to search the gloomy Cave of Spleen.
Swift on his sooty pinions flits the Gnome,
And in a vapour reached the dismal dome.
No cheerful breeze this sullen region knows,
The dreaded East is all the wind that blows. 20
Here in a grotto, sheltered close from air,
And screened in shades from day's detested glare,
She sighs forever on her pensive bed,
Pain at her side, and Megrim at her head.
Two handmaids wait the throne: alike in place,
But diff'ring far in figure and in face.
Here stood Ill-nature like an ancient maid,
Her wrinkled form in black and white arrayed;
With store of prayers, for mornings, nights, and noons,
Her hand is filled; her bosom with lampoons. 30
There Affectation, with a sickly mien,
Shows in her cheek the roses of eighteen,
Practised to lisp, and hang the head aside,

Faints into airs, and languishes with pride,
On the rich quilt sinks with becoming woe,
Wrapt in a gown, for sickness, and for show.
The fair ones feel such maladies as these,
When each new night-dress gives a new disease.
  A constant Vapor o'er the palace flies;
Strange phantoms rising as the mists arise; 40
Dreadful, as hermit's dreams in haunted shades,
Or bright, as visions of expiring maids.
Now glaring fiends, and snakes on rolling spires,
Pale specters, gaping tombs, and purple fires:
Now lakes of liquid gold, Elysian scenes,
And crystal domes, and angels in machines.
  Unnumbered throngs on every side are seen,
Of bodies changed to various forms by Spleen.
Here living Tea-pots stand, one arm held out,
One bent; the handle this, and that the spout: 50
A Pipkin there, like Homer's Tripod walks;
Here sighs a Jar, and there a Goose-pie talks;
Men prove with child, as powerful fancy works,
And maids turned bottles, call aloud for corks.
  Safe past the Gnome through this fantastic band,
A branch of healing Spleenwort in his hand.
Then thus addressed the power: "Hail, wayward Queen!
Who rule the sex to fifty from fifteen:
Parent of vapors and of female wit,
Who give th' hysteric or poetic fit, 60
On various tempers act by various ways,
Make some take physic, others scribble plays;
Who cause the proud their visits to delay,
And send the godly in a pet to pray.
A nymph there is, that all thy power disdains,
And thousands more in equal mirth maintains.
But oh! if e'er thy Gnome could spoil a grace,
Or raise a pimple on a beauteous face,
Like Citron-waters matrons' cheeks inflame,
Or change complexions at a losing game; 70
If e'er with airy horns I planted heads,
Or rumpled petticoats, or tumbled beds,

Or caus'd suspicion when no soul was rude,
Or discomposed the head-dress of a Prude,
Or e'er to costive lap-dog gave disease,
Which not the tears of brightest eyes could ease:
Hear me, and touch Belinda with chagrin,
That single act gives half the world the spleen."
  The Goddess with a discontented air
Seems to reject him, though she grants his prayer. 80
A wondrous Bag with both her hands she binds,
Like that where once Ulysses held the winds;
There she collects the force of female lungs,
Sighs, sobs, and passions, and the war of tongues.
A Vial next she fills with fainting fears,
Soft sorrows, melting griefs, and flowing tears.
The Gnome rejoicing bears her gifts away,
Spreads his black wings, and slowly mounts to day.
  Sunk in Thalestris' arms the nymph he found,
Her eyes dejected and her hair unbound. 90
Full o'er their heads the swelling bag he rent,
And all the Furies issued at the vent.
Belinda burns with more than mortal ire,
And fierce Thalestris fans the rising fire.
"Oh wretched maid!" she spread her hands, and cried,
(While Hampton's echoes, "Wretched maid!" replied)
"Was it for this you took such constant care
The bodkin, comb, and essence to prepare?
For this your locks in paper durance bound,
For this with torturing irons wreathed around? 100
For this with fillets strained your tender head,
And bravely bore the double loads of lead?
Gods! shall the ravisher display your hair,
While the Fops envy, and the Ladies stare!
Honor forbid! at whose unrivaled shrine
Ease, pleasure, virtue, all our sex resign.
Methinks already I your tears survey,
Already hear the horrid things they say,
Already see you a degraded toast,
And all your honor in a whisper lost! 110
How shall I, then, your helpless fame defend?

'Twill then be infamy to seem your friend!
And shall this prize, th' inestimable prize,
Exposed through crystal to the gazing eyes,
And heightened by the diamond's circling rays,
On that rapacious hand forever blaze?
Sooner shall grass in Hyde-park Circus grow,
And wits take lodgings in the sound of Bow;
Sooner let earth, air, sea, to Chaos fall,
Men, monkeys, lap-dogs, parrots, perish all!" 120
She said; then raging to Sir Plume repairs,
And bids her Beau demand the precious hairs:
(Sir Plume of amber snuff-box justly vain,
And the nice conduct of a clouded cane)
With earnest eyes, and round unthinking face,
He first the snuff-box opened, then the case,
And thus broke out—"My Lord, why, what the devil?
Z—ds! damn the lock! 'fore Gad, you must be civil!
Plague on't! 'tis past a jest—nay prithee, pox!
Give her the hair"—he spoke, and rapped his box. 130
"It grives me much" (replied the Peer again)
"Who speaks so well should ever speak in vain.
But by this Lock, this sacred Lock I swear,
(Which never more shall join its parted hair;
Which never more its honors shall renew,
Clipped from the lovely head where late it grew)
That while my nostrils draw the vital air,
This hand, which won it, shall for ever wear."
He spoke, and speaking, in proud triumph spread
The long-contended honors of her head. 140
But Umbriel, hateful Gnome! forbears not so;
He breaks the Vial whence the sorrows flow.
Then see! the nymph in beauteous grief appears,
Her eyes half-languishing, half-drowned in tears;
On her heaved bosom hung her drooping head,
Which, with a sigh, she raised; and thus she said.
"Forever cursed be this detested day,
Which snatched my best, my fav'rite curl away!
Happy! ah ten times happy had I been,
If Hampton-Court these eyes had never seen! 150

Yet am not I the first mistaken maid,
By love of Courts to numerous ills betrayed.
Oh had I rather un-admired remained
In some lone isle, or distant Northern land;
Where the gilt Chariot never marks the way,
Where none learn Ombre, none e'er taste Bohea!
There kept my charms concealed from mortal eye,
Like roses, that in deserts bloom and die.
What moved my mind with youthful Lords to roam?
Oh had I stayed, and said my prayers at home! 160
'Twas this, the morning omens seemed to tell,
Thrice from my trembling hand the patch-box fell;
The tott'ring China shook without a wind,
Nay, Poll sat mute, and Shock was most unkind!
A Sylph too warned me of the threats of fate,
In mystic visions, now believed too late!
See the poor remnants of these slighted hairs!
My hands shall rend what even thy rapine spares:
These in two sable ringlets taught to break,
Once gave new beauties to the snowy neck; 170
The sister-lock now sits uncouth, alone,
And in its fellow's fate foresees its own;
Uncurled it hangs, the fatal shears demands,
And tempts once more, thy sacrilegious hands.
Oh hadst thou, cruel! been content to seize
Hairs less in sight, or any hairs but these!"

CANTO V

She said: the pitying audience melt in tears.
But Fate and Jove had stopped the Baron's ears.
In vain Thalestris with reproach assails,
For who can move when fair Belinda fails?
Not half so fixed the Trojan could remain,
While Anna begged and Dido raged in vain.
Then grave Clarissa graceful waved her fan;
Silence ensued, and thus the nymph began.
"Say why are Beauties praised and honored most,

The wise man's passion, and the vain man's toast? 10
Why decked with all that land and sea afford,
Why Angels called, and Angel-like adored?
Why round our coaches crowd the white-gloved Beaux,
Why bows the side-box from its inmost rows;
How vain are all these glories, all our pains,
Unless good sense preserve what beauty gains:
That men may say, when we the front-box grace:
'Behold the first in virtue as in face!'
Oh! if to dance all night, and dress all day,
Charmed the small-pox, or chased old-age away; 20
Who would not scorn what housewife's cares produce,
Or who would learn one earthly thing of use?
To patch, nay ogle, might become a Saint,
Nor could it sure be such a sin to paint.
But since, alas! frail beauty must decay,
Curled or uncurled, since Locks will turn to grey;
Since painted, or not painted, all shall fade,
And she who scorns a man, must die a maid;
What then remains but well our power to use,
And keep good-humor still whate'er we lose? 30
And trust me, dear! good-humor can prevail,
When airs, and flights, and screams, and scolding fail.
Beauties in vain their pretty eyes may roll;
Charms strike the sight, but merit wins the soul."
So spoke the Dame, but no applause ensued;
Belinda frowned, Thalestris called her Prude.
"To arms, to arms!" the fierce Virago cries,
And swift as lightning to the combat flies.
All side in parties, and begin th' attack;
Fans clap, silks rustle, and tough whalebones crack; 40
Heroes' and Heroines' shouts confus'dly rise,
And bass and treble voices strike the skies.
No common weapons in their hands are found,
Like Gods they fight, nor dread a mortal wound.
So when bold Homer makes the Gods engage,
And heavenly breasts with human passions rage;
'Gainst Pallas, Mars; Latona, Hermes arms;
And all Olympus rings with loud alarms:

Jove's thunder roars, heaven trembles all around,
Blue Neptune storms, the bellowing deeps resound: 50
Earth shakes her nodding towers, the ground gives way,
And the pale ghosts start at the flash of day!
Triumphant Umbriel on a sconce's height
Clapped his glad wings, and sat to view the fight:
Propped on their bodkin spears, the Sprites survey
The growing combat, or assist the fray.
While through the press enraged Thalestris flies,
And scatters death around from both her eyes,
A Beau and Witling perished in the throng,
One died in metaphor, and one in song. 60
"O cruel nymph! a living death I bear,"
Cried Dapperwit, and sunk beside his chair.
A mournful glance Sir Fopling upwards cast,
"Those eyes are made so killing"—was his last.
Thus on Mæander's flowery margin lies
Th' expiring Swan, and as he sings he dies.
When bold Sir Plume had drawn Clarissa down,
Chloe stepped in, and killed him with a frown;
She smiled to see the doughty hero slain,
But, at her smile, the Beau revived again. 70
Now Jove suspends his golden scales in air,
Weighs the Men's wits against the Lady's hair;
The doubtful beam long nods from side to side;
At length the wits mount up, the hairs subside.
See, fierce Belinda on the Baron flies,
With more than usual lightning in her eyes:
Nor feared the Chief th' unequal fight to try,
Who sought no more than on his foe to die.
But this bold Lord with manly strength endued,
She with one finger and a thumb subdued: 80
Just where the breath of life his nostrils drew,
A charge of Snuff the wily virgin threw;
The Gnomes direct, to every atom just,
The pungent grains of titillating dust.
Sudden, with starting tears each eye o'erflows,
And the high dome re-echoes to his nose.
Now meet thy fate, incensed Belinda cried,

And drew a deadly bodkin from her side.
(The same, his ancient personage to deck,
Her great great grandsire wore about his neck,
In three seal-rings; which after, melted down,
Formed a vast buckle for his widow's gown:
Her infant grandame's whistle next it grew,
The bells she jingled, and the whistle blew;
Then in a bodkin graced her mother's hairs,
Which long she wore, and now Belinda wears.)
"Boast not my fall" (he cried) "insulting foe!
Thou by some other shalt be laid as low,
Nor think, to die dejects my lofty mind:
All that I dread is leaving you behind! 100
Rather than so, ah let me still survive,
And burn in Cupid's flames—but burn alive."
"Restore the Lock!" she cries; and all around
"Restore the Lock!" the vaulted roofs rebound.
Not fierce Othello in so loud a strain
Roared for the handkerchief that caused his pain.
But see how oft ambitious aims are crossed,
And chiefs contend till all the prize is lost!
The Lock, obtained with guilt, and kept with pain,
In every place is sought, but sought in vain: 110
With such a prize no mortal must be blest,
So heaven decrees! with heaven who can contest?
Some thought it mounted to the Lunar sphere,
Since all things lost on earth are treasured there.
There Hero's wits are kept in pond'rous vases,
And beau's in snuff-boxes and tweezer-cases.
There broken vows and death-bed alms are found,
And lovers' hearts with ends of riband bound,
The courtier's promises, and sick man's prayers,
The smiles of harlots, and the tears of heirs, 120
Cages for gnats, and chains to yoke a flea,
Dried butterflies, and tomes of casuistry.
But trust the Muse—she saw it upward rise,
Though marked by none but quick, poetic eyes:
(So Rome's great founder to the heavens withdrew,
To Proculus alone confessed in view)

A sudden Star, it shot through liquid air,
And drew behind a radiant trail of hair.
Not Berenice's Locks first rose so bright,
The heavens bespangling with disheveled light. 130
The Sylphs behold it kindling as it flies,
And pleased pursue its progress through the skies.
This is the Beau monde shall from the Mall survey,
And hail with music its propitious ray.
This the blest Lover shall for Venus take,
And send up vows from Rosamonda's lake.
This Partridge soon shall view in cloudless skies,
When next he looks through Galileo's eyes;
And hence th' egregious wizard shall foredoom
The fate of Louis, and the fall of Rome. 140
Then cease, bright Nymph! to mourn thy ravished hair,
Which adds new glory to the shining sphere!
Not all the tresses that fair head can boast,
Shall draw such envy as the Lock you lost.
For, after all the murders of your eye,
When, after millions slain, yourself shall die:
When those fair suns shall set, as set they must,
And all those tresses shall be laid in dust,
This Lock, the Muse shall consecrate to fame,
And 'midst the stars inscribe Belinda's name. 150

THE COXCOMB BIRD

ALEXANDER POPE

The coxcomb bird, so talkative and grave,
That from his cage cries Cuckold, Whore, and Knave,
Though many a passenger he rightly call,
You hold him no Philosopher at all.

¶ ELEGY WRITTEN IN A COUNTRY CHURCHYARD

THOMAS GRAY

The Curfew tolls the knell of parting day,
  The lowing herd winds slowly o'er the lea,
The plowman homeward plods his weary way,
  And leaves the world to darkness and to me.

Now fades the glimmering landscape on the sight,
  And all the air a solemn stillness holds,
Save where the beetle wheels his droning flight,
  And drowsy tinklings lull the distant folds;

Save that from yonder ivy-mantled tower
  The moping owl does to the moon complain 10
Of such, as wand'ring near her secret bower,
  Molest her ancient solitary reign.

Beneath those rugged elms, that yew-tree's shade,
  Where heaves the turf in many a mold'ring heap,
Each in his narrow cell for ever laid,
  The rude Forefathers of the hamlet sleep.

The breezy call of incense-breathing Morn,
  The swallow twitt'ring from the straw-built shed,
The cock's shrill clarion, or the echoing horn,
  No more shall rouse them from their lowly bed. 20

For them no more the blazing hearth shall burn,
  Or busy housewife ply her evening care:
No children run to lisp their sire's return,
  Or climb his knees the envied kiss to share.

Oft did the harvest to their sickle yield,
  Their furrow oft the stubborn glebe has broke;
How jocund did they drive their team afield!
  How bowed the woods beneath their sturdy stroke!

Let not Ambition mock their useful toil,
  Their homely joys, and destiny obscure; 30
Nor Grandeur hear with a disdainful smile,
  The short and simple annals of the poor.

The boast of heraldry, the pomp of power,
  And all that beauty, all that wealth e'er gave,
Await alike th' inevitable hour.
  The paths of glory lead but to the grave.

Nor you, ye proud, impute to these the fault,
  If Memory o'er their tomb no trophies raise,
Where through the long-drawn aisle and fretted vault
  The pealing anthem swells the note of praise. 40

Can storied urn or animated bust
  Back to its mansion call the fleeting breath?
Can Honor's voice provoke the silent dust,
  Or Flattery soothe the dull cold ear of Death?

Perhaps in this neglected spot is laid
  Some heart once pregnant with celestial fire;
Hands that the rod of empire might have swayed,
  Or waked to ecstasy the living lyre.

But Knowledge to their eyes her ample page
  Rich with the spoils of time did ne'er unroll; 50
Chill Penury repressed their noble rage,
  And froze the genial current of the soul.

Full many a gem of purest ray serene,
  The dark unfathomed caves of ocean bear:
Full many a flower is born tc blush unseen,
  And waste its sweetness on the desert air.

Some village Hampden, that, with dauntless breast
  The little tyrant of his fields withdstood;
Some mute inglorious Milton here may rest,
  Some Cromwell guiltless of his country's blood. 60

Th' applause of listening senates to command,
  The threats of pain and ruin to despise,
To scatter plenty o'er a smiling land,
  And read their history in a nation's eyes,

Their lot forbade: nor circumscribed alone
  Their growing virtues, but their crimes confined;
Forbade to wade through slaughter to a throne,
  And shut the gates of mercy on mankind.

The struggling pangs of conscious truth to hide,
  To quench the blushes of ingenuous shame, 70
Or heap the shrine of Luxury and Pride
  With incense kindled at the Muse's flame.

Far from the madding crowd's ignoble strife,
  Their sober wishes never learned to stray;
Along the cool requestered vale of life
  They kept the noiseless tenor of their way.

Yet ev'n these bones from insult to protect
  Some frail memorial still erected nigh,
With uncouth rimes and shapeless sculpture decked,
  Implores the passing tribute of a sigh. 80

Their name, their years, spelt by th' unlettered muse,
  The place of fame and elegy supply:
And many a holy text around she strews,
  That teach the rustic moralist to die.

For who to dumb Forgetfulness a prey,
  This pleasing anxious being e'er resigned,
Left the warm precincts of the cheerful day,
  Nor cast one longing ling'ring look behind?

On some fond breast the parting soul relies,
  Some pious drops the closing eye requires; 90
Ev'n from the tomb the voice of Nature cries,
  Ev'n in our Ashes live their wonted Fires.

For thee, who mindful of th' unhonored Dead
  Dost in these lines their artless tale relate;
If chance, by lonely contemplation led,
  Some kindred Spirit shall inquire thy fate,

Haply some hoary-headed Swain may say,
  "Oft have we seen him at the peep of dawn
Brushing with hasty steps the dews away
  To meet the sun upon the upland lawn. 100

"There at the foot of yonder nodding beech
  That wreathes its old fantastic roots so high,
His listless length at noontide would he stretch,
  And pore upon the brook that babbles by.

"Hard by yon wood, now smiling as in scorn,
  Mutt'ring his wayward fancies he would rove,
Now drooping, woeful wan, like one forlorn,
  Or crazed with care, or crossed in hopeless love.

"One morn I missed him on the customed hill,
  Along the heath and near his fav'rite tree; 110
Another came; nor yet beside the rill,
  Nor up the lawn, nor at the wood was he;

"The next with dirges due in sad array
  Slow through the church-way path we saw him borne.
Approach and read (for thou canst read) the lay
  Graved on the stone beneath yon agèd thorn."

THE EPITAPH

Here rests his head upon the lap of Earth
  A youth, to Fortune and to Fame unknown;
Fair Science frown'd not on his humble birth
  And Melancholy mark'd him for her own. 120

Large was his bounty, and his soul sincere;
  Heav'n did a recompense as largely send:

He gave to Mis'ry all he had, a tear,
He gain'd from Heav'n ('twas all he wish'd) a friend.

No farther seek his merits to disclose,
Or draw his frailties from their dread abode
(There they alike in trembling hope repose),
The bosom of his Father and his God.

ODE TO EVENING

WILLIAM COLLINS

If aught of oaten stop, or pastoral song,
May hope, chaste Eve, to soothe thy modest ear,
Like thy own solemn springs,
Thy springs and dying gales,

O nymph reserved, while now the bright-haired sun
Sits in yon western tent, whose cloudy skirts,
With brede ethereal wove,
O'erhang his wavy bed:

Now air is hushed, save where the weak-eyed bat,
With short shrill shriek, flits by on leathern wing, 10
Or where the beetle winds
His small but sullen horn,

As oft he rises 'midst the twilight path,
Against the pilgrim borne in heedless hum:
Now teach me, maid composed,
To breathe some softened strain,

Whose numbers, stealing through thy dark'ning vale,
May not unseemly with its stillness suit,
As, musing slow, I hail
Thy genial loved return! 20

For when thy folding-star arising shows
His paly circlet, at his warning lamp

The fragrant Hours, and elves
Who slept in flowers the day,

And many a nymph who wreaths her brows with sedge,
And sheds the fresh'ning dew, and, lovelier still,
The pensive Pleasures sweet,
Prepare thy shadowy car.

Then lead, calm vot'ress, where some sheety lake
Cheers the lone heath, or some time-hallowed pile 30
Or upland fallows gray
Reflect its last cool gleam.

But when chill blust'ring winds, or driving rain,
Forbid my willing feet, be mine the hut
That from the mountain's side
Views wilds, and swelling floods,

And hamlets brown, and dim-discovered spires,
And hears their simple bell, and marks o'er all
Thy dewy fingers draw
The gradual dusky veil. 40

While Spring shall pour his show'rs, as oft he wont,
And bathe thy breathing tresses, meekest Eve;
While Summer loves to sport
Beneath thy ling'ring light;

While sallow Autumn fills thy lap with leaves;
Or Winter, yelling through the troublous air,
Affrights thy shrinking train,
And rudely rends thy robes;

So long, sure-found beneath the sylvan shed,
Shall Fancy, Friendship, Science, rose-lipped Health, 50
Thy gentlest influence own,
And hymn thy fav'rite name!

A SONG FROM SHAKESPEARE'S CYMBELINE

Sung by Guiderus and Arviragus
over Fidele, supposed to be dead

WILLIAM COLLINS

To fair Fidele's grassy tomb
  Soft maids and village hinds shall bring
Each opening sweet, of earliest bloom,
  And rifle all the breathing Spring.

No wailing ghost shall dare appear
  To vex with shrieks this quiet grove:
But shepherd lads assemble here,
  And melting virgins own their love.

No withered witch shall here be seen,
  No goblins lead their nightly crew:
The female fays shall haunt the green,
  And dress thy grave with pearly dew!

The red-breast oft at evening hours
  Shall kindly lend his little aid:
With hoary moss, and gathered flowers,
  To deck the ground where thou art laid.

When howling winds, and beating rain,
  In tempests shake the sylvan cell:
Or midst the chace on every plain,
  The tender thought on thee shall dwell.

Each lonely scene shall thee restore,
  For thee the tear be duly shed:
Beloved till life can charm no more,
  And mourned, till Pity's self be dead.

TO MARY UNWIN

WILLIAM COWPER

Mary! I want a lyre with other strings,
Such aid from Heaven as some have feign'd they drew,
An eloquence scarce given to mortals, new
And undebased by praise of meaner things,
That ere through age or woe I shed my wings
I may record thy worth with honour due,
In verse as musical as thou art true,
And that immortalizes whom it sings:—
But thou hast little need. There is a Book
By seraphs writ with beams of heavenly light,
On which the eyes of God not rarely look,
A chronicle of actions just and bright—
There all thy deeds, my faithful Mary, shine;
And since thou own'st that praise, I spare thee mine.

THE POPLAR FIELD

WILLIAM COWPER

The poplars are felled; farewell to the shade
And the whispering sound of the cool colonnade;
The winds play no longer and sing in the leaves,
Nor Ouse on his bosom their image receives.

Twelve years have elapsed since I first took a view
Of my favourite field, and the bank where they grew;
And now in the grass behold they are laid,
And the tree is my seat that once lent me a shade.

The blackbird has fled to another retreat
Where the hazels afford him a screen from the heat,
And the scene where his melody charmed me before
Resounds with his sweet-flowing ditty no more.

My fugitive years are all hasting away,
And I must ere long lie as lowly as they

With a turf on my breast, and a stone at my head,
Ere another such grove shall arise in its stead.

'Tis a sight to engage me, if anything can,
To muse on the perishing pleasures of man;
Though his life be a dream, his enjoyments, I see,
Have a being less durable even than he.

THE INDIAN BURYING GROUND

PHILIP FRENEAU

In spite of all the learned have said,
I still my old opinion keep;
The posture that we give the dead
Points out the soul's eternal sleep.

Not so the ancients of these lands—
The Indian, when from life released,
Again is seated with his friends,
And shares again the joyous feast.

His imaged birds, and painted bowl,
And venison, for a journey dressed, 10
Bespeak the nature of the soul,
Activity, that knows no rest.

His bow, for action ready bent,
And arrows, with a head of stone,
Can only mean that life is spent,
And not the old ideas gone.

Thou, stranger, that shalt come this way,
No fraud upon the dead commit—
Observe the swelling turf, and say
They do not lie, but here they sit. 20

Here still a lofty rock remains,
On which the curious eye may trace

(Now wasted, half, by wearing rains)
The fancies of a ruder race.

Here still an aged elm aspires,
Beneath whose far-projecting shade
(And which the shepherd still admires)
The children of the forest played!

There oft a restless Indian queen
(Pale Shebah, with her braided hair) 30
And many a barbarous form is seen
To chide the man that lingers there.

By midnight moons, o'er moistening dews,
In habit for the chase arrayed,
The hunter still the deer pursues,
The hunter and the deer, a shade!

And long shall timorous fancy see
The painted chief, and pointed spear,
And Reason's self shall bow the knee
To shadows and delusions here. 40

❰ THE WILD HONEY-SUCKLE

PHILIP FRENEAU

Fair flower, that dost so comely grow,
Hid in this silent, dull retreat,
Untouched thy honied blossoms blow,
Unseen thy little branches greet;
No roving foot shall crush thee here,
No busy hand provoke a tear.

By Nature's self in white arrayed,
She bade thee shun the vulgar eye,
And planted here the guardian shade,
And sent soft waters murmuring by;
Thus quietly thy summer goes,
Thy days declining to repose.

Smit with those charms, that must decay,
I grieve to see your future doom;
They died—nor were those flowers more gay,
The flowers that did in Eden bloom;
  Unpitying frosts, and Autumn's power
  Shall leave no vestige of this flower.

From morning suns and evening dews
At first thy little being came:
If nothing once, you nothing lose,
For when you die you are the same;
  The space between, is but an hour,
  The frail duration of a flower.

THE LITTLE BLACK BOY

WILLIAM BLAKE

My mother bore me in the southern wild,
And I am black, but O! my soul is white;
White as an angel is the English child,
But I am black, as if bereav'd of light.

My mother taught me underneath a tree,
And sitting down before the heat of day,
She took me on her lap and kissed me,
And pointing to the East, began to say:

"Look on the rising sun: there God does live,
And gives his light, and gives his heat away,
And flowers and trees and beasts and men receive
Comfort in morning, joy in the noonday.

"And we are put on earth a little space,
That we may learn to bear the beams of love;
And these black bodies and this sunburnt face
Is but a cloud, and like a shady grove.

"For when our souls have learn'd the heat to bear,
The cloud will vanish, we shall hear his voice,

Saying, 'Come out from the grove, my love & care,
And round my golden tent like lambs rejoice.' "

Thus did my mother say, and kissed me,
And thus I say to little English boy:
When I from black, and he from white cloud free,
And round the tent of God like lambs we joy,

I'll shade him from the heat till he can bear
To lean in joy upon our Father's knee;
And then I'll stand and stroke his silver hair,
And be like him, and he will then love me.

THE TYGER

WILLIAM BLAKE

Tyger! Tyger! burning bright
In the forests of the night,
What immortal hand or eye
Could frame thy fearful symmetry?

In what distant deeps or skies
Burnt the fire of thine eyes?
On what wings dare he aspire?
What the hand dare seize the fire?

And what shoulder, & what art,
Could twist the sinews of thy heart?
And when thy heart began to beat,
What dread hand? & what dread feet?

What the hammer? what the chain?
In what furnace was thy brain?
What the anvil? what dread grasp
Dare its deadly terrors clasp?

When the stars threw down their spears,
And water'd heaven with their tears,

Did he smile his work to see?
Did he who made the Lamb make thee?

Tyger! Tyger! burning bright
In the forests of the night,
What immortal hand or eye,
Dare frame thy fearful symmetry?

AH! SUN-FLOWER

WILLIAM BLAKE

Ah, Sun-flower! weary of time,
Who countest the steps of the Sun;
Seeking after that sweet golden clime
Where the traveller's journey is done;

Where the Youth pined away with desire,
And the pale Virgin shrouded in snow,
Arise from their graves, and aspire
Where my Sun-flower wishes to go.

LONDON

WILLIAM BLAKE

I wander through each charter'd street,
Near where the charter'd Thames does flow,
And mark in every face I meet
Marks of weakness, marks of woe.

In every cry of every Man,
In every Infant's cry of fear,
In every voice, in every ban,
The mind-forg'd manacles I hear.

How the chimney-sweeper's cry
Every black'ning church appals;
And the hapless soldier's sigh
Runs in blood down palace walls.

But most through midnight streets I hear
How the youthful harlot's curse
Blasts the new-born infant's tear,
And blights with plagues the marriage hearse.

THE SCOFFERS

WILLIAM BLAKE

Mock on, mock on, Voltaire, Rousseau,
Mock on, mock on; 'tis all in vain;
You throw the sand against the wind
And the wind blows it back again.

And every sand becomes a gem
Reflected in the beams divine;
Blown back, they blind the mocking eye,
But still in Israel's paths they shine.

The atoms of Democritus
And Newton's particles of light
Are sands upon the Red Sea shore,
Where Israel's tents do shine so bright.

AUGURIES OF INNOCENCE

WILLIAM BLAKE

To see a World in a Grain of Sand
And a Heaven in a Wild flower,
Hold Infinity in the palm of your hand,
And Eternity in an hour.

A Robin Redbreast in a Cage
Puts all Heaven in a Rage.
A dove-house filled with Doves & Pigeons
Shudders Hell through all its regions.
A dog starved at his Master's Gate
Predicts the ruin of the State. 10

A Horse misused upon the Road
Calls to Heaven for Human blood.
Each outcry of the hunted Hare
A fibre from the Brain does tear.
A Skylark wounded in the wing,
A Cherubim does cease to sing;
The Game Cock clipped and armed for fight
Does the Rising Sun affright.
Every Wolf's & Lion's howl
Raises from Hell a Human Soul. 20
The wild Deer, wandering here & there,
Keeps the Human Soul from Care.
The Lamb misused breeds Public Strife
And yet forgives the Butcher's knife.
The Bat that flits at close of Eve
Has left the Brain that won't Believe.
The Owl that calls upon the Night
Speaks the Unbeliever's fright.
He who shall hurt the little Wren
Shall never be beloved by Men. 30
He who the Ox to wrath has moved
Shall never be by Woman loved.
The wanton Boy that kills the Fly
Shall feel the Spider's enmity.
He who torments the Chafer's Sprite
Weaves a Bower in endless Night.
The Caterpillar on the Leaf
Repeats to thee thy Mother's grief.
Kill not the Moth nor Butterfly,
For the Last Judgment draweth nigh. 40
He who shall train the Horse to war
Shall never pass the Polar Bar.
The Beggar's Dog & Widow's Cat,
Feed them & thou wilt grow fat.
The Gnat that sings his Summer's Song
Poison gets from Slander's tongue.
The poison of the Snake & Newt
Is the sweat of Envy's Foot.
The poison of the Honey Bee

Is the Artist's Jealousy. 50
The Prince's Robes & Beggar's Rags
Are Toadstools on the Miser's Bags.
A Truth that's told with bad intent
Beats all the Lies you can invent.
It is right it should be so;
Man was made for Joy & Woe;
And when this we rightly know,
Through the World we safely go.
Joy & Woe are woven fine,
A Clothing for the Soul divine. 60
Under every grief & pine
Runs a joy with silken twine.
The Babe is more than Swadling Bands;
Throughout all these Human Lands
Tools were made, & Born were hands,
Every Farmer understands.
Every Tear from Every Eye
Becomes a Babe in Eternity;
This is caught by Females bright,
And returned to its own delight. 70
The Bleat, the Bark, Bellow, & Roar
Are Waves that beat on Heaven's Shore.
The Babe that weeps the Rod beneath
Writes Revenge in realms of Death.
The Beggar's Rags, fluttering in Air,
Does to Rags the Heavens tear.
The Soldier, armed with Sword & Gun,
Palsied strikes the Summer's Sun.
The poor Man's Farthing is worth more
Than all the Gold on Afric's Shore. 80
One Mite wrung from the Lab'rer's hands
Shall buy & sell the Miser's Lands;
Or, if protected from on high,
Does that whole Nation sell & buy.
He who mocks the Infant's Faith
Shall be mocked in Age & Death.
He who shall teach the Child to Doubt
The rotting Grave shall never get out.

He who respects the Infant's faith
Triumphs over Hell & Death. 90
The Child's Toys and the Old Man's Reasons
Are the Fruits of the Two Seasons.
The Questioner, who sits so sly,
Shall never know how to Reply.
He who replies to words of Doubt
Doth put the Light of Knowledge out.
The Strongest Poison ever known
Came from Caesar's Laurel Crown.
Naught can Deform the Human Race
Like to the Armour's iron brace. 100
When Gold and Gems adorn the Plow
To peaceful Arts shall Envy bow.
A Riddle, or the Cricket's Cry,
Is to Doubt a fit Reply.
The Emmet's Inch & Eagle's Mile
Make Lame Philosophy to smile.
He who Doubts from what he sees
Will ne'er Believe, do what you Please.
If the Sun & Moon should Doubt,
They'd immediately Go Out. 110
To be in a Passion you Good may do,
But no Good if a Passion is in you.
The Whore & Gambler, by the State
Licensed, build that Nation's Fate.
The Harlot's cry from Street to Street
Shall weave Old England's winding Sheet.
The Winner's shout, the Loser's Curse,
Dance before dead England's Hearse.
Every Night and every Morn
Some to Misery are Born. 120
Every Morn and every Night
Some are Born to Sweet Delight.
Some are Born to Sweet Delight,
Some are Born to Endless Night.
We are led to Believe a Lie
When we see not Through the Eye,
Which was Born in a Night to perish in a Night,

When the Soul slept in Beams of Light.
God appears, & God is light,
To those poor souls who dwell in Night, 130
But does a Human Form Display
To those who Dwell in Realms of Day.

THE NEW JERUSALEM

WILLIAM BLAKE

And did those feet in ancient time
Walk upon England's mountains green?
And was the holy Lamb of God
On England's pleasant pastures seen?

And did the Countenance Divine
Shine forth upon our clouded hills?
And was Jerusalem builded here
Among those dark Satanic Mills?

Bring me my bow of burning gold!
Bring me my arrows of desire!
Bring me my spear! O clouds, unfold!
Bring me my chariot of fire!

I will not cease from mental fight,
Nor shall my sword sleep in my hand
Till we have built Jerusalem
In England's green and pleasant land.

JOHN ANDERSON, MY JO

ROBERT BURNS

John Anderson, my jo, John,
When we were first acquent,
Your locks were like the raven,
Your bonie brow was brent:
But now your brow is beld, John,

Your locks are like the snaw;
But blessings on your frosty pow,
John Anderson, my jo!

John Anderson, my jo, John,
We clamb the hill thegither;
And monie a cantie day, John,
We've had wi' ane anither:
Now we maun totter down, John,
And hand in hand we'll go,
And sleep thegither at the foot,
John Anderson, my jo!

FOR A' THAT AND A' THAT

ROBERT BURNS

Is there, for honest poverty,
That hings his head, and a' that?
The coward-slave, we pass him by,
We dare be poor for a' that!
For a' that, and a' that,
Our toils obscure, and a' that,
The rank is but the guinea's stamp;
The man's the gowd for a' that.

What though on hamely fare we dine,
Wear hodden-gray, and a' that; 10
Gie fools their silks, and knaves their wine,
A man's a man for a' that.
For a' that, and a' that,
Their tinsel show, and a' that,
The honest man, though e'er sae poor,
Is King o' men for a' that.

Ye see yon birkie, ca'd a lord,
Wha struts, and stares, and a' that;
Though hundreds worship at his word,
He's but a coof for a' that: 20

For a' that, and a' that,
His riband, star, and a' that.
The man of independent mind,
He looks and laughs at a' that.

A prince can mak a belted knight,
A marquis, duke, and a' that;
But an honest man's aboon his might,
Guid faith, he mauna fa' that!
For a' that, and a' that,
Their dignities, and a' that, 30
The pith o' sense, and pride o' worth,
Are higher rank than a' that.

Then let us pray that come it may,
As come it will, for a' that,
That sense and worth o'er a' the earth
Shall bear the gree, and a' that!
For a' that and a' that,
It's comin yet, for a' that,
That man to man the warld o'er,
Shall brothers be for a' that. 40

TAM O' SHANTER

ROBERT BURNS

When chapman billies [1] leave the street,
And drouthy neibors neibors meet,
As market-days are wearing late,
An' folk begin to tak the gate;
While we sit bousing at the nappy,[2]
An' getting fou and unco happy,
We think na on the slang Scots miles,
The mosses, waters, slaps,[3] and styles,
That lie between us and our hame,
Whare sits our sulky sullen dame, 10

[1] chapman billies—*pedlar fellows* [2] nappy—*ale* [3] slaps—*gates*

Gathering her brows like gathering storm,
Nursing her wrath to keep it warm.
  This truth fand honest Tam o' Shanter,
As he frae Ayr ae night did canter—
(Auld Ayr, wham ne'er a town surpasses
For honest men and bonnie lasses).
  O Tam! hadst thou but been sae wise
As ta'en thy ain wife Kate's advice!
She tauld thee weel thou was a skellum,[4]
A bletherin', blusterin', drunken blellum;[5] 20
That frae November till October,
Ae market-day thou was na sober;
That ilka melder[6] wi' the miller
Thou sat as lang as thou had siller;
That every naig was ca'd a shoe on,
The smith and thee gat roarin' fou on;
That at the Lord's house, even on Sunday,
Thou drank wi' Kirkton Jean till Monday.
She prophesied that, late or soon,
Thou would be found deep drown'd in Doon; 30
Or catch'd wi' warlocks[7] in the mirk[8]
By Alloway's auld haunted kirk.
  Ah, gentle dames! It gars me greet[9]
To think how mony counsels sweet,
How mony lengthen'd sage advices,
The husband frae the wife despises!
  But to our tale: Ae market night,
Tam had got planted unco right,
Fast by an ingle, bleezing finely,
Wi' reaming swats,[10] that drank divinely; 40
And at his elbow, Souter[11] Johnny,
His ancient, trusty, drouthy crony;
Tam lo'ed him like a very brither;
They had been fou for weeks thegither.
The night drave on wi' sangs and clatter,

[4] skellum—*rascal* [5] blellum—*babbler* [6] ilka melder—*each grinding time*
[7] warlocks—*wizards* [8] mirk—*dark* [9] gars me greet—*makes me cry*
[10] reaming swats—*foaming tankards* [11] Souter—*cobbler*

And aye the ale was growing better:
The landlady and Tam grew gracious,
Wi' favours secret, sweet, and precious;
The souter tauld his queerest stories;
The landlord's laugh was ready chorus: 50
The storm without might rair and rustle
Tam did na mind the storm a whistle.
Care, mad to see a man sae happy,
E'en drown'd himsel amang the nappy.
As bees flee hame wi' lades o' treasure,
The minutes wing'd their way wi' pleasure;
Kings may be blest, but Tam was glorious,
O'er a' the ills o' life victorious!
But pleasures are like poppies spread—
You seize the flow'r, its bloom is shed; 60
Or like the snow falls in the river—
A moment white, then melts for ever;
Or like the borealis race,
That flit ere you can point their place;
Or like the rainbow's lovely form
Evanishing amid the storm.
Nae man can tether time or tide;
The hour approaches Tam maun ride;
That hour, o' night's black arch the key-stane,
That dreary hour, he mounts his beast in; 70
And sic a night he taks the road in,
As ne'er poor sinner was abroad in.
The wind blew as 'tward blawn its last;
The rattling show'rs rose on the blast;
The speedy gleams the darkness swallow'd;
Loud, deep, and lang, the thunder bellow'd:
That night, a child might understand,
The Deil had business on his hand.
Weel mounted on his gray mare, Meg,
A better never lifted leg, 80
Tam skelpit[12] on thro' dub and mire,
Despising wind, and rain, and fire;
Whiles holding fast his gude blue bonnet;

[12] skelpit—*skedaddled*

Whiles crooning o'er some auld Scots sonnet;[13]
Whiles glow'ring round wi' prudent cares,
Lest bogles[14] catch him unawares.
Kirk-Alloway was drawing nigh,
Whare ghaists and houlets[15] nightly cry.
  By this time he was cross the ford,
Whare in the snaw the chapman smoor'd;[16] 90
And past the birks[17] and meikle stane,
Whare drunken Charlie brak 's neck-bane;
And thro' the whins,[18] and by the cairn,
Whare hunters fand the murder'd bairn;
And near the thorn, aboon the well,
Whare Mungo's mither hang'd hersel.
Before him Doon pours all his floods;
The doubling storm roars thro' the woods;
The lightnings flash from pole to pole;
Near and more near the thunders roll: 100
When, glimmering thro' the groaning trees,
Kirk-Alloway seem'd in a bleeze;
Thro' ilka bore[19] the beams were glancing;
And loud resounded mirth and dancing.
  Inspiring bold John Barleycorn!
What dangers thou canst make us scorn!
Wi' tippenny,[20] we fear nae evil;
Wi' usquabae,[21] we'll face the devil!
The swats sae ream'd[22] in Tammie's noddle,
Fair play, he car'd na deils a boddle![23] 110
But Maggie stood right sair astonish'd,
Till, by the heel and hand admonish'd,
She ventur'd forward on the light;
And, vow! Tam saw an unco sight!
Warlocks and witches in a dance!
Nae cotillon brent new frae France,
But hornpipes, jigs, strathspeys, and reels,

[13] sonnet—*ballad or song* [14] bogles—*goblins* [15] houlets—*owlets*
[16] smoored—*smothered* [17] birks—*birch trees* [18] whins—*furze bushes*
[19] ilka bore—*every crack* [20] tippenny—*twopenny ale* [21] usquabae—*whiskey*
[22] swats sae reamed—*ale so foamed* [23] boddle—*farthing*

Put life and mettle in their heels.
A winnock-bunker[24] in the east,
There sat auld Nick, in shape o' beast— 120
A touzie tyke, black, grim, and large!
To gie them music was his charge:
He screw'd the pipes and gart them skirl,
Till roof and rafters a' did dirl.
Coffins stood round like open presses,
That shaw'd the dead in their last dresses;
And by some devilish cantraip sleight[25]
Each in its cauld hand held a light,
By which heroic Tam was able
To note upon the haly table 130
A murderer's banes in gibbet-airns;
Twa span-lang, wee, unchristen'd bairns;
A thief new-cutted frae a rape—
Wi' his last gasp his gab[26] did gape;
Five tomahawks, wi' blude red-rusted;
Five scymitars, wi' murder crusted;
A garter, which a babe had strangled;
A knife, a father's throat had mangled,
Whom his ain son o' life bereft—
The gray hairs yet stack to the heft; 140
Wi' mair of horrible and awefu',
Which even to name wad be unlawfu'.
As Tammie glowr'd, amaz'd, and curious,
The mirth and fun grew fast and furious:
The piper loud and louder blew;
The dancers quick and quicker flew;
They reel'd, they set, they cross'd, they cleekit,
Till ilka carlin[27] swat[28] and reekit,[29]
And coost her duddies[30] to the wark,
And linkit at it in her sark![31] 150
Now Tam, O Tam! had thae been queans,[32]

[24] winnock-bunker—*window seat* [25] contraip sleight—*magic trick*
[26] gab—*mouth* [27] carlin—*hag* [28] swat—*sweated* [29] reekit—*reeked*
[30] coost her duddies—*threw off her clothes* [31] sark—*shirt*
[32] queans—*sturdy wenches*

A' plump and strapping in their teens;
Their sarks, instead o' creeshie flannen,[33]
Been snaw-white seventeen hunder linen!
Thir[34] breeks o' mine, my only pair,
That ance were plush, o' gude blue hair,
I wad hae gi'en them off my hurdies,[35]
For ae blink o' the bonnie burdies![36]
But wither'd beldams, auld and droll,
Ridgwoodie[37] hags wad spean[38] a foal, 160
Louping and flinging on a crummock,[39]
I wonder didna turn thy stomach.
But Tam kend what was what fu' brawlie
There was ae winsome wench and wawlie[40]
That night enlisted in the core,
Lang after kend on Carrick shore!
(For mony a beast to dead she shot,
And perish'd mony a bonnie boat,
And shook baith meikle corn and bear,[41]
And kept the country-side in fear.) 170
Her cutty sark,[42] o' Paisley harn,
That while a lassie she had worn,
In longitude tho' sorely scanty,
It was her best, and she was vauntie.[43]
Ah! little kend thy reverend grannie
That sark she coft[44] for her wee Nannie
Wi' twa pund Scots ('twas a' her riches)
Wad ever grac'd a dance of witches!
But here my Muse her wing maun cour;[45]
Sic flights are far beyond her pow'r— 180
To sing how Nannie lap and flang,
(A souple jade she was, and strang),
And how Tam stood, like ane bewitch'd,
And thought his very een enrich'd;

[33] creeshie flannen—*greasy flannel* [34] Thir—*these* [35] hurdies—*haunches*
[36] burdies—*girls* [37] Rigwoodie—*withered* [38] spean—*wean*
[39] crummock—*crooked staff* [40] wawlie—*buxom*
[41] corn and bear—*wheat and barley* [42] cutty sark—*short shift or chemise*
[43] vauntie—*proud of it* [44] coft—*bought* [45] cour—*lower*

Even Satan glowr'd, and fidg'd fu' fain,[46]
And hotch'd and blew wi' might and main:
Till first ae caper, syne anither,
Tam tint his reason a' thegither,
And roars out "Weel done, Cutty-sark!"
And in an instant all was dark! 190
And scarcely had he Maggie rallied,
When out the hellish legion sallied.
As bees bizz out wi' angry fyke
When plundering herds assail their byke,
As open pussie's[47] mortal foes
When pop! she starts before their nose,
As eager runs the market-crowd,
When "Catch the thief!" resounds aloud,
So Maggie runs; the witches follow,
Wi' money an eldritch skriech and hollow. 200
Ah, Tam! ah, Tam! thou'll get thy fairin'!
In hell they'll roast thee like a herrin'!
In vain thy Kate awaits thy comin'!
Kate soon will be a woefu' woman!
Now do thy speedy utmost, Meg,
And win the key-stane of the brig:
There at them thou thy tail may toss,
A running stream they darena cross.
But ere the key-stane she could make,
The fient a tail she had to shake! 210
For Nannie, far before the rest,
Hard upon noble Maggie prest,
And flew at Tam wi' furious ettle;[48]
But little wist she Maggie's mettle!
Ae spring brought off her master hale,
But left behind her ain gray tail:
The carlin claught her by the rump,
And left poor Maggie scarce a stump.
Now, wha this tale o' truth shall read,
Ilk man and mother's son, take heed; 220

[46] fidg'd fu' fain—*fidgeted with pleasure* [47] pussie—*the hare*
[48] ettle—*attempt*

Whene'er to drink you are inclin'd,
Or cutty-sarks run in your mind,
Think! ye may buy the joys o'er dear;
Remember Tam o'Shanter's mare.

THE SOLITARY REAPER

WILLIAM WORDSWORTH

Behold her, single in the field,
Yon solitary Highland Lass!
Reaping and singing by herself;
Stop here, or gently pass!
Alone she cuts and binds the grain,
And sings a melancholy strain;
O listen! for the Vale profound
Is overflowing with the sound.

No Nightingale did ever chant
More welcome notes to weary bands
Of travellers in some shady haunt,
Among Arabian sands:
A voice so thrilling ne'er was heard
In spring-time from the Cuckoo-bird,
Breaking the silence of the seas
Among the farthest Hebrides.

Will no one tell me what she sings?—
Perhaps the plaintive numbers flow
For old, unhappy, far-off things,
And battles long ago:
Or is it some more humble lay,
Familiar matter of to-day?
Some natural sorrow, loss, or pain,
That has been, and may be again?

Whate'er the theme, the maiden sang
As if her song could have no ending;
I saw her singing at her work,

And o'er the sickle bending;—
I listened, motionless and still;
And, as I mounted up the hill,
The music in my heart I bore
Long after it was heard no more.

A SLUMBER DID MY SPIRIT SEAL

WILLIAM WORDSWORTH

A slumber did my spirit seal;
I had no human fears:
She seemed a thing that could not feel
The touch of earthly years.

No motion has she now, no force;
She neither hears nor sees;
Rolled round in earth's diurnal course,
With rocks, and stones, and trees.

COMPOSED UPON WESTMINSTER BRIDGE
September 3, 1802

WILLIAM WORDSWORTH

Earth has not anything to show more fair;
Dull would he be of soul who could pass by
A sight so touching in its majesty:
This City now doth, like a garment, wear
The beauty of the morning; silent, bare,
Ships, towers, domes, theaters, and temples lie
Open unto the fields, and to the sky;
All bright and glittering in the smokeless air.
Never did sun more beautifully steep
In his first splendor, valley, rock, or hill;
Ne'er saw I, never felt, a calm so deep!
The river glideth at his own sweet will:
Dear God! the very houses seem asleep;
And all that mighty heart is lying still!

❡ LONDON, 1802

WILLIAM WORDSWORTH

Milton! thou shouldst be living at this hour;
England hath need of thee; she is a fen
Of stagnant waters: altar, sword, and pen,
Fireside, the heroic wealth of hall and bower,
Have forfeited their ancient English dower
Of inward happiness. We are selfish men;
Oh! raise us up, return to us again;
And give us manners, virtue, freedom, power.
Thy soul was like a Star, and dwelt apart:
Thou hadst a voice whose sound was like the sea:
Pure as the naked heavens, majestic, free,
So didst thou travel on life's common way,
In cheerful godliness; and yet thy heart
The lowliest duties on herself did lay.

❡ ODE: INTIMATIONS OF IMMORTALITY FROM RECOLLECTIONS OF EARLY CHILDHOOD

WILLIAM WORDSWORTH

The Child is father of the Man,
And I could wish my days to be
Bound each to each by natural piety.

I

There was a time when meadow, grove, and stream,
The earth, and every common sight,
To me did seem
Apparelled in celestial light,
The glory and the freshness of a dream.
It is not now as it hath been of yore;—
Turn wheresoe'er I may,
By night or day,
The things which I have seen I now can see no more.

2

The Rainbow comes and goes, 10
And lovely is the Rose;
The Moon doth with delight
Look round her when the heavens are bare;
Waters on a starry night
Are beautiful and fair;
The sunshine is a glorious birth;
But yet I know, where'er I go,
That there hath past away a glory from the earth.

3

Now, while the birds thus sing a joyous song,
And while the young lambs bound 20
As to the tabor's sound,
To me alone there came a thought of grief:
A timely utterance gave that thought relief,
And I again am strong:
The cataracts blow their trumpets from the steep;
No more shall grief of mine the season wrong;
I hear the Echoes through the mountains throng,
The Winds come to me from the fields of sleep,
And all the earth is gay;
Land and sea 30
Give themselves up to jollity,
And with the heart of May
Doth every Beast keep holiday;—
Thou Child of Joy,
Shout round me, let me hear thy shouts, thou
happy Shepherd-boy!

4

Ye blessed Creatures, I have heard the call
Ye to each other make; I see
The heavens laugh with you in your jubilee;

My heart is at your festival, 40
My head hath its coronal,
The fulness of your bliss, I feel—I feel it all.
Oh evil day! if I were sullen
While Earth herself is adorning,
This sweet May-morning,
And the Children are culling
On every side,
In a thousand valleys far and wide,
Fresh flowers; while the sun shines warm,
And the Babe leaps up on his Mother's arm:— 50
I hear, I hear, with joy I hear!
—But there's a Tree, of many, one,
A single Field which I have looked upon,
Both of them speak of something that is gone;
The Pansy at my feet
Doth the same tale repeat:
Whither is fled the visionary gleam?
Where is it now, the glory and the dream?

5

Our birth is but a sleep and a forgetting:
The Soul that rises with us, our life's Star, 60
Hath had elsewhere its setting,
And cometh from afar:
Not in entire forgetfulness,
And not in utter nakedness,
But trailing clouds of glory do we come
From God, who is our home:
Heaven lies about us in our infancy!
Shades of the prison-house begin to close
Upon the growing Boy,
But he beholds the light, and whence it flows, 70
He sees it in his joy;
The Youth, who daily farther from the east
Must travel, still is Nature's Priest,
And by the vision splendid

Is on his way attended;
At length the Man perceives it die away,
And fade into the light of common day.

6

Earth fills her lap with pleasures of her own;
Yearnings she hath in her own natural kind,
And, even with something of a Mother's mind, 80
And no unworthy aim,
The homely Nurse doth all she can
To make her Foster-child, her Inmate Man,
Forget the glories he hath known,
And that imperial palace whence he came.

7

Behold the Child among his new-born blisses,
A six years' Darling of a pigmy size!
See, where 'mid work of his own hand he lies,
Fretted by sallies of his mother's kisses,
With light upon him from his father's eyes! 90
See, at his feet, some little plan or chart,
Some fragment from his dream of human life,
Shaped by himself with newly-learned art;
A wedding or a festival,
A mourning or a funeral;
And this hath now his heart,
And unto this he frames his song:
Then will he fit his tongue
To dialogues of business, love, or strife;
But it will not be long 100
Ere this be thrown aside,
And with new joy and pride
The little Actor cons another part;
Filling from time to time his "humorous stage"
With all the Persons, down to palsied Age,
That Life brings with her in her equipage;

As if his whole vocation
Were endless imitation.

8

Thou, whose exterior semblance doth belie
Thy Soul's immensity; 110
Thou best Philosopher, who yet does keep
Thy heritage, thou Eye among the blind,
That, deaf and silent, read'st the eternal deep,
Haunted for ever by the eternal mind,—
Mighty Prophet! Seer blest!
On whom those truths do rest,
Which we are toiling all our lives to find,
In darkness lost, the darkness of the grave;
Thou, over whom thy Immortality
Broods like the Day, a Master o'er a Slave, 120
A Presence which is not to be put by;
To whom the grave
Is but a lonely bed without the sense or sight
Of day or the warm light,
A place of thought where we in waiting lie;
Thou little Child, yet glorious in the might
Of heaven-born freedom on thy being's height,
Why with such earnest pains dost thou provoke
The years to bring the inevitable yoke,
Thus blindly with thy blessedness at strife? 130
Full soon thy Soul shall have her earthly freight,
And custom lie upon thee with a weight,
Heavy as frost, and deep almost as life!

9

O joy! that in our embers
Is something that doth live,
That nature yet remembers
What was so fugitive!
The thought of our past years in me doth breed

Perpetual benediction: not indeed
For that which is most worthy to be blest; 140
Delight and liberty, the simple creed
Of childhood, whether busy or at rest,
With new-fledged hope still fluttering in his breast:—
Not for these I raise
The song of thanks and praise;
But for those obstinate questionings
Of sense and outward things,
Fallings from us, vanishings;
Blank misgivings of a Creature
Moving about in worlds not realized, 150
High instincts before which our mortal nature
Did tremble like a guilty thing surprised:
But for those first affections,
Those shadowy recollections,
Which, be they what they may,
Are yet the fountain-light of all our day,
Are yet a master-light of all our seeing;
Uphold us, cherish, and have power to make
Our noisy years seem moments in the being
Of the Eternal Silence: truths that wake, 160
To perish never:
Which neither listlessness, nor mad endeavor,
Nor man nor boy,
Nor all that is at enmity with joy,
Can utterly abolish or destroy!
Hence in a season of calm weather
Though inland far we be,
Our souls have sight of that immortal sea
Which brought us hither,
Can in a moment travel thither, 170
And see the children sport upon the shore,
And hear the mighty waters rolling evermore.

10

Then sing, ye Birds, sing, sing a joyous song!
And let the young Lambs bound

As to the tabor's sound!
We in thought will join your throng,
Ye that pipe and ye that play,
Ye that through your hearts to-day
Feel the gladness of the May!
What though the radiance which was once so bright 180
Be now forever taken from my sight,
Though nothing can bring back the hour
Of splendor in the grass, of glory in the flower;
We will grieve not, rather find
Strength in what remains behind;
In the primal sympathy
Which having been must ever be;
In the soothing thoughts that spring
Out of human suffering;
In the faith that looks through death, 190
In years that bring the philosophic mind.

II

And O, ye Fountains, Meadows, Hills, and Groves,
Forebode not any severing of our loves!
Yet in my heart of hearts I feel your might;
I only have relinquished one delight
To live beneath your more habitual sway.
I love the Brooks which down their channels fret,
Even more than when I tripped lightly as they;
The innocent brightness of a new-born Day
Is lovely yet; 200
The Clouds that gather round the setting sun
Do take a sober coloring from an eye
That hath kept watch o'er man's mortality;
Another race hath been, and other palms are won.
Thanks to the human heart by which we live,
Thanks to its tenderness, its joys, and fears,
To me the meanest flower that blows can give
Thoughts that do often lie too deep for tears.

MUTABILITY

WILLIAM WORDSWORTH

From low to high doth dissolution climb,
And sink from high to low, along a scale
Of awful notes, whose concord shall not fail;
A musical but melancholy chime,
Which they can hear who meddle not with crime,
Nor avarice, nor over-anxious care.
Truth fails not; but her outward forms that bear
The longest date do melt like frosty rime
That in the morning whiten'd hill and plain
And is no more; drop like the tower sublime
Of yesterday, which royally did wear
His crown of weeds, but could not even sustain
Some casual shout that broke the silent air,
Or the unimaginable touch of Time.

IT IS A BEAUTEOUS EVENING

WILLIAM WORDSWORTH

It is a beauteous evening, calm and free;
The holy time is quiet as a nun
Breathless with adoration; the broad sun
Is sinking down in its tranquility;
The gentleness of heaven broods o'er the sea:
Listen! the mighty Being is awake,
And doth with his eternal motion make
A sound like thunder—everlastingly.
Dear child! dear girl! that walkest with me here,
If thou appear untouched by solemn thought,
Thy nature is not therefore less divine:
Thou liest in Abraham's bosom all the year,
And worship'st at the Temple's inner shrine,
God being with thee when we know it not.

THE RIME OF THE ANCIENT MARINER

SAMUEL TAYLOR COLERIDGE

PART THE FIRST

An ancient Mariner meeteth three Gallants bidden to a wedding-feast, and detaineth one.

It is an ancient Mariner,
And he stoppeth one of three.
"By thy long grey beard and glittering eye,
Now wherefore stopp'st thou me?

The Bridegroom's doors are opened wide,
And I am next of kin;
The guests are met, the feast is set:
May'st hear the merry din."

He holds him with his skinny hand,
"There was a ship," quoth he. 10
"Hold off! unhand me, greybeard loon!"
Eftsoons his hand dropt he.

The Wedding-Guest is spell-bound by the eye of the old sea-faring man, and constrained to hear his tale.

He holds him with his glittering eye—
The Wedding-Guest stood still,
And listens like a three years' child:
The Mariner hath his will.

The Wedding-Guest sat on a stone:
He cannot choose but hear;
And thus spake on that ancient man,
The bright-eyed Mariner. 20

"The ship was cheered, the harbour cleared,
Merrily did we drop
Below the kirk, below the hill,
Below the lighthouse top.

The Mariner tells how the ship sailed southward with a good wind and fair weather, till it reached the line.

The Sun came up upon the left,
Out of the sea came he!
And he shone bright, and on the right
Went down into the sea.

Higher and higher every day,
Till over the mast at noon—" 30

The Wedding-Guest heareth the bridal music; but the Mariner continueth his tale.

The Wedding-Guest here beat his breast,
For he heard the loud bassoon.

The Bride hath paced into the hall,
Red as a rose is she;
Nodding their heads before her goes
The merry minstrelsy.

The Wedding-Guest he beat his breast,
Yet he cannot choose but hear;
And thus spake on that ancient man,
The bright-eyed Mariner. 40

The ship drawn by a storm toward the South Pole.

"And now the storm-blast came, and he
Was tyrannous and strong:
He struck with his o'ertaking wings,
And chased us south along.

With sloping masts and dipping prow,
As who pursued with yell and blow
Still treads the shadow of his foe
And forward bends his head,
The ship drove fast, loud roared the blast,
And southward aye we fled. 50

And now there came both mist and snow
And it grew wondrous cold:
And ice, mast-high, came floating by,
As green as emerald.

The land of ice, and of fearful sounds, where no living thing was to be seen.

And through the drifts the snowy clifts
Did send a dismal sheen:
Nor shapes of men nor beasts we ken—
The ice was all between.

The ice was here, the ice was there,
The ice was all around: 60

It cracked and growled, and roared and howled,
Like noises in a swound!

Till a great sea-bird, called the Albatross, came through the snow-fog, and was received with great joy and hospitality.

At length did cross an Albatross:
Thorough the fog it came;
As if it had been a Christian soul,
We hailed it in God's name.

It ate the food it ne'er had eat,
And round and round it flew.
The ice did split with a thunder-fit;
The helmsman steered us through! 70

And lo! the Albatross proveth a bird of good omen, and followeth the ship as it returned northward through fog and floating ice.

And a good south wind sprung up behind;
The Albatross did follow,
And every day, for food or play,
Came to the mariners' hollo!

In mist or cloud, on mast or shroud,
It perched for vespers nine;
Whiles all the night, through fog-smoke white,
Glimmered the white moonshine."

The ancient Mariner inhospitably killeth the pious bird of good omen.

"God save thee, ancient Mariner!
From the fiends that plague thee thus!— 80
Why look'st thou so?"—"With my crossbow
I shot the Albatross.

PART THE SECOND

"The Sun now rose upon the right:
Out of the sea came he,
Still hid in mist, and on the left
Went down into the sea.

And the good south wind still blew behind,
But no sweet bird did follow,

Nor any day for food or play
Came to the mariners' hollo! 90

His shipmates cry out against the ancient Mariner for killing the bird of good luck.

And I had done a hellish thing,
And it would work 'em woe:
For all averred, I had killed the bird
That made the breeze to blow.
Ah wretch! said they, the bird to slay,
That made the breeze to blow!

But when the fog cleared off, they justify the same, and thus make themselves accomplices in the crime.

Nor dim nor red, like God's own head,
The glorious Sun uprist:
Then all averred, I had killed the bird
That brought the fog and mist. 100
'Twas right, said they, such birds to slay,
That bring the fog and mist.

The fair breeze continues; the ship enters the Pacific Ocean and sails northward, even till it reaches the Line.

The fair breeze blew, the white foam flew,
The furrow followed free;
We were the first that ever burst
Into that silent sea.

The ship hath been suddenly becalmed.

Down dropt the breeze, the sails dropt down,
'Twas sad as sad could be;
And we did speak only to break
The silence of the sea! 110

All in a hot and copper sky,
The bloody Sun, at noon,
Right up above the mast did stand,
No bigger than the Moon.

Day after day, day after day,
We stuck, nor breath nor motion;
As idle as a painted ship
Upon a painted ocean.

And the Albatross begins to be avenged.

Water, water, everywhere,
And all the boards did shrink; 120

Water, water, everywhere,
Nor any drop to drink.

The very deep did rot: O Christ!
That ever this should be!
Yea, slimy things did crawl with legs
Upon the slimy sea.

About, about, in reel and rout
The death-fires danced at night;
The water, like a witch's oils,
Burnt green, and blue, and white. 130

And some in dreams assurèd were
Of the Spirit that plagued us so;
Nine fathom deep he had followed us
From the land of mist and snow.

A Spirit had followed them; one of the invisible inhabitants of this planet, neither departed souls nor angels; concerning whom the learned Jew, Josephus, and the Platonic Constantinopolitan, Michael Psellus, may be consulted. They are very numerous, and there is no climate or element without one or more.

And every tongue, through utter drought,
Was withered at the root;
We could not speak, no more than if
We had been choked with soot.

The shipmates, in their sore distress, would fain throw the whole guilt on the ancient Mariner: in sign whereof they hang the dead sea-bird round his neck.

Ah! well-a-day! what evil looks
Had I from old and young! 140
Instead of the cross, the Albatross
About my neck was hung.

PART THE THIRD

"There passed a weary time. Each throat
Was parched, and glazed each eye.
A weary time! a weary time!
How glazed each weary eye!
When looking westward, I beheld
A something in the sky.

The ancient Mariner beholdeth a sign in the element afar off.

At first it seemed a little speck,
And then it seemed a mist; 150
It moved and moved, and took at last
A certain shape, I wist.

A speck, a mist, a shape, I wist!
And still it neared and neared:
As if it dodged a watersprite,
It plunged and tacked and veered.

At its nearer approach it seemeth him to be a ship; and at a dear ransom he freeth his speech from the bonds of thirst.

With throats unslaked, with black lips baked,
We could not laugh nor wail;
Through utter drought all dumb we stood!
I bit my arm, I sucked the blood, 160
And cried, A sail! a sail!

A flash of joy;

With throats unslaked, with black lips baked,
Agape they heard me call:
Gramercy! they for joy did grin,
And all at once their breath drew in,
As they were drinking all.

And horror follows. For can it be a ship that comes onward without wind or tide?

See! See! (I cried) she tacks no more!
Hither to work us weal;
Without a breeze, without a tide,
She steadies with upright keel! 170

The western wave was all a-flame.
The day was well-nigh done!
Almost upon the western wave
Rested the broad bright Sun;
When that strange shape drove suddenly
Betwixt us and the Sun.

It seemeth him but the skeleton of a ship.

And straight the Sun was flecked with bars,
(Heaven's Mother send us grace!)
As if through a dungeon-grate he peered
With broad and burning face. 180

Alas! (thought I, and my heart beat loud)
How fast she nears and nears!
Are those her sails that glance in the Sun,
Like restless gossameres!

Are those her ribs through which the Sun
Did peer, as through a grate?
And is that Woman all her crew?
Is that a Death? and are there two?
Is Death that woman's mate?

And its ribs are seen as bars on the face of the setting Sun. The Spectre-Woman and her Death-mate, and no other on board the skeleton ship.

Her lips were red, her looks were free, 190
Her locks were yellow as gold:
Her skin was as white as leprosy,
The Nightmare Life-in-Death was she,
Who thicks man's blood with cold.

Like vessel, like crew!

The naked hulk alongside came
And the twain were casting dice;
"The game is done! I've won, I've won!"
Quoth she, and whistles thrice.

Death and Life-in-Death have diced for the ship's crew, and she (the latter) winneth the ancient Mariner.

The Sun's rim dips; the stars rush out:
At one stride comes the dark; 200
With far-heard whisper, o'er the sea,
Off shot the spectre-bark.

No twilight within the courts of the Sun.

We listened and looked sideways up!
Fear at my heart, as at a cup,
My life-blood seemed to sip!
The stars were dim, and thick the night,
The steersman's face by his lamp gleamed white;
From the sails the dew did drip—
Till clomb above the eastern bar
The hornèd Moon, with one bright star 210
Within the nether tip.

At the rising of the Moon,

One after another,

One after one, by the star-dogged Moon,
Too quick for groan or sigh,
Each turned his face with a ghastly pang,
And cursed me with his eye.

His shipmates drop down dead;

Four times fifty living men,
(And I heard nor sigh nor groan)
With heavy thump, a lifeless lump,
They dropped down one by one.

But Life-in-Death begins her work on the ancient Mariner.

The souls did from their bodies fly,— 220
They fled to bliss or woe!
And every soul, it passed me by,
Like the whizz of my crossbow!"

PART THE FOURTH

The Wedding-Guest feareth that a spirit is talking to him;

"I fear thee, ancient Mariner!
I fear thy skinny hand!
And thou art long, and lank, and brown,
As is the ribbed sea-sand.

I fear thee and thy glittering eye,
And thy skinny hand, so brown"—

But the ancient Mariner assureth him of his bodily life, and proceedeth to relate his horrible penance.

"Fear not, fear not, thou Wedding-Guest! 230
This body dropt not down.

Alone, alone, all, all alone,
Alone on a wide wide sea!
And never a saint took pity on
My soul in agony.

He despiseth the creatures of the calm.

The many men, so beautiful!
And they all dead did lie:
And a thousand thousand slimy things
Lived on; and so did I.

And envieth that they should live, and so many lie dead.

I looked upon the rotting sea, 240
And drew my eyes away;
I looked upon the rotting deck,
And there the dead men lay.

I looked to Heaven, and tried to pray;
But or ever a prayer had gusht,
A wicked whisper came, and made
My heart as dry as dust.

I closed my lids, and kept them close,
And the balls like pulses beat;
For the sky and the sea, and the sea and the sky, 250
Lay like a load on my weary eye,
And the dead were at my feet.

But the curse liveth for him in the eye of the dead men.

The cold sweat melted from their limbs,
Nor rot nor reek did they;
The look with which they looked on me
Had never passed away.

An orphan's curse would drag to hell
A spirit from on high;
But oh! more horrible than that
Is a curse in a dead man's eye! 260
Seven days, seven nights, I saw that curse,
And yet I could not die.

In his loneliness and fixedness he yearneth towards the journeying Moon, and the Stars that still sojourn, yet still move onward; and everywhere the blue sky belongs to them, and is their appointed rest, and their native country and their own natural homes, which they enter unannounced, as lords that are certainly expected and yet there is a silent joy at their arrival.

The moving Moon went up the sky,
And nowhere did abide:
Softly she was going up,
And a star or two beside—

Her beams bemocked the sultry main,
Like April hoar-frost spread;
But where the ship's huge shadow lay,
The charmèd water burnt alway
A still and awful red.

By the light of the Moon he beholdeth God's creatures of the great calm.

Beyond the shadow of the ship,
I watched the water-snakes:
They moved in tracks of shining white,
And when they reared, the elfish light
Fell off in hoary flakes.

Within the shadow of the ship
I watched their rich attire:
Blue, glossy green, and velvet black,
They coiled and swam; and every track 280
Was a flash of golden fire.

Their beauty and their happiness.

O happy living things! no tongue
Their beauty might declare:
A spring of love gushed from my heart,

He blesseth them in his heart.

And I blessed them unaware:
Sure my kind saint took pity on me,
And I blessed them unaware.

The spell begins to break.

The selfsame moment I could pray;
And from my neck so free
The Albatross fell off, and sank 290
Like lead into the sea.

PART THE FIFTH

'O sleep! it is a gentle thing,
Beloved from pole to pole!
To Mary Queen the praise be given!
She sent the gentle sleep from Heaven,
That slid into my soul.

By grace of the holy Mother, the ancient Mariner is refreshed with rain.

The silly buckets on the deck,
That had so long remained,
I dreamt that they were filled with dew;
And when I awoke, it rained. 300

My lips were wet, my throat was cold,
My garments all were dank;
Sure I had drunken in my dreams,
And still my body drank.

I moved, and could not feel my limbs:
I was so light—almost
I thought that I had died in sleep,
And was a blessèd ghost.

He heareth sounds and seeth strange sights and commotions in the sky and the element.

And soon I heard a roaring wind:
It did not come anear; 310
But with its sound it shook the sails,
That were so thin and sere.

The upper air burst into life!
And a hundred fire-flags sheen,
To and fro they were hurried about!
And to and fro, and in and out,
The wan stars danced between.

And the coming wind did roar more loud,
And the sails did sigh like sedge;
And the rain poured down from one black cloud; 320
The Moon was at its edge.

The thick black cloud was cleft, and still
The Moon was at its side:
Like waters shot from some high crag,
The lightning fell with never a jag,
A river steep and wide.

The bodies of the ship's crew are inspired, and the ship moves on;

The loud wind never reached the ship,
Yet now the ship moved on!
Beneath the lightning and the Moon
The dead men gave a groan. 330

They groaned, they stirred, they all uprose,
Nor spake, nor moved their eyes;

It had been strange, even in a dream,
To have seen those dead men rise.

The helmsman steered, the ship moved on;
Yet never a breeze up blew;
The mariners all 'gan work the ropes,
Where they were wont to do;
They raised their limbs like lifeless tools—
We were a ghastly crew. 340

The body of my brother's son
Stood by me, knee to knee:
The body and I pulled at one rope,
But he said nought to me."

"I fear thee, ancient Mariner!"
"Be calm, thou Wedding-Guest!
'Twas not those souls that fled in pain,
Which to their corses came again,
But a troop of spirits blest:

But not by the souls of the men, nor by daemons of earth or middle air, but by a blessed troop of angelic spirits, sent down by the invocation of the guardian saint.

For when it dawned—they dropt their arms, 350
And clustered round the mast;
Sweet sounds rose slowly through their mouths,
And from their bodies passed.

Around, around, flew each sweet sound,
Then darted to the Sun;
Slowly the sounds came back again,
Now mixed, now one by one.

Sometimes a-dropping from the sky
I heard the skylark sing;
Sometimes all little birds that are, 360
How they seemed to fill the sea and air
With their sweet jargoning!

And now 'twas like all instruments,
Now like a lonely flute;

And now it is an angel's song,
That makes the Heavens be mute.

It ceased; yet still the sails made on
A pleasant noise till noon,
A noise like of a hidden brook
In the leafy month of June, 370
That to the sleeping woods all night
Singeth a quiet tune.

Till noon we quietly sailed on,
Yet never a breeze did breathe:
Slowly and smoothly went the ship,
Moved onward from beneath.

The lonesome Spirit from the South Pole carries on the ship as far as the Line, in obedience to the angelic troop, but still requireth vengeance.

Under the keel nine fathom deep,
From the land of mist and snow,
The Spirit slid: and it was he
That made the ship to go. 380
The sails at noon left off their tune,
And the ship stood still also.

The Sun, right up above the mast,
Had fixed her to the ocean:
But in a minute she 'gan stir,
With a short uneasy motion—
Backwards and forwards half her length
With a short uneasy motion.

Then, like a pawing horse let go,
She made a sudden bound: 390
It flung the blood into my head,
And I fell down in a swound.

The Polar Spirit's fellow daemons, the invisible inhabitants of the element, take part in his wrong; and two of them relate, one to

How long in that same fit I lay,
I have not to declare;
But ere my living life returned,
I heard and in my soul discerned
Two voices in the air.

the other, that penance long and heavy for the ancient Mariner hath been accorded to the Polar Spirit, who returneth southward.

'Is it he?' quoth one, 'Is this the man?
By Him who died on cross,
With his cruel bow he laid full low 400
The harmless Albatross.

The Spirit who bideth by himself
In the land of mist and snow,
He loved the bird that loved the man
Who shot him with his bow.'

The other was a softer voice,
As soft as honeydew:
Quoth he, 'The man hath penance done,
And penance more will do.'

PART THE SIXTH

First Voice

" 'But tell me, tell me! speak again, 410
Thy soft response renewing—
What makes that ship drive on so fast?
What is the ocean doing?'

Second Voice

'Still as a slave before his lord,
The Ocean hath no blast;
His great bright eye most silently
Up to the Moon is cast—

If he may know which way to go;
For she guides him smooth or grim.
See, brother, see! how graciously 420
She looketh down on him.'

First Voice

The Mariner hath been cast into a trance;

'But why drives on that ship so fast,
Without or wave or wind?'

for the angelic power causeth the vessel to drive northward faster than human life could endure.

Second Voice

'The air is cut away before,
And closes from behind.

Fly, brother, fly! more high, more high!
Or we shall be belated:
For slow and slow that ship will go,
When the Mariner's trance is abated.'

The supernatural motion is retarded; the Mariner awakes, and his penance begins anew.

I woke, and we were sailing on 430
As in a gentle weather:
'Twas night, calm night, the Moon was high;
The dead men stood together.

All stood together on the deck,
For a charnel-dungeon fitter:
All fixed on me their stony eyes,
That in the Moon did glitter.

The pang, the curse, with which they died,
Had never passed away:
I could not draw my eyes from theirs, 440
Nor turn them up to pray.

The curse is finally expiated.

And now this spell was snapt: once more
I viewed the ocean green,
And looked far forth, yet little saw
Of what had else been seen—

Like one that on a lonesome road
Doth walk in fear and dread,
And having once turned round walks on,
And turns no more his head;
Because he knows a frightful fiend 450
Doth close behind him tread.

But soon there breathed a wind on me,
Nor sound nor motion made:

Its path was not upon the sea,
In ripple or in shade.

It raised my hair, it fanned my cheek
Like a meadow-gale of spring—
It mingled strangely with my fears,
Yet it felt like a welcoming.

Swiftly, swiftly flew the ship, 460
Yet she sailed softly too:
Sweetly, sweetly blew the breeze—
On me alone it blew.

And the ancient Mariner beholdeth his native country.

Oh! dream of joy! is this indeed
The lighthouse top I see?
Is this the hill? is this the kirk?
Is this mine own countree?

We drifted o'er the harbour-bar,
And I with sobs did pray—
O let me be awake, my God! 470
Or let me sleep alway.

The harbour-bay was clear as glass,
So smoothly was it strewn!
And on the bay the moonlight lay,
And the shadow of the Moon.

The rock shone bright, the kirk no less,
That stands above the rock:
The moonlight steeped in silentness
The steady weathercock.

And the bay was white with silent light, 480
Till rising from the same,
Full many shapes, that shadows were,
In crimson colours came.

The angelic spirits leave the dead bodies, and appear in their own forms of light.

A little distance from the prow
Those crimson shadows were:

I turned my eyes upon the deck—
O, Christ! what saw I there!

Each corse lay flat, lifeless and flat,
And, by the holy rood!
A man all light, a seraph-man, 490
On every corse there stood.

This seraph-band, each waved his hand:
It was a heavenly sight!
They stood as signals to the land,
Each one a lovely light;

This seraph-band, each waved his hand,
No voice did they impart—
No voice; but oh! the silence sank
Like music on my heart.

But soon I heard the dash of oars, 500
I heard the Pilot's cheer;
My head was turned perforce away,
And I saw a boat appear.

The Pilot and the Pilot's boy,
I heard them coming fast:
Dear Lord in Heaven! it was a joy
That dead men could not blast.

I saw a third—I heard his voice:
It is the Hermit good!
He singeth loud his godly hymns 510
That he makes in the wood.
He'll shrieve my soul, he'll wash away
The Albatross's blood.

PART THE SEVENTH

The Hermit of the Wood

"This Hermit good lives in that wood
Which slopes down to the sea.

How loudly his sweet voice he rears!
He loves to talk with the marineres
That come from a far countree.

He kneels at morn, and noon, and eve—
He hath a cushion plump: 520
It is the moss that wholly hides
The rotted old oak-stump.

The skiff-boat neared: I heard them talk,
'Why this is strange, I trow!
Where are those lights so many and fair,
That signal made but now?'

Approacheth the ship with wonder.

'Strange, by faith!' the Hermit said—
'And they answered not our cheer!
The planks look warped! and see those sails,
How thin they are and sere! 530
I never saw aught like to them,
Unless perchance it were
Brown skeletons of leaves that lag
My forest-brook along;
When the ivy-tod is heavy with snow,
And the owlet whoops to the wolf below,
That eats the she-wolf's young.'

'Dear Lord! it hath a fiendish look—'
(The Pilot made reply)
'I am a-feared'—'Push on, push on!' 540
Said the Hermit cheerily.

The boat came closer to the ship,
But I nor spake nor stirred;
The boat came close beneath the ship,
And straight a sound was heard.

Under the water it rumbled on,
Still louder and more dread:

The ship suddenly sinketh.

It reached the ship, it split the bay;
The ship went down like lead.

Stunned by that loud and deadful sound, 550
Which sky and ocean smote,
Like one that hath been seven days drowned
My body lay afloat;
But swift as dreams, myself I found
Within the Pilot's boat.

The ancient Mariner is saved in the Pilot's boat.

Upon the whirl, where sank the ship,
The boat spun round and round;
And all was still, save that the hill
Was telling of the sound.

I moved my lips—the Pilot shrieked 560
And fell down in a fit;
The holy Hermit raised his eyes,
And prayed where he did sit.

I took the oars: the Pilot's boy,
Who now doth crazy go,
Laughed loud and long, and all the while
His eyes went to and fro.
'Ha! ha!' quoth he, 'full plain I see,
The Devil knows how to row.'

And now, all in my own countree, 570
I stood on the firm land!
The Hermit stepped forth from the boat,
And scarcely he could stand.

The ancient Mariner earnestly entreateth the Hermit to shrive him; and the penance of life falls on him.

'O shrieve me, shrieve me, holy man!'
The Hermit crossed his brow.
'Say quick,' quoth he, 'I bid thee say—
What manner of man are thou?'

Forthwith this frame of mine was wrenched
With a woeful agony,

Which forced me to begin my tale; 580
And then it left me free.

And ever and anon throughout his future life an agony constraineth him to travel from land to land,

Since then, at an uncertain hour,
That agony returns:
And till my ghastly tale is told,
This heart within me burns.

I pass, like night, from land to land;
I have strange power of speech;
That moment that his face I see,
I know the man that must hear me:
To him my tale I teach. 590

What loud uproar bursts from that door!
The wedding-guests are there:
But in the garden-bower the Bride
And Bride-maids singing are:
And hark the little vesper bell,
Which biddeth me to prayer!

O Wedding-Guest! this soul hath been
Alone on a wide wide sea:
So lonely 'twas, that God Himself
Scarce seemèd there to be. 600

O sweeter than the marriage-feast,
'Tis sweeter far to me,
To walk together to the kirk
With a goodly company!—

To walk together to the kirk,
And all together pray,
While each to his great Father bends,
Old men, and babes, and loving friends,
And youths and maidens gay!

And to teach, by his own example, love and reverence to all

Farewell, farewell! but this I tell 610
To thee, thou Wedding-Guest!

things that God made and loveth.

He prayeth well, who loveth well
Both man and bird and beast.

He prayeth best, who loveth best
All things both great and small;
For the dear God who loveth us,
He made and loveth all."

The Mariner, whose eye is bright,
Whose beard with age is hoar,
Is gone: and now the Wedding-Guest 620
Turned from the Bridegroom's door.

He went like one that hath been stunned,
And is of sense forlorn:
A sadder and a wiser man,
He rose the morrow morn.

¶ KUBLA KHAN; Or, a Vision in a Dream

SAMUEL TAYLOR COLERIDGE

In Xanadu did Kubla Khan
A stately pleasure-dome decree:
Where Alph, the sacred river, ran
Through caverns measureless to man
Down to a sunless sea.
So twice five miles of fertile ground
With walls and towers were girdled round:
And here were gardens bright with sinuous rills,
Where blossomed many an incense-bearing tree;
And here were forests ancient as the hills, 10
Enfolding sunny spots of greenery.

But oh! that deep romantic chasm which slanted
Down the green hill athwart a cedarn cover!
A savage place! as holy and enchanted
As e'er beneath a waning moon was haunted
By woman wailing for her demon-lover!

And from this chasm, with ceaseless turmoil seething,
As if this earth in fast thick pants were breathing,
A mighty fountain momently was forced;
Amid whose swift half-intermitted burst 20
Huge fragments vaulted like rebounding hail,
Or chaffy grain beneath the thresher's flail:
And 'mid these dancing rocks at once and ever
It flung up momently the sacred river.
Five miles meandering with a mazy motion
Through wood and dale the sacred river ran,
Then reached the caverns measureless to man,
And sank in tumult to a lifeless ocean:
And 'mid this tumult Kubla heard from far
Ancestral voices prophesying war! 30
The shadow of the dome of pleasure
Floated midway on the waves;
Where was heard the mingled measure
From the fountain and the caves.
It was a miracle of rare device,
A sunny pleasure-dome with caves of ice!

A damsel with a dulcimer
In a vision once I saw:
It was an Abyssinian maid,
And on her dulcimer she played, 40
Singing of Mount Abora.
Could I revive within me
Her symphony and song,
To such a deep delight 'twould win me,
That with music loud and long,
I would build that dome in air,
That sunny dome! those caves of ice!
And all who heard should see them there,
And all should cry, Beware! Beware!
His flashing eyes, his floating hair! 50
Weave a circle round him thrice.
And close your eyes with holy dread,
For he on honey-dew hath fed,
And drunk the milk of Paradise.

PAST RUIN'D ILION . . .

WALTER SAVAGE LANDOR

Past ruin'd Ilion Helen lives,
  Alcestis rises from the shades;
Verse calls them forth; 'tis verse that gives
  Immortal youth to mortal maids.

Soon shall Oblivion's deepening veil
  Hide all the peopled hills you see,
The gay, the proud, while lovers hail
  In distant ages you and me.

The tear for fading beauty check,
  For passing glory cease to sigh;
One form shall rise above the wreck,
  One name, Ianthe, shall not die.

ROSE AYLMER

WALTER SAVAGE LANDOR

Ah what avails the sceptred race,
  Ah what the form divine!
What every virtue, every grace!
  Rose Aylmer, all were thine.

Rose Aylmer, whom these wakeful eyes
  May weep, but never see,
A night of memories and sighs
  I consecrate to thee.

ON SEEING A HAIR OF LUCRETIA BORGIA

WALTER SAVAGE LANDOR

Borgia, thou once were almost too august
And high for adoration;—now thou'rt dust;
All that remains of thee these plaits infold,
Calm hair, meandering with pellucid gold!

TO A PAINTER

WALTER SAVAGE LANDOR

Conceal not Time's misdeeds, but on my brow
Retrace his mark:
Let the retiring hair be silvery now
That once was dark:
Eyes that reflected images too bright
Let clouds o'ercast,
And from the tablet be abolished quite
The cheerful past.
Yet care's deep lines should one from wakened mirth
Steal softly o'er,
Perhaps on me the fairest of the earth
May glance once more.

LATELY OUR POETS

WALTER SAVAGE LANDOR

Lately our poets loiter'd in green lanes,
Content to catch the ballads of the plains;
I fancied I had strength enough to climb
A loftier station at no distant time,
And might securely from intrusion doze
Upon the flowers thro' which Ilissus flows.
In those pale olive grounds all voices cease,
And from afar dust fills the paths of Greece.
My slumber broken and my doublet torn,
I find the laurel also bears a thorn.

STANZAS FOR MUSIC

GEORGE GORDON, LORD BYRON

There's not a joy the world can give like that it takes away,
When the glow of early thought declines in Feeling's dull decay;

'Tis not on Youth's smooth cheek the blush alone, which fades so fast,
But the tender bloom of heart is gone, ere Youth itself be past.

Then the few whose spirits float above the wreck of happiness
Are driven o'er the shoals of guilt or ocean of excess:
The magnet of their course is gone, or only points in vain
The shore to which their shivered sail shall never stretch again.

Then the mortal coldness of the soul like Death itself comes down;
It cannot feel for others' woes, it dare not dream its own;
That heavy chill has frozen o'er the fountain of our tears,
And though the eye may sparkle still, 'tis where the ice appears.

Though wit may flash from fluent lips, and mirth distract the breast,
Through midnight hours that yield no more their former hope of rest;
'Tis but as ivy-leaves around the ruined turret wreath,
All green and wildly fresh without, but worn and grey beneath.

Oh could I feel as I have felt,—or be what I have been,
Or weep as I could once have wept, o'er many a vanished scene;
As springs, in deserts found, seem sweet, all brackish though they be,
So, midst the withered waste of life, those tears would flow to me.

STANZAS FOR MUSIC

GEORGE GORDON, LORD BYRON

There be none of beauty's daughters
With a magic like thee;
And like music on the waters
Is thy sweet voice to me:
When, as if its sound were causing
The charmed ocean's pausing,
The waves lie still and gleaming,
And the lulled winds seem dreaming;

And the midnight moon is weaving
Her bright chain o'er the deep;

Whose breast is gently heaving,
  As an infant's asleep:
So the spirit bows before thee,
To listen and adore thee;
With a full but soft emotion,
Like the swell of Summer's ocean.

THE ISLES OF GREECE
from *Don Juan*

GEORGE GORDON, LORD BYRON

The isles of Greece, the isles of Greece!
  Where burning Sappho loved and sung,
Where grew the arts of War and Peace,—
  Where Delos rose, and Phoebus sprung!
Eternal summer gilds them yet,
But all, except their Sun, is set.

The Scian and the Teian muse,
  The Hero's harp, the Lover's lute,
Have found the fame your shores refuse:
  Their place of birth alone is mute 10
To sounds which echo further west
Than your Sires' "Islands of the Blest."

The mountains look on Marathon—
  And Marathon looks on the sea;
And musing there an hour alone,
  I dreamed that Greece might still be free;
For standing on the Persians' grave,
I could not deem myself a slave.

A King sate on the rocky brow
  Which looks o'er sea-born Salamis; 20
And ships, by thousands, lay below,
  And men in nations;—all were his!
He counted them at break of day—
And when the Sun set, where were they?

And where are they? and where art thou,
  My country? On thy voiceless shore
The heroic lay is tuneless now—
  The heroic bosom beats no more!
And must thy Lyre, so long divine,
Degenerate into hands like mine? 30

'Tis something, in the dearth of Fame,
  Though linked among a fettered race,
To feel at least a patriot's shame,
  Even as I sing, suffuse my face;
For what is left the poet here?
For Greeks a blush—for Greece a tear.

Must *we* but weep o'er days more blest?
  Must *we* but blush?—Our fathers bled.
Earth! render back from out thy breast
  A remnant of our Spartan dead! 40
Of the three hundred grant but three,
To make a new Thermopylae!

What, silent still? and silent all?
  Ah! no;—the voices of the dead
Sound like a distant torrent's fall,
  And answer, "Let one living head,
But one arise,—we come, we come!"
'Tis but the living who are dumb.

In vain—in vain: strike other chords:
  Fill high the cup with Samian wine! 50
Leave battles to the Turkish hordes,
  And shed the blood of Scio's vine!
Hark! rising to the ignoble call—
How answers each bold Bacchanal!

You have the Pyrrhic dance as yet;
  Where is the Pyrrhic phalanx gone?
Of two such lessons, why forget
  The nobler and the manlier one?

You have the letters Cadmus gave—
Think ye he meant them for a slave? 60

Fill high the bowl with Samian wine!
  We will not think of themes like these!
It made Anacreon's song divine:
  He served—but served Polycrates—
A Tyrant; but our masters then
Were still, at least, our countrymen.

The Tyrant of the Chersonese
  Was Freedom's best and bravest friend;
That tyrant was Miltiades!
  Oh! that the present hour would lend 70
Another despot of the kind!
Such chains as his were sure to bind.

Fill high the bowl with Samian wine!
  On Suli's rock, and Parga's shore,
Exists the remnant of a line
  Such as the Doric mothers bore;
And there, perhaps, some seed is sown,
The Heracleidan blood might own.

Trust not for freedom to the Franks—
  They have a king who buys and sells; 80
In native swords and native ranks,
  The only hope of courage dwells;
But Turkish force, and Latin fraud,
Would break your shield, however broad.

Fill high the bowl with Samian wine!
  Our virgins dance beneath the shade—
I see their glorious black eyes shine;
  But gazing on each glowing maid,
My own the burning tear-drop laves,
To think such breasts must suckle slaves. 90

Place me on Sunium's marbled steep,
  Where nothing, save the waves and I,

May hear our mutual murmurs sweep;
  There, swan-like, let me sing and die:
A land of slaves shall ne'er be mine—
Dash down yon cup of Samian wine!

* * *

Thus sung, or would, or could, or should have sung,
  The modern Greek, in tolerable verse:
If not like Orpheus quite, when Greece was young,
  Yet in these times he might have done much worse: 100
His strain displayed some feeling—right or wrong;
  And feeling, in a poet, is the source
Of others' feeling; but they are such liars,
And take all colours—like the hands of dyers.

But words are things, and a small drop of ink,
  Falling like dew, upon a thought, produces
That which makes thousands, perhaps millions, think;
  'Tis strange, the shortest letter which man uses
Instead of speech, may form a lasting link
  Of ages; to what straits old Time reduces 110
Frail man when paper—even a rag like this,
Survives himself, his tomb, and all that's his!

And when his bones are dust, his grave a blank,
  His station, generation, even his nation,
Become a thing, or nothing, save to rank
  In chronological commemoration,
Some dull MS. oblivion long has sank,
  Or graven stone found in a barrack's station
In digging the foundation of a closet,
May turn his name up, as a rare deposit. 120

And glory long has made the sages smile;
  'Tis something, nothing, words, illusion, wind—
Depending more upon the historian's style
  Than on the name a person leaves behind:
Troy owes to Homer what whist owes to Hoyle;

The present century was growing blind
To the great Marlborough's skill in giving knocks,
Until his late Life by Archdeacon Coxe.

Milton's the prince of poets—so we say;
A little heavy, but no less divine: 130
An independent being in his day—
Learn'd, pious, temperate in love and wine;
But his life falling into Johnson's way,
We're told this great high priest of all the Nine
Was whipt at college—a harsh sire—odd spouse,
For the first Mrs. Milton left his house.

All these are, *certes,* entertaining facts,
Like Shakespeare's stealing deer, Lord Bacon's bribes;
Like Titus' youth, and Cæsar's earliest acts;
Like Burns (whom Doctor Currie well describes); 140
Like Cromwell's pranks;—but although truth exacts
These amiable descriptions from the scribes,
As most essential to their hero's story,
They do not much contribute to his glory.

All are not moralists, like Southey, when
He prated to the world of "Pantisocrasy":
Or Wordsworth unexcised, unhired, who then
Season'd his pedlar poems with democracy;
Or Coleridge, long before his flighty pen
Lent to the Morning Post its aristocracy; 150
When he and Southey, following the same path,
Espoused two partners (milliners of Bath).

Such names at present cut a convict figure,
The very Botany Bay in moral geography;
Their royal treason, renegado rigor,
Are good manure for their more bare biography.
Wordsworth's last quarto, by the way, is bigger
Than any since the birthday of typography;
A drowsy frowzy poem, call'd the "Excursion,"
Writ in a manner which is my aversion. 160

He there builds up a formidable dyke
  Between his own and others' intellect;
But Wordsworth's poem, and his followers, like
  Joanna Southcote's Shiloh, and her sect,
Are things which in this century don't strike
  The public mind,—so few are the elect;
And the new births of both their stale virginities
Have proved but dropsies, taken for divinities.

But let me to my story: I must own,
  If I have any fault, it is digression, 170
Leaving my people to proceed alone,
  While I soliloquize beyond expression:
But these are my addresses from the throne,
  Which put off business to the ensuing session:
Forgetting each omission is a loss to
The world, not quite so great as Ariosto.

I know that what our neighbors call *"longueurs,"*
  (We've not so good a *word,* but have the *thing,*
In that complete perfection which insures
  An epic from Bob Southey every Spring—) 180
Form not the true temptation which allures
  The reader; but 't would not be hard to bring
Some fine examples of the *epopée.*
To prove its grand ingredient is *ennui.*

We learn from Horace, "Homer sometimes sleeps;"
  We feel without him, Wordsworth sometimes wakes,—
To show with what complacency he creeps,
  With his dear *"Wagoners,"* around his lakes.
He wishes for "a boat" to sail the deeps—
  Of ocean?—No, of air; and then he makes 190
Another outcry for "a little boat,"
And drivels seas to set it well afloat.

If he must fain sweep o'er the ethereal plain,
  And Pegasus runs restive in his "Wagon,"
Could he not beg the loan of Charles's Wain?

Or pray Medea for a single dragon?
Or if, too classic for his vulgar brain,
He fear'd his neck to venture such a nag on,
And he must needs mount nearer to the moon,
Could not the blockhead ask for a balloon? 200

"Pedlars," and "Boats," and "Wagons!" Oh! ye shades
Of Pope and Dryden, are we come to this?
That trash of such sort not alone evades
Contempt, but from the bathos' vast abyss
Floats scumlike uppermost, and these Jack Cades
Of sense and song above your graves may hiss—
The "little boatman" and his "Peter Bell"
Can sneer at him who drew "Achitophel!"

ODE TO THE WEST WIND

PERCY BYSSHE SHELLEY

I

O wild West Wind, thou breath of Autumn's being,
Thou, from whose unseen presence the leaves dead
Are driven, like ghosts from an enchanter fleeing,

Yellow, and black, and pale, and hectic red,
Pestilence-stricken multitudes: O thou,
Who chariotest to their dark wintry bed

The wingèd seeds, where they lie cold and low,
Each like a corpse within its grave, until
Thine azure sister of the Spring shall blow

Her clarion o'er the dreaming earth, and fill 10
(Driving sweet buds like flocks to feed in air)
With living hues and odors plain and hill:

Wild Spirit, which art moving everywhere;
Destroyer and preserver; hear! oh, hear!

2

Thou on whose stream, mid the steep sky's commotion,
Loose clouds like earth's decaying leaves are shed,
Shook from the tangled boughs of Heaven and Ocean,

Angels of rain and lightning: there are spread
On the blue surface of thine airy surge,
Like the bright hair uplifted from the head 20

Of some fierce Mænad, even from the dim verge
Of the horizon to the zenith's height,
The locks of the approaching storm. Thou dirge

Of the dying year, to which this closing night
Will be the dome of a vast sepulcher,
Vaulted with all thy congregated might

Of vapors, from whose solid atmosphere
Black rain, and fire, and hail will burst: oh, hear!

3

Thou who didst waken from his summer dreams
The blue Mediterranean, where he lay, 30
Lulled by the coil of his crystàlline streams,

Beside a pumice isle in Baiæ's bay,
And saw in sleep old palaces and towers
Quivering within the wave's intenser day,

All overgrown with azure moss and flowers
So sweet, the sense faints picturing them! thou
For whose path the Atlantic's level powers

Cleave themselves into chasms, while far below
The sea-blooms and the oozy woods which wear
The sapless foliage of the ocean, know 40

Thy voice, and suddenly grow gray with fear,
And tremble and despoil themselves: oh, hear!

4

If I were a dead leaf thou mightest bear;
If I were a swift cloud to fly with thee;
A wave to pant beneath thy power, and share

The impulse of thy strength, only less free
Than thou, O uncontrollable! If even
I were as in my boyhood, and could be

The comrade of thy wanderings over heaven,
As then, when to outstrip thy skiey speed 50
Scarce seemed a vision; I would ne'er have striven

As thus with thee in prayer in my sore need.
Oh lift me as a wave, a leaf, a cloud!
I fall upon the thorns of life! I bleed!

A heavy weight of hours has chained and bowed
One too like thee: tameless, and swift, and proud.

5

Make me thy lyre, even as the forest is:
What if my leaves are falling like its own!
The tumult of thy mighty harmonies

Will take from both a deep, autumnal tone, 60
Sweet though in sadness. Be thou, spirit fierce,
My spirit! Be thou me, impetuous one!

Drive my dead thoughts over the universe
Like withered leaves to quicken a new birth!
And, by the incantation of this verse,

Scatter, as from an unextinguished hearth
Ashes and sparks, my words among mankind!
Be through my lips to unawakened earth

The trumpet of a prophecy! Oh, wind,
If Winter comes, can Spring be far behind? 70

OZYMANDIAS

PERCY BYSSHE SHELLEY

I met a traveller from an antique land
Who said: "Two vast and trunkless legs of stone
Stand in the desert. Near them, on the sand,
Half sunk, a shattered visage lies, whose frown,
And wrinkled lip, and sneer of cold command,
Tell that its sculptor well those passions read
Which yet survive, stamped on these lifeless things,
The hand that mocked them and the heart that fed;
And on the pedestal these words appear:
'My name is Ozymandias, king of kings;
Look on my works, ye Mighty, and despair!'
Nothing beside remains. Round the decay
Of that colossal wreck, boundless and bare
The lone and level sands stretch far away."

chorus from *HELLAS*

PERCY BYSSHE SHELLEY

The world's great age begins anew,
  The golden years return,
The earth doth like a snake renew
  Her winter weeds outworn:
Heaven smiles, and faiths and empires gleam,
Like wrecks of a dissolving dream.

A brighter Hellas rears its mountains
  From waves serener far:

A new Peneus rolls his fountains
  Against the morning star. 10
Where fairer Tempes bloom, there sleep
Young Cyclads on a sunnier deep.

A loftier Argo cleaves the main,
  Fraught with a later prize;
Another Orpheus sings again,
  And loves, and weeps, and dies.
A new Ulysses leaves once more
Calypso for his native shore.

O, write no more the tale of Troy,
  If Earth Death's scroll must be! 20
Nor mix with Laian rage the joy
  Which dawns upon the free:
Although a subtler Sphinx renew
Riddles of death Thebes never knew.

Another Athens shall arise,
  And to remoter time
Bequeath, like sunset to the skies,
  The splendour of its prime;
And leave, if nought so bright may live,
All earth can take or Heaven can give. 30

Saturn and Love their long repose
  Shall burst, more bright and good
Than all who fell, than One who rose,
  Than many unsubdued:
Not gold, not blood, their altar dowers,
But votive tears and symbol flowers.

Oh, cease! Must hate and death return?
  Cease! Must men kill and die?
Cease! drain not to its dregs the urn
  Of bitter prophecy. 40
The world is weary of the past,
Oh, might it die, or rest at last!

LINES: "WHEN THE LAMP IS SHATTERED"

PERCY BYSSHE SHELLEY

When the lamp is shattered,
The light in the dust lies dead—
When the cloud is scattered
The rainbow's glory is shed.
When the lute is broken,
Sweet tones are remembered not;
When the lips have spoken,
Loved accents are soon forgot.

As music and splendor
Survive not the lamp and the lute,
The heart's echoes render
No song when the spirit is mute:—
No song but sad dirges,
Like the wind through a ruined cell,
Or the mournful surges
That ring the dead seaman's knell.

When hearts have once mingled
Love first leaves the well-built nest;
The weak one is singled
To endure what it once possessed.
O Love! who bewailest
The frailty of all things here,
Why choose you the frailest
For your cradle, your home, and your bier?

Its passions will rock thee
As the storms rock the ravens on high;
Bright reason will mock thee,
Like the sun from a wintry sky.
From thy nest every rafter
Will rot, and thine eagle home
Leave thee naked to laughter,
When leaves fall and cold winds come.

TO A WATERFOWL

WILLIAM CULLEN BRYANT

Whither, midst falling dew,
While glow the heavens with the last steps of day,
Far, through their rosy depths, dost thou pursue
Thy solitary way?

Vainly the fowler's eye
Might mark thy distant flight to do thee wrong,
As, darkly seen against the crimson sky,
Thy figure floats along.

Seek'st thou the plashy brink
Of weedy lake, or marge of river wide,
Or where the rocking billows rise and sink
On the chafed ocean-side?

There is a Power whose care
Teaches thy way along that pathless coast—
The desert and illimitable air—
Lone wandering, but not lost.

All day thy wings have fanned,
At that far height, the cold, thin atmosphere,
Yet stoop not, weary, to the welcome land,
Though the dark night is near.

And soon that toil shall end;
Soon shalt thou find a summer home, and rest,
And scream among thy fellows; reeds shall bend,
Soon, o'er thy sheltered nest.

Thou'rt gone, the abyss of heaven
Hath swallowed up thy form; yet, on my heart
Deeply hath sunk the lesson thou hast given,
And shall not soon depart.

He who, from zone to zone,
Guides through the boundless sky thy certain flight,
In the long way that I must tread alone,
Will lead my steps aright.

THE DEATH OF LINCOLN

WILLIAM CULLEN BRYANT

Oh, slow to smite and swift to spare,
Gentle and merciful and just!
Who, in the fear of God, didst bear
The sword of power, a nation's trust!

In sorrow by thy bier we stand,
Amid the awe that hushes all,
And speak the anguish of a land
That shook with horror at thy fall.

Thy task is done; the bond are free:
We bear thee to an honored grave,
Whose proudest monument shall be
The broken fetters of the slave.

Pure was thy life; its bloody close
Hath placed thee with the sons of light,
Among the noble host of those
Who perished in the cause of Right.

THE EVE OF ST. AGNES

JOHN KEATS

(There was a belief in medieval times that on St. Anges' Eve, January 20th, a girl, with proper preparation, might dream of her future husband, who would appear to her as in a vision and kiss her and feast with her.)

St. Agnes' Eve—Ah, bitter chill it was!
The owl, for all his feathers, was a-cold;
The hare limped trembling through the frozen grass,
And silent was the flock in woolly fold:
Numb were the Beadsman's fingers while he told
His rosary, and while his frosted breath,
Like pious incense from a censer old,
Seemed taking flight for heaven, without a death,
Past the sweet Virgin's picture, while his prayer he saith.

2

His prayer he saith, this patient, holy man; 10
Then takes his lamp, and riseth from his knees,
And back returneth, meager, barefoot, wan,
Along the chapel aisle by slow degrees:
The sculptured dead, on each side, seem to freeze,
Imprisoned in black, purgatorial rails:
Knights, ladies, praying in dumb orat'ries,
He passeth by, and his weak spirit fails
To think how they may ache in icy hoods and mails.

3

Northward he turneth through a little door,
And scarce three steps, ere Music's golden tongue 20
Flattered to tears this aged man and poor;
But no—already had his death-bell rung:
The joys of all his life were said and sung;
His was harsh penance on St. Agnes' Eve:
Another way he went, and soon among
Rough ashes sat he for his soul's reprieve,
And all night kept awake, for sinners' sake to grieve.

4

That ancient Beadsman heard the prelude soft;
And so it chanced, for many a door was wide,

From hurry to and fro. Soon, up aloft, 30
The silver, snarling trumpets 'gan to chide:
The level chambers, ready with their pride,
Were glowing to receive a thousand guests:
The carved angels, ever eager-eyed,
Stared, where upon their heads the cornice rests,
With hair blown back and wings put crosswise on their breasts.

5

At length burst in the argent revelry,
With plume, tiara, and all rich array,
Numerous as shadows haunting faerily
The brain new-stuffed, in youth, with triumphs gay 40
Of old romance. These let us wish away,
And turn, sole-thoughted, to one Lady there,
Whose heart had brooded, all that wintry day,
On love, and winged St. Agnes' saintly care,
As she had heard old dames full many times declare.

6

They told her how, upon St. Agnes' Eve,
Young virgins might have visions of delight,
And soft adorings from their loves receive
Upon the honeyed middle of the night,
If ceremonies due they did aright; 50
As, supperless to bed they must retire,
And couch supine their beauties, lily white;
Nor look behind, nor sideways, but require
Of Heaven with upward eyes for all that they desire.

7

Full of this whim was thoughtful Madeline:
The music, yearning like a God in pain,
She scarcely heard: her maiden eyes divine,
Fixed on the floor, saw many a sweeping train
Pass by—she heeded not at all: in vain

Came many a tiptoe, amorous cavalier, 60
And back retired; not cooled by high disdain,
But she saw not: her heart was otherwhere;
She sighed for Agnes' dreams, the sweetest of the year.

8

She danced along with vague, regardless eyes,
Anxious her lips, her breathing quick and short:
The hallowed hour was near at hand: she sighs
Amid the timbrels, and the thronged resort
Of whisperers in anger or in sport;
'Mid looks of love, defiance, hate, and scorn,
Hoodwinked with faery fancy; all amort, 70
Save to St. Agnes and her lambs unshorn,
And all the bliss to be before to-morrow morn.

9

So, purposing each moment to retire,
She lingered still. Meantime, across the moors,
Had come young Porphyro, with heart on fire
For Madeline. Beside the portal doors,
Buttressed from moonlight, stands he, and implores
All saints to give him sight of Madeline,
But for one moment in the tedious hours,
That he might gaze and worship all unseen; 80
Perchance speak, kneel, touch, kiss—in sooth such things have been.

10

He ventures in: let no buzzed whisper tell:
All eyes be muffled, or a hundred swords
Will storm his heart, Love's fev'rous citadel:
For him, those chambers held barbarian hordes,
Hyena foemen, and hot-blooded lords,
Whose very dogs would execrations howl
Against his lineage: not one breast affords

Him any mercy, in that mansion foul,
Save one old beldame, weak in body and in soul. 90

11

Ah, happy chance! the aged creature came,
Shuffling along with ivory-headed wand,
To where he stood, hid from the torch's flame,
Behind a broad hall-pillar, far beyond
The sound of merriment and chorus bland:
He startled her; but soon she knew his face,
And grasped his fingers in her palsied hand,
Saying, "Mercy, Porphyro! hie thee from this place;
They are all here to-night, the whole bloodthirsty race!

12

"Get hence! get hence! there's dwarfish Hildebrand: 100
He had a fever late, and in the fit
He cursed thee and thine, both house and land:
Then there's that old Lord Maurice, not a whit
More tame for his gray hairs—Alas me! flit!
Flit like a ghost away."—"Ah, Gossip dear,
We're safe enough; here in this arm-chair sit,
And tell me how—" "Good saints! not here, not here!
Follow me, child, or else these stones will be thy bier."

13

He followed through a lowly arched way,
Brushing the cobwebs with his lofty plume; 110
And as she muttered "Well-a—well-a-day!"
He found him in a little moonlight room,
Pale, latticed, chill, and silent as a tomb.
"Now tell me where is Madeline," said he,
"O tell me, Angela, by the holy loom
Which none but secret sisterhood may see,
When they St. Agnes' wool are weaving piously."

14

"St. Agnes! Ah! it is St. Agnes' Eve—
Yet men will murder upon holy days.
Thou must hold water in a witch's sieve, 120
And be liege-lord of all the Elves and Fays
To venture so: it fills me with amaze
To see thee, Porphyro!—St. Agnes' Eve!
God's help! my lady fair the conjurer plays
This very night: good angels her deceive!
But let me laugh awhile,—I've mickle time to grieve."

15

Feebly she laugheth in the languid moon,
While Porphyro upon her face doth look,
Like puzzled urchin on an aged crone
Who keepeth closed a wondrous riddle-book, 130
As spectacled she sits in chimney nook.
But soon his eyes grew brilliant, when she told
His lady's purpose; and he scarce could brook
Tears, at the thought of those enchantments cold,
And Madeline asleep in lap of legends old.

16

Sudden a thought came like a full-blown rose,
Flushing his brow, and in his pained heart
Made purple riot: then doth he propose
A stratagem, that makes the beldame start:
"A cruel man and impious thou art: 140
Sweet lady, let her pray, and sleep, and dream
Alone with her good angels, far apart
From wicked men like thee. Go, go! I deem
Thou canst not surely be the same that thou didst seem."

17

"I will not harm her, by all saints I swear,"
Quoth Porphyro: "O may I ne'er find grace

When my weak voice shall whisper its last prayer,
If one of her soft ringlets I displace,
Or look with ruffian passion in her face:
Good Angela, believe me by these tears; 150
Or I will, even in a moment's space,
Awake, with horrid shout, my foemen's ears,
And beard them, though they be more fanged than wolves and
bears."

18

"Ah! why wilt thou affright a feeble soul?
A poor, weak, palsy-stricken, churchyard thing,
Whose passing-bell may ere the midnight toll;
Whose prayers for thee, each morn and evening,
Were never missed." Thus plaining, doth she bring
A gentler speech from burning Porphyro;
So woeful, and of such deep sorrowing, 160
That Angela gives promise she will do
Whatever he shall wish, betide her weal or woe.

19

Which was, to lead him, in close secrecy,
Even to Madeline's chamber, and there hide
Him in a closet, of such privacy
That he might see her beauty unespied,
And win perhaps that night a peerless bride,
While legioned fairies paced the coverlet,
And pale enchantment held her sleepy-eyed.
Never on such a night have lovers met, 170
Since Merlin paid his Demon all the monstrous debt.

20

"It shall be as thou wishest," said the Dame:
"All cates and dainties shall be stored there
Quickly on this feast-night: by the tambour frame
Her own lute thou wilt see: no time to spare,

For I am slow and feeble, and scarce dare
On such a catering trust my dizzy head.
Wait here, my child, with patience; kneel in prayer
The while. Ah! thou must needs the lady wed,
Or may I never leave my grave among the dead." 180

21

So saying she hobbled off with busy fear.
The lover's endless minutes slowly passed;
The dame returned, and whispered in his ear
To follow her; with aged eyes aghast
From fright of dim espial. Safe at last
Through many a dusky gallery, they gain
The maiden's chamber, silken, hushed and chaste;
Where Porphyro took covert, pleased amain.
His poor guide hurried back with agues in her brain.

22

Her faltering hand upon the balustrade, 190
Old Angela was feeling for the stair,
When Madeline, St. Agnes' charmed maid,
Rose, like a missioned spirit, unaware:
With silver taper's light, and pious care,
She turned, and down the aged gossip led
To a safe level matting. Now prepare,
Young Porphyro, for gazing on that bed;
She comes, she comes again, like ring-dove frayed and fled.

23

Out went the taper as she hurried in;
Its little smoke, in pallid moonshine, died: 200
She closed the door, she panted, all akin
To spirits of the air, and visions wide:
No uttered syllable, or, woe betide!
But to her heart, her heart was voluble,
Paining with eloquence her balmy side;

As though a tongueless nightingale should swell
Her throat in vain, and die, heart-stifled, in her dell.

24

A casement high and triple-arched there was,
All garlanded with carven imageries,
Of fruits, and flowers, and bunches of knot-grass, **210**
And diamonded with panes of quaint device,
Innumerable of stains and splendid dyes,
As are the tiger-moth's deep-damasked wings;
And in the midst, 'mong thousand heraldries,
And twilight saints, and dim emblazonings,
A shielded scutcheon blushed with blood of queens and kings.

25

Full on this casement shone the wintry moon,
And threw warm gules on Madeline's fair breast,
As down she knelt for Heaven's grace and boon;
Rose-bloom fell on her hands, together prest, **220**
And on her silver cross soft amethyst,
And on her hair a glory, like a saint:
She seemed a splendid angel, newly drest,
Save wings, for heaven:—Porphyro grew faint:
She knelt, so pure a thing, so free from mortal taint.

26

Anon his heart revives: her vespers done,
Of all its wreathed pearls her hair she frees;
Unclasps her warmed jewels one by one;
Loosens her fragrant bodice; by degrees
Her rich attire creeps rustling to her knees: **230**
Half-hidden, like a mermaid in sea-weed,
Pensive awhile she dreams awake, and sees,
In fancy, fair St. Agnes in her bed,
But dares not look behind, or all the charm is fled.

27

Soon, trembling in her soft and chilly nest,
In sort of wakeful swoon, perplexed she lay,
Until the poppied warmth of sleep oppressed
Her soothed limbs, and soul fatigued away;
Flown, like a thought, until the morrow-day;
Blissfully havened both from joy and pain; 240
Clasped like a missal where swart Paynims pray;
Blinded alike from sunshine and from rain,
As though a rose should shut, and be a bud again.

28

Stolen to this paradise, and so entranced,
Porphyro gazed upon her empty dress,
And listened to her breathing, if it chanced
To wake into a slumberous tenderness;
Which when he heard, that minute did he bless,
And breathed himself: then from the closet crept,
Noiseless as fear in a wide wilderness, 250
And over the hushed carpet, silent, stept,
And 'tween the curtains peeped, where, lo!—how fast she slept.

29

Then by the bed-side, where the faded moon
Made a dim, silver twilight, soft he set
A table, and, half anguished, threw thereon
A cloth of woven crimson, gold, and jet—
O for some drowsy Morphean amulet!
The boisterous, midnight, festive clarion,
The kettle-drum, and far-heard clarinet,
Affray his ears, though but in dying tone:— 260
The hall-door shuts again, and all the noise is gone.

30

And still she slept an azure-lidded sleep,
In blanched linen, smooth, and lavendered,

While he from forth the closet brought a heap
Of candied apple, quince, and plum, and gourd;
With jellies soother than the creamy curd,
And lucent syrops, tinct with cinnamon;
Manna and dates, in argosy transferred
From Fez; and spiced dainties, every one,
From silken Samarcand to cedared Lebanon. 270

31

These delicates he heaped with glowing hand
On golden dishes and in baskets bright
Of wreathed silver: sumptuous they stand
In the retired quiet of the night,
Filling the chilly room with perfume light.—
"And now, my love, my seraph fair, awake!
Thou art my heaven, and I thine eremite:
Open thine eyes, for meek St. Agnes' sake,
Or I shall drowse beside thee, so my soul doth ache."

32

Thus whispering, his warm, unnerved arm 280
Sank in her pillow. Shaded was her dream
By the dusk curtains:—'twas a midnight charm
Impossible to melt as iced stream:
The lustrous salvers in the moonlight gleam;
Broad golden fringe upon the carpet lies:
It seemed he never, never could redeem
From such a stedfast spell his lady's eyes;
So mused awhile, entoiled in woofed phantasies.

33

Awakening up, he took her hollow lute,—
Tumultuous,—and, in chords that tenderest be, 290
He played an ancient ditty, long since mute,
In Provence called, "La belle dame sans mercy:"
Close to her ear touching the melody;—

Wherewith disturbed, she uttered a soft moan:
He ceased—she panted quick—and suddenly
Her blue affrayed eyes wide open shone:
Upon his knees he sank, pale as smooth-sculptured stone.

34

Her eyes were open, but she still beheld,
Now wide awake, the vision of her sleep:
There was a painful change, that nigh expelled 300
The blisses of her dream so pure and deep
At which fair Madeline began to weep,
And moan forth witless words with many a sigh,
While still her gaze on Porphyro would keep;
Who knelt, with joined hands and piteous eye,
Fearing to move or speak, she looked so dreamingly.

35

"Ah, Porphyro!" said she, "but even now
Thy voice was at sweet tremble in mine ear,
Made tuneable with every sweetest vow;
And those sad eyes were spiritual and clear: 310
How changed thou art! how pallid, chill, and drear!
Give me that voice again, my Porphyro,
Those looks immortal, those complainings dear!
Oh, leave me not in this eternal woe,
For if thou diest, my Love, I know not where to go."

36

Beyond a mortal man impassioned far
At these voluptuous accents, he arose,
Ethereal, flushed, and like a throbbing star
Seen 'mid the sapphire heaven's deep repose;
Into her dream he melted, as the rose 320
Blendeth its odor with the violet,—
Solution sweet: meantime the frost-wind blows
Like Love's alarum, pattering the sharp sleet
Against the window-panes; St. Agnes' moon hath set.

37

'Tis dark: quick pattereth the flaw-blown sleet.
"This is no dream, my bride, my Madeline!"
'Tis dark: the iced gusts still rave and beat:
"No dream, alas! alas! and woe is mine!
Porphyro will leave me here to fade and pine.
Cruel! what traitor could thee hither bring? 330
I curse not, for my heart is lost in thine,
Though thou forsakest a deceived thing;—
A dove forlorn and lost with sick unpruned wing."

38

"My Madeline! sweet dreamer! lovely bride!
Say, may I be for aye thy vassal blest?
Thy beauty's shield, heart-shaped and vermeil-dyed?
Ah, silver shrine, here will I take my rest
After so many hours of toil and quest,
A famished pilgrim,—saved by miracle.
Though I have found, I will not rob thy nest, 340
Saving of thy sweet self; if thou think'st well
To trust, fair Madeline, to no rude infidel.

39

"Hark! 'tis an elfin-storm from faery land,
Of haggard seeming, but a boon indeed:
Arise—arise! the morning is at hand;—
The bloated wassailers will never heed;—
Let us away, my love, with happy speed;
There are no ears to hear, or eyes to see,—
Drowned all in Rhenish and the sleepy mead:
Awake! arise! my love, and fearless be, 350
For o'er the southern moors I have a home for thee."

40

She hurried at his words, beset with fears,
For there were sleeping dragons all around,

At glaring watch, perhaps, with ready spears—
Down the wide stairs a darkling way they found;
In all the house was heard no human sound.
A chain-drooped lamp was flickering by each door;
The arras, rich with horseman, hawk, and hound,
Fluttered in the besieging wind's uproar;
And the long carpets rose along the gusty floor. 360

41

They glide, like phantoms, into the wide hall;
Like phantoms, to the iron porch they glide,
Where lay the Porter, in uneasy sprawl,
With a huge empty flagon by his side:
The wakeful bloodhound rose, and shook his hide,
But his sagacious eye an inmate owns:
By one, and one, the bolts full easy slide:—
The chains lie silent on the footworn stones;
The key turns, and the door upon its hinges groans.

42

And they are gone: aye, ages long ago 370
These lovers fled away into the storm.
That night the Baron dreamt of many a woe,
And all his warrior-guests with shade and form
Of witch, and demon, and large coffin-worm,
Were long be-nightmared. Angela the old
Died palsy-twitched, with meager face deform;
The Beadsman, after thousand aves told,
For aye unsought-for slept among his ashes cold.

LA BELLE DAME SANS MERCI

JOHN KEATS

O WHAT can ail thee, Knight at arms,
Alone and palely loitering?
The sedge has withered from the Lake
And no birds sing!

O what can ail thee, Knight at arms,
So haggard, and so woe begone?
The Squirrel's granary is full
And the harvest's done.

I see a lily on thy brow
With anguish moist and fever dew, 10
And on thy cheeks a fading rose
Fast withereth too—

I met a Lady in the Meads,
Full beautiful, a faery's child
Her hair was long, her foot was light
And her eyes were wild—

I made a Garland for her head,
And bracelets too, and fragrant Zone
She look'd at me as she did love
And made sweet moan— 20

I set her on my pacing steed
And nothing else saw all day long
For sidelong would she bend and sing
A faery's song—

She found me roots of relish sweet
And honey wild and manna dew
And sure in language strange she said
I love thee true—

She took me to her elfin grot
And there she wept and sigh'd full sore, 30
And there I shut her wild wild eyes
With kisses four.

And there she lulled me asleep
And there I dream'd, Ah Woe betide!
The latest dream I ever dreamt
On the cold hill side.

I saw pale Kings, and Princes too
  Pale warriors, death pale were they all;
They cried, La belle dame sans merci
  Thee hath in thrall. 40

I saw their starv'd lips in the gloam
  With horrid warning gaped wide,
And I awoke, and found me here
  On the cold hill's side.

And this is why I sojourn here
  Alone and palely loitering;
Though the sedge is withered from the Lake
  And no birds sing——

¶ ODE ON A GRECIAN URN

JOHN KEATS

1

Thou still unravish'd bride of quietness,
  Thou foster-child of silence and slow time,
Sylvan historian, who canst thus express
  A flowery tale more sweetly than our rhyme:
What leaf-fring'd legend haunts about thy shape
  Of deities or mortals, or of both,
    In Tempe or the dales of Arcady?
  What men or gods are these? What maidens loth?
What mad pursuit? What struggle to escape?
    What pipes and timbrels? What wild ecstasy? 10

2

Heard melodies are sweet, but those unheard
  Are sweeter; therefore, ye soft pipes, play on;
Not to the sensual ear, but, more endear'd,
  Pipe to the spirit ditties of no tone:
Fair youth, beneath the trees, thou canst not leave

Thy song, nor ever can those trees be bare;
Bold Lover, never, never canst thou kiss,
Though winning near the goal—yet, do not grieve;
She cannot fade, though thou hast not thy bliss,
For ever wilt thou love, and she be fair! 20

3

Ah, happy, happy boughs! that cannot shed
Your leaves, nor ever bid the Spring adieu;
And, happy melodist, unwearièd,
For ever piping songs for ever new;
More happy love! more happy, happy love!
For ever warm and still to be enjoy'd,
For ever panting, and for ever young;
All breathing human passion far above,
That leaves a heart high-sorrowful and cloy'd,
A burning forehead, and a parching tongue. 30

4

Who are these coming to the sacrifice?
To what green altar, O mysterious priest,
Lead'st thou that heifer lowing at the skies,
And all her silken flanks with garlands drest?
What little town by river or sea shore,
Or mountain-built with peaceful citadel,
Is emptied of this folk, this pious morn?
And, little town, thy streets for evermore
Will silent be; and not a soul to tell
Why thou art desolate, can e'er return. 40

5

O Attic shape! Fair attitude! with brede
Of marble men and maidens overwrought,
With forest branches and the trodden weed;
Thou, silent form, dost tease us out of thought
As doth eternity: Cold Pastoral!

When old age shall this generation waste,
Thou shalt remain, in midst of other woe
Than ours, a friend to man, to whom thou say'st,
"Beauty is truth, truth beauty,"—that is all
Ye know on earth, and all ye need to know. 50

ODE TO A NIGHTINGALE

JOHN KEATS

1

My heart aches, and a drowsy numbness pains
My sense, as though of hemlock I had drunk,
Or emptied some dull opiate to the drains
One minute past, and Lethe-wards had sunk:
'Tis not through envy of thy happy lot,
But being too happy in thine happiness,—
That thou, light-wingèd Dryad of the trees,
In some melodious plot
Of beechen green, and shadows numberless,
Singest of summer in full-throated ease. 10

2

O, for a draught of vintage! that hath been
Cool'd a long age in the deep-delved earth,
Tasting of Flora and the country green,
Dance, and Provençal song, and sunburnt mirth!
O for a beaker full of the warm South,
Full of the true, the blushful Hippocrene,
With beaded bubbles winking at the brim,
And purple-stained mouth;
That I might drink, and leave the world unseen,
And with thee fade away into the forest dim: 20

3

Fade far away, dissolve, and quite forget
What thou among the leaves hast never known,

The weariness, the fever, and the fret
  Here, where men sit and hear each other groan;
Where palsy shakes a few, sad, last gray hairs,
  Where youth grows pale, and spectre-thin, and dies;
    Where but to think is to be full of sorrow
      And leaden-eyed despairs,
  Where Beauty cannot keep her lustrous eyes,
    Or new Love pine at them beyond tomorrow. 30

4

Away! away! for I will fly to thee,
  Not charioted by Bacchus and his pards,
But on the viewless wings of Poesy,
  Though the dull brain perplexes and retards:
Already with thee! tender is the night,
  And haply the Queen-Moon is on her throne,
    Cluster'd around by all her starry fays;
      But here there is no light,
  Save what from heaven is with the breezes blown
    Through verdurous glooms and winding mossy ways. 40

5

I cannot see what flowers are at my feet,
  Nor what soft incense hangs upon the boughs,
But, in embalmèd darkness, guess each sweet
  Wherewith the seasonable month endows
The grass, the thicket, and the fruit-tree wild;
  White hawthorn, and the pastoral eglantine;
    Fast fading violets cover'd up in leaves;
      And mid-May's eldest child,
  The coming musk-rose, full of dewy wine,
    The murmurous haunt of flies on summer eves. 50

6

Darkling I listen; and, for many a time
  I have been half in love with easeful Death,

Call'd him soft names in many a musèd rhyme,
  To take into the air my quiet breath;
Now more than ever seems it rich to die,
  To cease upon the midnight with no pain,
    While thou art pouring forth thy soul abroad
      In such an ecstasy!
  Still wouldst thou sing, and I have ears in vain—
    To thy high requiem become a sod. 60

7

Thou wast not born for death, immortal Bird!
  No hungry generations tread thee down;
The voice I hear this passing night was heard
  In ancient days by emperor and clown:
Perhaps the self-same song that found a path
  Through the sad heart of Ruth, when, sick for home,
    She stood in tears amid the alien corn;
      The same that oft-times hath
  Charm'd magic casements, opening on the foam
    Of perilous seas, in faery lands forlorn. 70

8

Forlorn! the very word is like a bell
  To toll me back from thee to my sole self!
Adieu! the fancy cannot cheat so well
  As she is fam'd to do, deceiving elf.
Adieu! adieu! thy plaintive anthem fades
  Past the near meadows, over the still stream,
    Up the hill-side; and now 'tis buried deep
      In the next valley-glades:
  Was it a vision, or a waking dream?
    Fled is that music:—Do I wake or sleep? 80

ODE ON MELANCHOLY

JOHN KEATS

1

No, no, go not to Lethe, neither twist
  Wolf's-bane, tight-rooted, for its poisonous wine;
Nor suffer thy pale forehead to be kissed
  By nightshade, ruby grape of Proserpine;
Make not your rosary of yew-berries,
  Nor let the beetle, nor the death-moth be
    Your mournful Psyche, nor the downy owl
A partner in your sorrow's mysteries;
  For shade to shade will come too drowsily,
    And drown the wakeful anguish of the soul.

2

But when the melancholy fit shall fall
  Sudden from heaven like a weeping cloud,
That fosters the droop-headed flowers all,
  And hides the green hill in an April shroud;
Then glut thy sorrow on a morning rose,
  Or on the rainbow of the salt sand-wave,
    Or on the wealth of globèd peonies;
Or if thy mistress some rich anger shows,
  Emprison her soft hand, and let her rave,
    And feed deep, deep upon her peerless eyes.

3

She dwells with Beauty—Beauty that must die;
  And Joy, whose hand is ever at his lips
Bidding adieu; and aching Pleasure nigh,
  Turning to poison while the bee-mouth sips:
Ay, in the very temple of Delight
  Veiled Melancholy has her sovran shrine,
    Though seen of none save him whose strenuous tongue

Can burst Joy's grape against his palate fine:
His soul shall taste the sadness of her might,
And be among her cloudy trophies hung.

FATE

RALPH WALDO EMERSON

Deep in the man sits fast his fate
To mould his fortunes mean or great:
Unknown to Cromwell as to me
Was Cromwell's measure or degree;
Unknown to him, as to his horse,
If he than his groom be better or worse.
He works, plots, fights, in rude affairs,
With squires, lords, kings, his craft compares,
Till late he learned, through doubt and fear,
Broad England harboured not his peer:
Obeying Time, the last to own
The Genius from its cloudy throne.
For the prevision is allied
Unto the thing so signified;
Or say, the foresight that awaits
Is the same Genius that creates.

COMPENSATION

RALPH WALDO EMERSON

The wings of Time are black and white,
Pied with morning and with night.
Mountain tall and ocean deep
Trembling balance duly keep.
In changing moon, in tidal wave,
Glows the feud of Want and Have.
Gauge of more and less through space.
Electric star or pencil plays,
The lonely Earth amid the balls
That hurry through the eternal halls,

A makeweight flying to the void,
Supplemental asteroid,
Or compensatory spark,
Shoots across the neutral Dark.

Man's the elm, and Wealth the vine;
Stanch and strong the tendrils twine:
Though the frail ringlets thee deceive,
None from its stock that vine can reave.
Fear not, then, thou child infirm,
There's no god dare wrong a worm;
Laurel crowns cleave to deserts,
And power to him who power exerts.
Hast not thy share? On winged feet,
Lo! it rushes thee to meet;
And all that Nature made thy own,
Floating in air or pent in stone,
Will rive the hills and swim the sea
And, like thy shadow, follow thee.

⸿ BACCHUS

RALPH WALDO EMERSON

Bring me wine, but wine which never grew
In the belly of the grape,
Or grew on vine whose tap-roots, reaching through
Under the Andes to the Cape,
Suffered no savor of the earth to scape.

Let its grapes the morn salute
From a nocturnal root,
Which feels the acrid juice
Of Styx and Erebus;
And turns the woe of Night,— 10
By its own craft, to a more rich delight.

We buy ashes for bread;
We buy diluted wine;

Give me of the true,—
Whose ample leaves and tendrils curled
Among the silver hills of heaven,
Draw everlasting dew;
Wine of wine,
Blood of the world,
Form of forms, and mould of statures, 20
That I intoxicated,
And by the draught assimilated,
May float at pleasure through all natures;
The bird-language rightly spell,
And that which roses say so well.

Wine that is shed
Like the torrents of the sun
Up the horizon walls,
Or like the Atlantic streams, which run
When the South Sea calls. 30

Water and bread,
Food which needs no transmuting,
Rainbow-flowering, wisdom-fruiting,
Wine which is already man,
Food which teach and reason can.

Wine which Music is,—
Music and wine are one,—
That I, drinking this,
Shall hear far Chaos talk with me;
Kings unborn shall walk with me; 40
And the poor grass shall plot and plan
What it will do when it is man.
Quickened so, will I unlock
Every crypt of every rock.

I thank the joyful juice
For all I know;—
Winds of remembering
Of the ancient being blow,

And seeming-solid walls of use
Open and flow. 50

Pour, Bacchus! the remembering wine;
Retrieve the loss of me and mine!
Vine for vine be antidote,
And the grape requite the lote!
Haste to cure the old despair,—
Reason in Nature's lotus drenched,
The memory of ages quenched;
Give them again to shine;
Let wine repair what this undid;

And where the infection slid, 60
A dazzling memory revive;
Refresh the faded tints,
Recut the aged prints,
And write my old adventures with the pen
Which on the first day drew,
Upon the tablets blue,
The dancing Pleiads and eternal men.

❡ from SONNETS FROM THE PORTUGUESE

ELIZABETH BARRETT BROWNING

38

First time he kissed me, he but only kissed
The fingers of this hand wherewith I write;
And, ever since, it more grew clean and white, . . .
Slow to world-greetings . . . quick with its "Oh, list,"
When the angels speak. A ring of amethyst
I could not wear here, plainer to my sight,
Than the first kiss. The second passed in height
The first, and sought the forehead, and half missed,
Half falling on the hair. O beyond meed!
That was the chrism of love, which love's own crown,
With sanctifying sweetness, did precede.

The third upon my lips was folded down
In perfect, purple state; since when, indeed,
I have been proud and said, "My love, my own."

THE JEWISH CEMETERY AT NEWPORT

HENRY WADSWORTH LONGFELLOW

How strange it seems! These Hebrews in their graves,
Close by the street of this fair seaport town,
Silent beside the never-silent waves,
At rest in all this moving up and down!

The trees are white with dust, that o'er their sleep
Wave their broad curtains in the south-wind's breath,
While underneath these leafy tents they keep
The long, mysterious Exodus of Death.

And these sepulchral stones, so old and brown,
That pave with level flags their burial-place, 10
Seem like the tablets of the Law, thrown down
And broken by Moses at the mountain's base.

The very names recorded here are strange,
Of foreign accent, and of different climes;
Alvares and Rivera interchange
With Abraham and Jacob of old times.

"Blessed be God! for he created Death!"
The mourner said, "and Death is rest and peace";
Then added, in the certainty of faith,
"And giveth Life that never more shall cease." 20

Closed are the portals of their Synagogue,
No Psalms of David now the silence break,
No Rabbi reads the ancient Decalogue
In the grand dialect the Prophets spake.

Gone are the living, but the dead remain,
And not neglected; for a hand unseen,

Scattering its bounty, like a summer rain,
  Still keeps their graves and their remembrance green.

How came they here? What burst of Christian hate,
  What persecution, merciless and blind, 30
Drove o'er the sea—that desert desolate—
  These Ishmaels and Hagars of mankind?

They lived in narrow streets and lanes obscure,
  Ghetto and Judenstrass, in mirk and mire;
Taught in the school of patience to endure
  The life of anguish and the death of fire.

All their lives long, with the unleavened bread
  And bitter herbs of exile and its fears,
The wasting famine of the heart that fed,
  And slaked its thirst with Marah of their tears. 40

Anathema maranatha! was the cry
  That rang from town to town, from street to street;
At every gate the accursed Mordecai
  Was mocked and jeered, and spurned by Christian feet.

Pride and humiliation hand in hand
  Walked with them through the world where'er they went;
Trampled and beaten were they as the sand,
  And yet unshaken as the continent.

For in the background figures vague and vast
  Of patriarchs and of prophets rose sublime, 50
And all the great traditions of the Past
  They saw reflected in the coming time.

And thus forever with reverted look
  The mystic volume of the world they read,
Spelling it backward, like a Hebrew book,
  Till life became a Legend of the Dead.

But ah! what once has been shall be no more!
  The groaning earth in travail and in pain

Brings forth its races, but does not restore,
And the dead nations never rise again. 60

❪ BREAK, BREAK, BREAK

ALFRED, LORD TENNYSON

Break, break, break,
On thy cold gray stones, O Sea!
And I would that my tongue could utter
The thoughts that arise in me.

O well for the fisherman's boy,
That he shouts with his sister at play!
O well for the sailor lad,
That he sings in his boat on the bay!

And the stately ships go on
To their haven under the hill;
But O for the touch of a vanished hand,
And the sound of a voice that is still!

Break, break, break
At the foot of thy crags, O Sea!
But the tender grace of a day that is dead
Will never come back to me.

❪ COME DOWN, O MAID

ALFRED, LORD TENNYSON

Come down, O maid, from yonder mountain height:
What pleasure lives in height (the shepherd sang)
In height and cold, the splendour of the hills?
But cease to move so near the heavens, and cease
To glide a sunbeam by the blasted Pine,
To sit a star upon the sparkling spire;
And come, for Love is of the valley, come,
For Love is of the valley, come thou down

And find him; by the happy threshold, he,
Or hand in hand with Plenty in the maize,
Or red with spirted purple of the vats,
Or foxlike in the vine; nor cares to walk
With Death and Morning on the silver horns,
Nor wilt thou snare him in the white ravine,
Nor find him dropt upon the firths of ice
That huddling slant in furrow-cloven falls
To roll the torrent out of dusky doors:
But follow; let the torrent dance thee down
To find him in the valley; let the wild
Lean-headed Eagles yelp alone, and leave
The monstrous ledges there to slope, and spill
Their thousand wreaths of dangling water-smoke
That like a broken purpose waste in air:
So waste not thou; but come; for all the vales
Await thee; azure pillars of the hearth
Arise to thee; the children call, and I
Thy shepherd pipe, and sweet is every sound,
Sweeter thy voice, but every sound is sweet;
Myriads of rivulets hurrying thro' the lawn,
The moan of doves in immemorial elms,
And murmuring of innumerable bees.

❡ IT IS THE MILLER'S DAUGHTER

ALFRED, LORD TENNYSON

It is the miller's daughter,
And she is grown so dear, so dear,
That I would be the jewel
That trembles at her ear:
For hid in ringlets day and night,
I'd touch her neck so warm and white.

And I would be the girdle
About her dainty dainty waist,
And her heart would beat against me,
In sorrow and in rest:

And I should know if it beat right,
I'd clasp it round so close and tight

And I would be the necklace,
And all day long to fall and rise
Upon her balmy bosom,
With her laughter or her sighs,
And I would lie so light, so light,
I scarce should be unclasp'd at night.

selections from IN MEMORIAM A. H. H.

ALFRED, LORD TENNYSON

PROLOGUE

Strong Son of God, immortal Love,
Whom we, that have not seen thy face,
By faith, and faith alone, embrace,
Believing where we cannot prove;

Thine are these orbs of light and shade;
Thou madest Life in man and brute;
Thou madest Death; and lo, thy foot
Is on the skull which thou hast made.

Thou wilt not leave us in the dust:
Thou madest man, he knows not why, 10
He thinks he was not made to die;
And thou hast made him: thou art just.

Thou seemest human and divine,
The highest, holiest manhood, thou:
Our wills are ours, we know not how;
Our wills are ours, to make them thine.

Our little systems have their day;
They have their day and cease to be:
They are but broken lights of thee,
And thou, O Lord, are more than they. 20

We have but faith: we cannot know;
For knowledge is of things we see;
And yet we trust it comes from thee,
A beam in darkness: let it grow.

Let knowledge grow from more to more,
But more of reverence in us dwell;
That mind and soul, according well,
May make one music as before,

But vaster. We are fools and slight;
We mock thee when we do not fear: 30
But help thy foolish ones to bear;
Help thy vain worlds to bear thy light.

Forgive what seem'd my sin in me;
What seem'd my worth since I began;
For merit lives from man to man,
And not from man, O Lord, to thee.

Forgive my grief for one removed,
Thy creature, whom I found so fair.
I trust he lives in thee, and there
I find him worthier to be loved. 40

Forgive these wild and wandering cries,
Confusions of a wasted youth;
Forgive them where they fail in truth,
And in thy wisdom make me wise.

21

I sing to him that rests below,
And, since the grasses round me wave,
I take the grasses of the grave,
And make them pipes whereon to blow.

The traveller hears me now and then,
And sometimes harshly will he speak: 50

"This fellow would make weakness weak,
And melt the waxen hearts of men."

Another answers, "Let him be,
He loves to make parade of pain,
That with his piping he may gain
The praise that comes to constancy."

A third is wroth: "Is this an hour
For private sorrow's barren song,
When more and more the people throng
The chairs and thrones of evil power? 60

"A time to sicken and to swoon,
When Science reaches forth her arms
To feel from world to world, and charms
Her secret from the latest moon?"

Behold, ye speak an idle thing:
Ye never knew the sacred dust:
I do but sing because I must,
And pipe but as the linnets sing:

And one is glad; her note is gay,
For now her little ones have ranged; 70
And one is sad; her note is changed,
Because her brood is stol'n away.

30

With trembling fingers did we weave
The holly round the Christmas hearth;
A rainy cloud possess'd the earth,
And sadly fell our Christmas-eve.

At our old pastimes in the hall
We gamboll'd, making vain pretence
Of gladness, with an awful sense
Of one mute Shadow watching all. 80

We paused: the winds were in the beech:
  We heard them sweep the winter land;
  And in a circle hand-in-hand
Sat silent, looking each at each.

Then echo-like our voices rang;
  We sung, tho' every eye was dim,
  A merry song we sang with him
Last year: impetuously we sang:

We ceased: a gentler feeling crept
  Upon us: surely rest is meet: 90
  "They rest," we said, "their sleep is sweet,"
And silence follow'd, and we wept.

Our voices took a higher range;
  Once more we sang: "They do not die
  Nor lose their mortal sympathy,
Nor change to us, altho' they change;

"Rapt from the fickle and the frail
  With gather'd power, yet the same,
  Pierces the keen seraphic flame
From orb to orb, from veil to veil." 100

Rise, happy morn, rise, holy morn,
  Draw forth the cheerful day from night:
  O Father, touch the east, and light
The light that shone when Hope was born.

52

I cannot love thee as I ought,
  For love reflects the thing beloved;
  My words are only words, and moved
Upon the topmost froth of thought.

"Yet blame not thou thy plaintive song,"
  The Spirit of true love replied; 110

"Thou canst not move me from thy side,
Nor human frailty do me wrong.

"What keeps a spirit wholly true
To that ideal which he bears?
What record? not the sinless years
That breathed beneath the Syrian blue:

"So fret not, like an idle girl,
That life is dash'd with flecks of sin.
Abide: thy wealth is gather'd in,
When Time hath sunder'd shell from pearl." 120

54

Oh yet we trust that somehow good
Will be the final goal of ill,
To pangs of nature, sins of will,
Defects of doubt, and taints of blood;

That nothing walks with aimless feet;
That not one life shall be destroy'd,
Or cast as rubbish to the void,
When God hath made the pile complete;

That not a worm is cloven in vain;
That not a moth with vain desire 130
Is shrivell'd in a fruitless fire,
Or but subserves another's gain.

Behold, we know not anything;
I can but trust that good shall fall
At last—far off—at last, to all,
And every winter change to spring.

So runs my dream; but what am I?
An infant crying in the night:
An infant crying for the light:
And with no language but a cry. 140

from EPILOGUE

And rise, O moon, from yonder down,
  Till over down and over dale
  All night the shining vapour sail
And pass the silent-lighted town,

The white-faced halls, the glancing rills,
  And catch at every mountain head,
  And o'er the friths that branch and spread
Their sleeping silver through the hills;

And touch with shade the bridal doors,
  With tender gloom the roof, the wall; 150
  And breaking let the splendour fall
To spangle all the happy shores

By which they rest, and ocean sounds,
  And, star and system rolling past,
  A soul shall draw from out the vast
And strike his being into bounds,

And, moved through life of lower phase,
  Result in man, be born and think,
  And act and love, a closer link
Betwixt us and the crowning race 160

Of those that, eye to eye, shall look
  On knowledge; under whose command
  Is Earth and Earth's, and in their hand
Is Nature like an open book;

No longer half-akin to brute,
  For all we thought and loved and did,
  And hoped, and suffered, is but seed
Of what in them is flower and fruit;

Whereof the man, that with me trod
  This planet, was a noble type 170

Appearing ere the times were ripe,
That friend of mine who lives in God,

That God, which ever lives and loves,
One God, one law, one element,
And one far-off divine event,
To which the whole creation moves.

THE LOTOS-EATERS

ALFRED, LORD TENNYSON

"Courage!" he said, and pointed toward the land,
"This mounting wave will roll us shoreward soon."
In the afternoon they came unto a land
In which it seemed always afternoon.
All round the coast the languid air did swoon,
Breathing like one that hath a weary dream.
Full-faced above the valley stood the moon;
And like a downward smoke, the slender stream
Along the cliff to fall and pause and fall did seem.

A land of streams! some, like a downward smoke, 10
Slow-dropping veils of thinnest lawn, did go;
And some through wavering lights and shadows broke,
Rolling a slumbrous sheet of foam below.
They saw the gleaming river seaward flow
From the inner land: far off, three mountain-tops,
Three silent pinnacles of aged snow,
Stood sunset-flushed: and, dewed with showery drops,
Up-clomb the shadowy pine above the woven copse.

The charmed sunset lingered low adown
In the red West: through mountain clefts the dale 20
Was seen far inland, and the yellow down
Bordered with palm, and many a winding vale
And meadow, set with slender galingale;
A land where all things always seemed the same!
And round about the keel with faces pale,

Dark faces pale against that rosy flame,
The mild-eyed melancholy Lotos-eaters came.

Branches they bore of that enchanted stem,
Laden with flower and fruit, whereof they gave
To each, but whoso did receive of them, 30
And taste, to him the gushing of the wave
Far far away did seem to mourn and rave
On alien shores; and if his fellow spake,
His voice was thin, as voices from the grave;
And deep-asleep he seemed, yet all awake,
And music in his ears his beating heart did make.

They sat them down upon the yellow sand,
Between the sun and moon upon the shore;
And sweet it was to dream of Fatherland,
Of child, and wife, and slave; but evermore 40
Most weary seemed the sea, weary the oar,
Weary the wandering fields of barren foam.
Then someone said, "We will return no more";
And all at once they sang, "Our island home
Is far beyond the wave; we will no longer roam."

CHORIC SONG

I

There is sweet music here that softer falls
Than petals from blown roses on the grass,
Or night-dews on still waters between walls
Of shadowy granite, in a gleaming pass;
Music that gentlier on the spirit lies, 50
Than tired eyelids upon tired eyes;
Music that brings sweet sleep down from the blissful skies.
Here are cool mosses deep,
And through the moss the ivies creep,
And in the stream the long-leaved flowers weep,
And from the craggy ledge the poppy hangs in sleep.

2

Why are we weighed upon with heaviness,
And utterly consumed with sharp distress,
While all things else have rest from weariness?
All things have rest: why should we toil alone, 60
We only toil, who are the first of things,
And make perpetual moan,
Still from one sorrow to another thrown:
Nor ever fold our wings,
And cease from wanderings,
Nor steep our brows in slumber's holy balm;
Nor hearken what the inner spirit sings,
"There is no joy but calm!"—
Why should we only toil, the roof and crown of things?

3

Lo! in the middle of the wood, 70
The folded leaf is wooed from out the bud
With winds upon the branch, and there
Grows green and broad, and takes no care,
Sun-steeped at noon, and in the moon
Nightly dew-fed; and turning yellow
Falls, and floats adown the air.
Lo! sweetened with the summer light,
The full-juiced apple, waxing over-mellow,
Drops in a silent autumn night.
All its allotted length of days, 80
The flower ripens in its place,
Ripens and fades, and falls, and hath no toil,
Fast-rooted in the fruitful soil.

4

Hateful is the dark-blue sky,
Vaulted o'er the dark-blue sea.
Death is the end of life; ah, why
Should life all labor be?

Let us alone. Time driveth onward fast,
And in a little while our lips are dumb.
Let us alone. What is it that will last? 90
All things are taken from us, and become
Portions and parcels of the dreadful past.
Let us alone. What pleasure can we have
To war with evil? Is there any peace
In ever climbing up the climbing wave?
All things have rest, and ripen toward the grave
In silence—ripen, fall and cease:
Give us long rest or death, dark death, or dreamful ease.

5

How sweet it were, hearing the downward stream,
With half-shut eyes ever to seem 100
Falling asleep in a half-dream!
To dream and dream, like yonder amber light,
Which will not leave the myrrh-bush on the height;
To hear each other's whispered speech;
Eating the Lotos day by day,
To watch the crisping ripples on the beach,
And tender curving lines of creamy spray;
To lend our hearts and spirits wholly
To the influence of mild-minded melancholy;
To muse and brood and live again in memory, 110
With those old faces of our infancy
Heaped over with a mound of grass,
Two handfuls of white dust, shut in an urn of brass!

6

Dear is the memory of our wedded lives,
And dear the last embraces of our wives
And their warm tears: but all hath suffered change;
For surely now our household hearths are cold:
Our sons inherit us: our looks are strange:
And we should come like ghosts to trouble joy.
Or else the island princes over-bold 120

Have eat our substance, and the minstrel sings
Before them of the ten-years' war in Troy,
And our great deeds, as half-forgotten things.
Is there confusion in the little isle?
Let what is broken so remain.
The Gods are hard to reconcile:
'Tis hard to settle order once again.
There *is* confusion worse than death,
Trouble on trouble, pain on pain,
Long labor unto aged breath, 130
Sore task to hearts worn out with many wars
And eyes grown dim with gazing on the pilot-stars.

7

But, propt on beds of amaranth and moly,
How sweet (while warm airs lull us, blowing lowly)
With half-dropt eyelids still,
Beneath a heaven dark and holy,
To watch the long bright river drawing slowly
His waters from the purple hill—
To hear the dewy echoes calling
From cave to cave through the thick-twined vine— 140
To watch the emerald-colored water falling
Through many a woven acanthus-wreath divine!
Only to hear and see the far-off sparkling brine,
Only to hear were sweet, stretched out beneath the pine.

8

The Lotos blooms below the barren peak:
The Lotos blows by every winding creek:
All day the wind breathes low with mellower tone:
Through every hollow cave and alley lone
Round and round the spicy downs the yellow Lotos-dust is
blown.
We have had enough of action, and of motion we, 150
Rolled to starboard, rolled to larboard, when the surge was
seething free,

Where the wallowing monster spouted his foam-fountains
in the sea.
Let us swear an oath, and keep it with an equal mind,
In the hollow Lotos-land to live and lie reclined
On the hills like Gods together, careless of mankind.
For they lie beside their nectar, and the bolts are hurled
Far below them in the valleys, and the clouds are lightly
curled
Round their golden houses, girdled with the gleaming
world:
Where they smile in secret, looking over wasted lands,
Blight and famine, plague and earthquake, roaring deeps
and fiery sands, 160
Clanging fights, and flaming towns, and sinking ships, and
praying hands.
But they smile, they find a music centered in a doleful song
Steaming up, a lamentation and an ancient tale of wrong,
Like a tale of little meaning though the words are strong;
Chanted from an ill-used race of men that cleave the soil,
Sow the seed, and reap the harvest with enduring toil,
Storing yearly little dues of wheat, and wine and oil;
Till they perish and they suffer—some, 'tis whispered—
down in hell
Suffer endless anguish, others in Elysian valleys dwell,
Resting weary limbs at last on beds of asphodel. 170
Surely, surely, slumber is more sweet than toil, the shore
Than labor in the deep mid-ocean, wind and wave and oar;
Oh, rest ye, brother mariners, we will not wander more.

¶ TO HELEN

EDGAR ALLAN POE

Helen, thy beauty is to me
Like those Nicèan barks of yore,
That gently, o'er a perfumed sea,
The weary, way-worn wanderer bore
To his own native shore.

On desperate seas long wont to roam,
Thy hyacinth hair, thy classic face,
Thy Naiad airs have brought me home
To the glory that was Greece,
And the grandeur that was Rome.

Lo! in yon brilliant window-niche
How statue-like I see thee stand,
The agate lamp within thy hand!
Ah! Psyche, from the regions which
Are Holy-Land!

THE CITY IN THE SEA

EDGAR ALLAN POE

Lo! Death has reared himself a throne
In a strange city lying alone
Far down within the dim West,
Where the good and the bad and the worst and the best
Have gone to their eternal rest.
There shrines and palaces and towers
(Time-eaten towers that tremble not!)
Resemble nothing that is ours.
Around, by lifting winds forgot,
Resignedly beneath the sky 10
The melancholy waters lie.
No rays from the holy heaven come down
On the long night-time of that town;
But light from out the lurid sea
Streams up the turrets silently,
Gleams up the pinnacles far and free:
Up domes, up spires, up kingly halls,
Up fanes, up Babylon-like walls,
Up shadowy long-forgotten bowers
Of sculptured ivy and stone flowers, 20
Up many and many a marvelous shrine
Whose wreathèd friezes intertwine
The viol, the violet, and the vine.

Resignedly beneath the sky
The melancholy waters lie.
So blend the turrets and shadows there
That all seem pendulous in air,
While from a proud tower in the town
Death looks gigantically down.

There open fanes and gaping graves 30
Yawn level with the luminous waves;
But not the riches there that lie
In each idol's diamond eye,—
Not the gayly-jeweled dead,
Tempt the waters from their bed;
For no ripples curl, alas,
Along that wilderness of glass;
No swellings tell that winds may be
Upon some far-off happier sea;
No heavings hint that winds have been 40
On seas less hideously serene!

But lo, a stir is in the air!
The wave—there is a movement there!
As if the towers had thrust aside,
In slightly sinking, the dull tide;
As if their tops had feebly given
A void within the filmy Heaven!
The waves have now a redder glow,
The hours are breathing faint and low;
And when, amid no earthly moans, 50
Down, down that town shall settle hence,
Hell, rising from a thousand thrones,
Shall do it reverence.

⁋ four stanzas from THE RUBAIYAT

EDWARD FITZGERALD

But leave the Wise to wrangle, and with me
The Quarrel of the Universe let be:

And, in some corner of the Hubbub couch'd,
Make game of that which makes as much of Thee.

* * *

And that inverted Bowl we call the Sky,
Whereunder crawling coop'd we live and die,
Lift not your hands to *It* for help—for it
As impotently moves as You or I.

* * *

Look to the blowing Rose about us. "Lo,
Laughing," she says, "into the world I blow,
At once the silken tassel of my Purse
Tear, and its Treasure on the Garden throw."

* * *

I sometimes think that never blows so red
The Rose as where some buried Caesar bled;
That every Hyacinth the Garden wears
Dropt in her Lap from some once lovely Head.

SOLILOQUY OF THE SPANISH CLOISTER

ROBERT BROWNING

Gr-r-r—there go, my heart's abhorrence!
Water your damned flower-pots, do!
If hate killed men, Brother Lawrence,
God's blood, would not mine kill you!
What? your myrtle-bush wants trimming?
Oh, that rose has prior claims—
Needs its leaden vase filled brimming?
Hell dry you up with its flames!

At the meal we sit together;
Salve tibi! I must hear 10

Wise talk of the kind of weather,
  Sort of season, time of year:
Not a plenteous cork-crop: scarcely
  Dare we hope oak-galls, I doubt;
What's the Latin name for "parsley?"
  What's the Greek name for Swine's Snout?

Whew! We'll have our platter burnished,
  Laid with care on our own shelf!
With a fire-new spoon we're furnished,
  And a goblet for ourself, 20
Rinsed like something sacrificial
  Ere 'tis fit to touch our chaps—
Marked with L. for our initial!
  (He-he! There his lily snaps!)

Saint, forsooth! While brown Dolores
  Squats outside the Convent bank
With Sanchicha, telling stories,
  Steeping tresses in the tank,
Blue-black, lustrous, thick like horsehairs,
  —Can't I see his dead eye glow, 30
Bright as 'twere a Barbary corsair's?
  (That is, if he'd let it show!)

When he finishes refection,
  Knife and fork he never lays
Cross-wise, to my recollection,
  As do I, in Jesu's praise.
I the Trinity illustrate,
  Drinking watered orange-pulp—
In three sips the Arian frustrate;
  While he drains his at one gulp. 40

Oh, those melons? If he's able
  We're to have a feast! so nice!
One goes to the Abbot's table,
  All of us get each a slice.
How go on your flowers? None double?

Not one fruit-sort can you spy?
Strange!—And I, too, at such trouble,
Keep them close-nipped on the sly!

There's a great text in Galatians, 50
Once you trip on it, entails
Twenty-nine distinct damnations,
One sure, if another fails:
If I trip him just a-dying,
Sure of heaven as sure as can be,
Spin him round and send him flying
Off to hell, a Manichee?

Or, my scrofulous French novel
On grey paper with blunt type!
Simply glance at it, you grovel
Hand and foot in Belial's gripe: 60
If I double down its pages
At the woeful sixteenth print,
When he gathers his greengages,
Ope a sieve and slip it in 't?

Or, there's Satan!—one might venture
Pledge one's soul to him, yet leave
Such a flaw in the indenture
As he'd miss till, past retrieve,
Blasted lay that rose-acacia
We're so proud of! *Hy, Zy, Hine* . . . 70
'St, there's Vespers! *Plena gratiâ*
Ave, Virgo! Gr-r-r—you swine!

❡ MY LAST DUCHESS

ROBERT BROWNING

Ferrara

That's my last Duchess painted on the wall,
Looking as if she were alive. I call

That piece a wonder, now: Frà Pandolf's hands
Worked busily a day, and there she stands.
Will't please you sit and look at her? I said
"Frà Pandolf" by design, for never read
Strangers like you that pictured countenance,
The depth and passion of its earnest glance,
But to myself they turned (since none puts by
The curtain I have drawn for you, but I) 10
And seemed as they would ask me, if they durst,
How such a glance came there; so, not the first
Are you to turn and ask thus. Sir, 'twas not
Her husband's presence only, called that spot
Of joy into the Duchess' cheek; perhaps
Frà Pandolf chanced to say, "Her mantle laps
Over my lady's wrist too much," or "Paint
Must never hope to reproduce the faint
Half-flush that dies along her throat": such stuff
Was courtesy, she thought, and cause enough 20
For calling up that spot of joy. She had
A heart—how shall I say?—too soon made glad,
Too easily impressed: she liked whate'er
She looked on, and her looks went everywhere.
Sir, 'twas all one! My favour at her breast,
The dropping of the daylight in the West,
The bough of cherries some officious fool
Broke in the orchard for her, the white mule
She rode with round the terrace—all and each
Would draw from her alike the approving speech, 30
Or blush, at least. She thanked men,—good! but thanked
Somehow—I know not how—as if she ranked
My gift of a nine-hundred-years-old name
With anybody's gift. Who'd stoop to blame
This sort of trifling? Even had you skill
In speech—(which I have not)—to make your will
Quite clear to such an one, and say, "Just this
Or that in you disgusts me; here you miss,
Or there exceed the mark"—and if she let
Herself be lessoned so, nor plainly set 40
Her wits to yours, forsooth, and made excuse,

—E'en then would be some stooping; and I choose
Never to stoop. Oh sir, she smiled, no doubt,
Whene'er I passed her; but who passed without
Much the same smile? This grew; I gave commands;
Then all smiles stopped together. There she stands
As if alive. Will't please you rise? We'll meet
The company below, then. I repeat,
The Count your master's known munificence
Is ample warrant that no just pretence 50
Of mine for dowry will be disallowed;
Though his fair daughter's self, as I avowed
At starting is my object. Nay, we'll go
Together down, sir. Notice Neptune, though,
Taming a sea-horse, thought a rarity,
Which Claus of Innsbruck cast in bronze for me!

❨ PROSPICE

ROBERT BROWNING

Fear death?—to feel the fog in my throat,
  The mist in my face,
When the snows begin, and the blasts denote
  I am nearing the place,
The power of the night, the press of the storm,
  The post of the foe;
Where he stands, the Arch Fear in a visible form,
  Yet the strong man must go:
For the journey is done and the summit attained,
  And the barriers fall,
Though a battle's to fight ere the guerdon be gained,
  The reward of it all.
I was ever a fighter, so—one fight more,
  The best and the last!
I would hate that death bandaged my eyes and forbore,
  And bade me creep past.
No! let me taste the whole of it, fare like my peers
  The heroes of old,
Bear the brunt, in a minute pay glad life's arrears

Of pain, darkness and cold.
For sudden the worst turns the best to the brave,
The black minute's at end,
And the elements' rage, the fiend-voices that rave,
Shall dwindle, shall blend,
Shall change, shall become first a peace, out of pain,
Then a light, then thy breast,
O thou soul of my soul! I shall clasp thee again
And with God be the rest!

THE LAST RIDE TOGETHER

ROBERT BROWNING

1

I said—Then, dearest, since 'tis so,
Since now at length my fate I know,
Since nothing all my love avails,
Since all, my life seemed meant for, fails,
Since this was written and needs must be—
My whole heart rises up to bless
Your name in pride and thankfulness!
Take back the hope you gave,—I claim
Only a memory of the same,
—And this beside, if you will not blame, 10
Your leave for one more last ride with me.

2

My mistress bent that brow of hers;
Those deep dark eyes where pride demurs
When pity would be softening through,
Fixed me a breathing-while or two
With life or death in the balance: right!
The blood replenished me again;
My last thought was at least not vain:
I and my mistress, side by side
Shall be together, breathe and ride, 20

So, one day more am I deified.
  Who knows but the world may end to-night?

3

Hush! if you saw some western cloud
All billowy-bosomed, over-bowed
By many benedictions—sun's
And moon's and evening-star's at once—
  And so, you, looking and loving best,
Conscious grew, your passion drew
Cloud, sunset, moonrise, star-shine too,
Down on you, near and yet more near, 30
Till flesh must fade for heaven was here!—
Thus leant she and lingered—joy and fear!
  Thus lay she a moment on my breast.

4

Then we began to ride. My soul
Smoothed itself out, a long-cramped scroll
Freshening and fluttering in the wind.
Past hopes already lay behind.
  What need to strive with a life awry?
Had I said that, had I done this,
So might I gain, so might I miss. 40
Might she have loved me? just as well
She might have hated, who can tell!
Where had I been now if the worst befell?
  And here we are riding, she and I.

5

Fail I alone, in words and deeds?
Why, all men strive, and who succeeds?
We rode; it seemed my spirit flew,
Saw other regions, cities new,
  As the world rushed by on either side.
I thought,—All labour, yet no less 50

Bear up beneath their unsuccess.
Look at the end of work, contrast
The petty done, the undone vast,
This present of theirs with the hopeful past!
  I hoped she would love; here we rode.

6

What hand and brain went ever paired?
What heart alike conceived and dared?
What act proved all its thought had been?
What will but felt the fleshly screen?
  We ride and I see her bosom heave. 60
There's many a crown for who can reach.
Ten lines, a statesman's life in each!
The flag stuck on a heap of bones,
A soldier's doing! what atones?
They scratch his name on the Abbey-stones.
  My riding is better, by their leave.

7

What does it all mean, poet? Well,
Your brains beat into rhythm, you tell
What we felt only; you expressed
You hold things beautiful the best, 70
  And pace them in rhyme so, side by side.
'Tis something, nay 'tis much: but then,
Have you yourself what's best for men?
Are you—poor, sick, old ere your time—
Nearer one whit your own sublime
Than we who never have turned a rhyme?
  Sing, riding's a joy! For me, I ride.

8

And you, great sculptor—so, you gave
A score of years to Art, her slave, 80
And that's your Venus, whence we turn

To yonder girl that fords the burn!
  You acquiesce, and shall I repine?
What, man of music, you grown grey
With notes and nothing else to say,
Is this your sole praise from a friend,
"Greatly his opera's strains intend,
But in music we know how fashions end!"
  I gave me youth; but we ride, in fine.

9

Who knows what's fit for us? Had fate 90
Proposed bliss here should sublimate
My being—had I signed the bond—
Still one must lead some life beyond,
  Have a bliss to die with, dim-descried.
This foot once planted on the goal,
This glory-garland round my soul,
Could I descry such? Try and test!
I sink back shuddering from the quest.
Earth being so good, would heaven seem best?
  Now, heaven and she are beyond this ride. 100

10

And yet—she has not spoke so long!
What if heaven be that, fair and strong
At life's best, with our eyes upturned
Whither life's flower is first discerned,
  We, fixed so, ever should so abide?
What if we still ride on, we two
With life for ever old yet new,
Changed not in kind but in degree,
The instant made eternity,—
And heaven just prove that I and she 110
  Ride, ride together, for ever ride?

❡ REMEMBRANCE

EMILY BRONTË

Cold in the earth—and the deep snow piled above
thee,
Far, far removed, cold in the dreary grave!
Have I forgot, my only Love, to love thee,
Severed at last by Time's all-severing wave?

Now, when alone, do my thoughts no longer hover
Over the mountains, on that northern shore,
Resting their wings where heath and fern-leaves
cover
Thy noble heart for ever, ever more?

Cold in the earth—and fifteen wild Decembers,
From those brown hills, have melted into spring:
Faithful, indeed, is the spirit that remembers
After such years of change and suffering!

Sweet Love of youth, forgive, if I forget thee,
While the world's tide is bearing me along;
Other desires and other hopes beset me,
Hopes which obscure, but cannot do thee wrong!

No later light has lightened up my heaven,
No second moon has ever shone for me;
All my life's bliss from thy dear life was given,
All my life's bliss is in the grave with thee.

But, when the days of golden dreams had perished,
And ev'n Despair was powerless to destroy;
Then did I learn how existence could be cherished,
Strengthened, and fed without the aid of joy.

Then did I check the tears of useless passion—
Weaned my young soul from yearning after thine;
Sternly denied its burning wish to hasten
Down to that tomb already more than mine.

And, even yet, I dare not let it languish,
Dare not indulge in memory's rapturous pain;
Once drinking deep of that divinest anguish,
How could I seek the empty world again?

THE LATEST DECALOGUE

ARTHUR HUGH CLOUGH

Thou shalt have one God only; who
Would be at the expense of two?
No graven images may be
Worshipped, except the currency.
Swear not at all; for, for thy curse
Thine enemy is none the worse.
At church on Sunday to attend
Will serve to keep the world thy friend.
Honor thy parents; that is, all
From whom advancement may befall.
Thou shalt not kill; but need'st not strive
Officiously to keep alive.
Do not adultery commit;
Advantage rarely comes of it.
Thou shalt not steal; an empty feat,
When it's so lucrative to cheat.
Bear not false witness; let the lie
Have time on its own wings to fly.
Thou shalt not covet, but tradition
Approves all forms of competition.

THE COLLEGE COLONEL

HERMAN MELVILLE

He rides at their head;
  A crutch by his saddle just slants in view,
One slung arm is in splints, you see,
  Yet he guides his strong steed—how coldly too.

He brings his regiment home—
  Not as they filed two years before,
But a remnant half-tattered, and battered, and worn,
Like castaway sailors, who—stunned
      By the surf's loud roar,
  Their mates dragged back and seen no more—
Again and again breast the surge,
  And at last crawl, spent, to shore.

A still rigidity and pale—
  An Indian aloofness lones his brow;
He has lived a thousand years
Compressed in battle's pains and prayers,
  Marches and watches slow.
There are welcoming shouts, and flags;
  Old men off hat to the Boy,
Wreaths from gay balconies fall at his feet,
  But to *him*—there comes alloy.

It is not that a leg is lost,
  It is not that an arm is maimed,
It is not that the fever has racked—
  Self he has long disclaimed.

But all through the Seven Days' Fight,
  And deep in the Wilderness grim,
And in the field-hospital tent,
  And Petersburg crater, and dim
Lean brooding in Libby, there came—
  Ah heaven!—what *truth* to him.

⁋ from SONG OF MYSELF

WALT WHITMAN

21

I am the poet of the Body and I am the poet of the Soul,
The pleasures of heaven are with me and the pains of hell are with
    me,

The first I graft and increase upon myself, the latter I translate into a
new tongue.

I am the poet of the woman the same as the man,
And I say it is as great to be a woman as to be a man,
And I say there is nothing greater than the mother of men.

I chant the chant of dilation or pride,
We have had ducking and deprecating about enough,
I show that size is only development.

Have you outstript the rest? are you the President?
It is a trifle, they will move more than arrive there every one, and still
pass on.

I am he that walks with the tender and growing night,
I call to the earth and sea half-held by the night.

Press close bare-bosom'd night—press close magnetic nourishing
night!
Night of south winds—night of the large few stars!
Still nodding night—mad naked summer night.

Smile O voluptuous cool-breath'd earth!
Earth of the slumbering and liquid trees!
Earth of the departed sunset—earth of the mountains misty-topt!
Earth of the vitreous pour of the full moon just tinged with blue!
Earth of shine and dark mottling the tide of the river!
Earth of the limpid gray of clouds brighter and clearer for my sake!
Far-swooping elbow'd earth—rich apple-blossom'd earth!
Smile, for your lover comes.

Prodigal, you have given me love—therefore I to you give love!
O unspeakable passionate love.

❡ WHEN LILACS LAST IN THE DOORYARD BLOOM'D

WALT WHITMAN

1

When lilacs last in the dooryard bloom'd,
And the great star early droop'd in the western sky in the night,
I mourn'd, and yet shall mourn with ever-returning spring.

Ever-returning spring, trinity sure to me you bring,
Lilac blooming perennial and drooping star in the west,
And thought of him I love.

2

O powerful western fallen star!
O shades of night—O moody, tearful night!
O great star disappear'd—O the black murk that hides the star!
O cruel hands that hold me powerless—O helpless soul of me! 10
O harsh surrounding cloud that will not free my soul.

3

In the dooryard fronting an old farm-house near the white-wash'd
palings,
Stands the lilac-bush tall-growing with heart-shaped leaves of rich
green,
With many a pointed blossom rising delicate, with the perfume strong
I love,
With every leaf a miracle—and from this bush in the dooryard,
With delicate-colour'd blossoms and heart-shaped leaves of rich green,
A sprig with its flower I break.

4

In the swamp in secluded recesses,
A shy and hidden bird is warbling a song.
Solitary the thrush, 20

The hermit withdrawn to himself, avoiding the settlements,
Sings by himself a song.

Song of the bleeding throat,
Death's outlet song of life (for well, dear brother, I know,
If thou wast not granted to sing thou would'st surely die).

5

Over the breast of the spring, the land, amid cities,
Amid lanes and through old woods, where lately the violets peep'd
from the ground, spotting the grey débris,
Amid the grass in the fields each side of the lanes, passing the end-
less grass,
Passing the yellow-spear'd wheat, every grain from its shroud in the
dark-brown fields uprisen, 30
Passing the apple-tree blows of white and pink in the orchards,
Carrying a corpse to where it shall rest in the grave,
Night and day journeys a coffin.

6

Coffin that passes through lanes and streets,
Through day and night with the great cloud darkening the land,
With the pomp of the inloop'd flags with the cities draped in black,
With the show of the States themselves as of crepe-veiled women
standing,
With processions long and winding and the flambeaus of the night,
With the countless torches lit, with the silent sea of faces and the un-
bared heads,
With the waiting depot, the arriving coffin, and the somber faces,
With dirges through the night, with the thousand voices rising strong
and solemn, 40
With all the mournful voices of the dirges poured around the coffin,
The dim-lit churches and the shuddering organs—where amid these
you journey,
With the tolling tolling bells' perpetual clang,
Here, coffin that slowly passes,
I give you my sprig of lilac.

7

(Nor for you, for one alone,
Blossoms and branches green to coffins all I bring,
For fresh as the morning, thus would I chant a song for you O sane
and sacred death.

All over bouquets of roses,
O death, I cover you over with roses and early lilies, 50
But mostly and now the lilac that blooms the first,
Copious I break, I break the sprigs from the bushes,
With loaded arms I come, pouring for you,
For you and the coffins all of you O death.)

8

O western orb sailing the heaven,
Now I know what you must have meant as a month since I walked,
As I walked in silence the transparent shadowy night,
As I saw you had something to tell as you bent to me night after
night,
As you drooped from the sky low down as if to my side (while the
other stars all looked on),
As we wandered together the solemn night (for something I know
not what kept me from sleep), 60
As the night advanced, and I saw on the rim of the west how full
you were of woe,
As I stood on the rising ground in the breeze in the cool transparent
night,
As I watched where you passed and was lost in the netherward black
of the night,
As my soul in its trouble dissatisfied sank, as where you sad orb,
Concluded, dropped in the night, and was gone.

9

Sing on there in the swamp,
O singer bashful and tender, I hear your notes, I hear your call,
I hear, I come presently, I understand you,

But a moment I linger, for the lustrous star has detained me,
The star my departing comrade holds and detains me. 70

10

O how shall I warble myself for the dead one there I loved?
And how shall I deck my song for the large sweet soul that has gone?
And what shall my perfume be for the grave of him I love?

Sea-winds blown from east and west,
Blown from the Eastern sea and blown from the Western sea, till
there on the prairies meeting,
These and with these and the breath of my chant,
I'll perfume the grave of him I love.

11

O what shall I hang on the chamber walls?
And what shall the pictures be that I hang on the walls,
To adorn the burial-house of him I love? 80

Pictures of growing spring and farms and homes,
With the Fourth-month eve at sundown, and the gray smoke lucid
and bright,
With floods of the yellow gold of the gorgeous, indolent, sinking
sun, burning, expanding the air,
With the fresh sweet herbage under foot, and the pale green leaves
of the trees prolific,
In the distance the flowing glaze, the breast of the river, with a
wind-dapple here and there,
With ranging hills on the banks, with many a line against the sky,
and shadows,
And the city at hand with dwellings so dense, and stacks of chimneys,
And all the scenes of life and the workshops, and the workmen
homeward returning.

12

Lo, body and soul—this land,
My own Manhattan with spires, and the sparkling and hurrying tides,
and the ships, 90

The varied and ample land, the South and the North in the light,
Ohio's shores and flashing Missouri,
And ever the far-spreading prairies covered with grass and corn.

Lo, the most excellent sun so calm and haughty,
The violet and purple morn with just-felt breezes,
The gentle soft-born measureless light,
The miracle spreading bathing all, the fulfilled noon,
The coming eve delicious, the welcome night and the stars,
Over my cities shining all, enveloping man and land.

13

Sing on, sing on you gray-brown bird,
Sing from the swamps, the recesses, pour your chant from the
bushes, 100
Limitless out of the dusk, out of the cedars and pines.

Sing on dearest brother, warble your reedy song,
Loud human song, with voice of uttermost woe.

O liquid and free and tender!
O wild and loose to my soul—O wondrous singer!
You only I hear—yet the star holds me (but will soon depart),
Yet the lilac with mastering odor holds me.

14

Now while I sat in the day and looked forth,
In the close of the day with its light and the fields of spring, and the
farmers preparing their crops,
In the large unconscious scenery of my land with its lakes and
forests 110
In the heavenly aerial beauty (after the perturbed winds and the
storms),
Under the arching heavens of the afternoon swift passing, and the
voices of children and women,
The many-moving sea-tides, and I saw the ships how they sailed,
And the summer approaching with richness, and the fields all busy
with labor,

And the infinite separate houses, how they all went on, each with
its meals and minutia of daily usages,
And the streets how their throbbings throbb'd, and the cities pent
—lo, then and there,
Falling upon them all and among them all, enveloping me with the
rest,
Appear'd the cloud, appear'd the long black trail,
And I knew death, its thought, and the sacred knowledge of death.

Then with the knowledge of death as walking one side of me, 120
And the thought of death close-walking the other side of me,
And I in the middle as with companions, and as holding the hands
of companions,
I fled forth to the hiding receiving night that talks not,
Down to the shores of the water, the path by the swamp in the
dimness,
To the solemn shadowy cedars and ghostly pines so still.

And the singer so shy to the rest receiv'd me,
The gray-brown bird I know receiv'd us comrades three,
And he sang the carol of death, and a verse for him I love.

From deep secluded recesses,
From the fragrant cedars and the ghostly pines so still, 130
Came the carol of the bird.

And the charm of the carol rapt me,
As I held as if by their hands my comrades in the night,
And the voice of my spirit tallied the song of the bird.

Come lovely and soothing death,
Undulate round the world, serenely arriving, arriving,
In the day, in the night, to all, to each,
Sooner or later delicate death.
Prais'd be the fathomless universe,
For life and joy, and for objects and knowledge curious, 140
And for love, sweet love—but praise! praise! praise!
For the sure-enwinding arms of cool-enfolding death.

Dark mother always gliding near with soft feet,
Have none chanted for thee a chant of fullest welcome?
Then I chant it for thee, I glorify thee above all,
I bring thee a song that when thou must indeed come, come unfalteringly.

Approach strong deliveress,
When it is so, when thou hast taken them I joyously sing the dead,
Lost in the loving floating ocean of thee,
Laved in the flood of thy bliss, O death. 150
From me to thee glad serenades,
Dances for thee I propose saluting thee, adornments and feastings for thee,
And the sights of the open landscape and the high-spread sky are fitting,
And life and the fields, and the huge and thoughtful night.

The night in silence under many a star,
The ocean shore and the husky whispering wave whose voice I know,
And the soul turning to thee, O vast and well-veil'd death,
And the body gratefully nestling close to thee.

Over the tree-tops I float thee a song,
Over the rising and sinking waves, over the myriad fields and the prairies wide, 160
Over the dense-pack'd cities all and the teeming wharves and ways,
I float this carol with joy, with joy to thee, O death.

15

To the tally of my soul,
Loud and strong kept up the gray-brown bird,
With pure deliberate notes spreading filling the night.

Loud in the pines and cedars dim,
Clear in the freshness moist and the swamp-perfume,
And I with my comrades there in the night.

While my sight that was bound in my eyes unclosed,
As to long panoramas of visions. 170

And I saw askant the armies,
I saw as in noiseless dreams hundreds of battle-flags,
Borne through the smoke of the battles and pierc'd with missiles
I saw them,
And carried hither and yon through the smoke, and torn and
bloody,
And at last but a few shreds left on the staffs (and all in silence),
And the staffs all splinter'd and broken.

I saw battle-corpses, myriads of them,
And the white skeletons of young men, I saw them,
I saw the débris and débris of all the slain soldiers of the war,
But I saw they were not as was thought, 180
They themselves were fully at rest, they suffered not,
The living remained and suffered, the mother suffered,
And the wife and the child and the musing comrade suffered,
And the armies that remained suffered.

16

Passing the visions, passing the night,
Passing, unloosing the hold of my comrades' hands,
Passing the song of the hermit bird and the tallying song of my soul,
Victorious song, death's outlet song, yet varying ever-altering song,
As low and wailing, yet clear the notes, rising and falling, flooding the
night,
Sadly sinking and fainting, as warning and warning, and yet again
bursting with joy, 190
Covering the earth and filling the spread of the heaven,
As that powerful psalm in the night I heard from recesses,
Passing, I leave thee lilac with heart-shaped leaves,
I leave thee there in the door-yard, blooming, returning with spring.

I cease from my song for thee,
From my gaze on thee in the west, fronting the west, communing
with thee,
O comrade lustrous with silver face in the night.

Yet each to keep and all, retrievements out of the night,
The song, the wondrous chant of the gray-brown bird,

And the tallying chant, the echo aroused in my soul, 200
With the lustrous and drooping star with the countenance full of woe,
With the holders holding my hand nearing the call of the bird,
Comrades mine and I in the midst, and their memory ever to keep,
for the dead I loved so well,
For the sweetest, wisest soul of all my days and lands—and this for
his dear sake,
Lilac and star and bird twined with the chant of my soul,
There in the fragrant pines and the cedars dusk and dim.

THE LAST INVOCATION

WALT WHITMAN

At the last, tenderly,
From the walls of the powerful fortress'd house,
From the clasp of the knitted locks, from the keep of the well-closed
doors,
Let me be wafted.

Let me glide noiselessly forth;
With the key of softness unlock the locks—with a whisper,
Set ope the doors O soul.

Tenderly—be not impatient,
(Strong is your hold O mortal flesh.
Strong is your hold O love.)

TO MARGUERITE

MATTHEW ARNOLD

Yes! in the sea of life enisled,
With echoing straits between us thrown,
Dotting the shoreless watery wild,
We mortal millions live *alone*.
The islands feel the enclasping flow,
And then their endless bounds they know.

But when the moon their hollows lights,
And they are swept by balms of spring,
And in their glens, on starry nights,
The nightingales divinely sing;
And lovely notes, from shore to shore,
Across the sounds and channels pour—

Oh! then a longing like despair
Is to their farthest caverns sent;
For surely once, they feel, we were
Parts of a single continent!
Now round us spreads the watery plain—
Oh, might our marges meet again!

Who ordered, that their longing's fire
Should be, as soon as kindled, cooled?
Who renders vain their deep desire?—
A god, a god their severance ruled!
And bade betwixt their shores to be
The unplumbed, salt, estranging sea.

REQUIESCAT

MATTHEW ARNOLD

Strew on her roses, roses,
And never a spray of yew!
In quiet she reposes;
Ah, would that I did too!

Her mirth the world required;
She bathed it in smiles of glee.
But her heart was tired, tired,
And now they let her be.

Her life was turning, turning,
In mazes of heat and sound.
But for peace her soul was yearning,
And now peace laps her round.

Her cabined, ample spirit,
It fluttered and failed for breath.
To-night it doth inherit
The vasty hall of death.

DOVER BEACH

MATTHEW ARNOLD

The sea is calm tonight,
The tide is full, the moon lies fair
Upon the straits;—on the French coast the light
Gleams and is gone; the cliffs of England stand,
Glimmering and vast, out in the tranquil bay.
Come to the window, sweet is the night-air!
Only, from the long line of spray
Where the sea meets the moon-blanched land,
Listen! you hear the grating roar 10
Of pebbles which the waves draw back, and fling,
At their return, up the high strand,
Begin, and cease, and then again begin,
With tremulous cadence slow, and bring
The eternal note of sadness in.

Sophocles long ago
Heard it on the Ægæan, and it brought
Into his mind the turbid ebb and flow
Of human misery; we
Find also in the sound a thought, 20
Hearing it by this distant northern sea.

The Sea of Faith
Was once, too, at the full, and round earth's shore
Lay like the folds of a bright girdle furled.
But now I only hear
Its melancholy, long, withdrawing roar,
Retreating, to the breath
Of the night-wind, down the vast edges drear
And naked shingles of the world.

Ah, love, let us be true 30
To one another! for the world, which seems
To lie before us like a land of dreams,
So various, so beautiful, so new,
Hath really neither joy, nor love, nor light,
Nor certitude, nor peace, nor help for pain;
And we are here as on a darkling plain
Swept with confused alarms of struggle and flight,
Where ignorant armies clash by night.

BRIDAL BIRTH

DANTE GABRIEL ROSSETTI

As when desire, long darkling, dawns, and first
  The mother looks upon the newborn child,
  Even so my Lady stood at gaze and smiled
When her soul knew at length the Love it nursed.
Born with her life, creature of poignant thirst
  And exquisite hunger, at her heart Love lay
  Quickening in darkness, till a voice that day
Cried on him, and the bonds of birth were burst.

Now, shielded in his wings, our faces yearn
  Together, as his full-grown feet now range
    The grove, and his warm hands our couch prepare:
Till to his song our bodiless souls in turn
  Be born his children, when Death's nuptial change
    Leaves us for light the halo of his hair.

SILENT NOON

DANTE GABRIEL ROSSETTI

Your hands lie open in the long fresh grass,—
  The finger-points look through like rosy blooms:
  Your eyes smile peace. The pasture gleams and glooms
'Neath billowing skies that scatter and amass.
All round our nest, far as the eye can pass,

Are golden kingcup-fields with silver edge
Where the cow-parsley skirts the hawthorn-hedge.
'Tis visible silence, still as the hour-glass.

Deep in the sun-searched growths the dragon-fly
Hangs like a blue thread loosened from the sky:—
So this wing'd hour is dropt to us from above.
Oh! clasp we to our hearts, for deathless dower,
This close-companioned inarticulate hour
When twofold silence was the song of love.

MARK WHERE THE PRESSING WIND

GEORGE MEREDITH

Mark where the pressing wind shoots javelin-like,
Its skeleton shadow on the broad-backed wave!
Here is a fitting spot to dig Love's grave;
Here where the ponderous breakers plunge and strike,
And dart their hissing tongues high up the sand:
In hearing of the ocean, and in sight
Of those ribbed wind-streaks running into white.
If I the death of Love had deeply planned,
I never could have made it half so sure,
As by the unblest kisses which upbraid
The full-waked senses; or failing that, degrade!
'Tis morning: but no morning can restore
What we have forfeited. I see no sin:
The wrong is mixed. In tragic life, God wot,
No villain need be! Passions spin the plot:
We are betrayed by what is false within.

LUCIFER IN STARLIGHT

GEORGE MEREDITH

On a starred night Prince Lucifer uprose.
Tired of his dark dominion, swung the fiend
Above the rolling ball, in cloud part screened,

Where sinners hugged their specter of repose.
Poor prey to his hot fit of pride were those.
And now upon his western wing he leaned,
Now his huge bulk o'er Afric's sands careened,
Now the black planet shadowed Arctic snows.
Soaring through wider zones that pricked his scars
With memory of the old revolt from Awe,
He reached a middle height, and at the stars,
Which are the brain of heaven, he looked, and sank.
Around the ancient track marched, rank on rank,
The army of unalterable law.

WEARY IN WELL-DOING

CHRISTINA ROSSETTI

I would have gone; God bade me stay:
  I would have worked; God bade me rest.
He broke my will from day to day,
  He read my yearnings unexprest,
    And said them nay.

Now I would stay; God bids me go:
  Now I would rest; God bids me work.
He breaks my heart tost to and fro;
  My soul is wrung with doubts that lurk
    And vex it so.

I go, Lord, where Thou sendest me;
  Day after day I plod and moil:
But, Christ my God, when will it be
  That I may let alone my toil
    And rest with Thee?

AFTER GREAT PAIN A FORMAL FEELING COMES

EMILY DICKINSON

After great pain a formal feeling comes—
The nerves sit ceremonious like tombs;
The stiff heart questions—was it He that bore?
And yesterday—or centuries before?

The feet mechanical go round
A wooden way,
Of ground or air of Ought,
Regardless grown;
A quartz contentment like a stone.

This is the hour of lead
Remembered if outlived
As freezing persons recollect
The snow—
First chill, then stupor, then
The letting go.

I HEARD A FLY BUZZ WHEN I DIED

EMILY DICKINSON

I heard a fly buzz when I died;
The stillness in the room
Was like the stillness in the air
Between the heaves of storm.

The eyes around had wrung them dry,
And breaths were gathering firm
For that last onset when the king
Be witnessed in the room.

I willed my keepsakes, signed away
What portion of me be

Assignable—and then it was
There interposed a fly,

With blue, uncertain, stumbling buzz
Between the light and me;
And then the windows failed, and then
I could not see to see.

’TWAS WARM AT FIRST, LIKE US

EMILY DICKINSON

’Twas warm at first, like us,
Until there crept thereon
A chill, like frost upon a glass,
Till all the scene be gone.

The forehead copied stone,
The fingers grew too cold
To ache, and like a skater’s brook
The busy eyes congealed.

It straightened—that was all—
It crowded cold to cold—
It multiplied indifference
As Pride were all it could.

And even when with cords
’Twas lowered like a freight,
It made no signal, nor demurred,
But dropped like adamant.

A LIGHT EXISTS IN SPRING

EMILY DICKINSON

A light exists in spring
Not present in the year

At any other period.
When March is scarcely here

A color stands abroad
On solitary hills
That science cannot overtake,
But human nature feels.

It waits upon the lawn;
It shows the furthest tree
Upon the furthest slope we know;
It almost speaks to me.

Then, as horizons step,
Or noons report away,
Without the formula of sound,
It passes, and we stay:

A quality of loss
Affecting our content,
As trade had suddenly encroached
Upon a sacrament.

❡ AS IMPERCEPTIBLY AS GRIEF

EMILY DICKINSON

As imperceptibly as grief
The Summer lapsed away,—
Too imperceptible, at last,
To seem like perfidy.

A quietness distilled,
As twilight long begun,
Or Nature, spending with herself
Sequestered Afternoon.

The dusk drew earlier in,
The morning foreign shone,—

A courteous, yet harrowing grace,
As guest who would be gone.

And thus, without a wing,
Or service of a keel,
Our summer made her light escape
Into the beautiful.

THERE'S A CERTAIN SLANT OF LIGHT

EMILY DICKINSON

There's a certain slant of light,
On winter afternoons,
That oppresses, like the weight
Of cathedral tunes.

Heavenly hurt it gives us;
We can find no scar,
But internal difference
Where the meanings are.

None may teach it anything,
'Tis the seal, despair,—
An imperial affliction
Sent us of the air.

When it comes, the landscape listens,
Shadows hold their breath;
When it goes, 'tis like the distance
On the look of death.

A CEMETERY

EMILY DICKINSON

This quiet Dust was Gentlemen and Ladies,
And Lads and Girls;

Was laughter and ability and sighing,
  And frocks and curls.

This passive place a Summer's nimble mansion,
  Where Bloom and Bees
Fulfilled their Oriental Circuit,
  Then ceased like these.

THE GARDEN OF PROSERPINE

ALGERNON CHARLES SWINBURNE

Here, where the world is quiet;
  Here, where all trouble seems
Dead winds' and spent waves' riot
  In doubtful dreams of dreams;
I watch the green field growing
For reaping folk and sowing,
For harvest-time and mowing,
  A sleepy world of streams.

I am tired of tears and laughter,
  And men that laugh and weep, 10
Of what may come hereafter
  For men that sow to reap;
I am weary of days and hours,
Blown buds of barren flowers,
Desires and dreams and powers
  And everything but sleep.

Here life has death for neighbor,
  And far from eye or ear
Wan waves and wet winds labor,
  Weak ships and spirits steer; 20
They drive adrift, and whither
They wot not who make thither;
But no such winds blow hither,
  And no such things grow here.

No growth of moor or coppice,
No heather-flower or vine,
But bloomless buds of poppies,
Green grapes of Proserpine,
Pale beds of blowing rushes
Where no leaf blooms or blushes 30
Save this whereout she crushes
For dead men deadly wine.

Pale, without name or number,
In fruitless fields of corn,
They bow themselves and slumber
All night till light is born;
And like a soul belated,
In hell and heaven unmated,
By cloud and mist abated
Comes out of darkness morn. 40

Though one were strong as seven,
He too with death shall dwell,
Nor wake with wings in heaven,
Nor weep for pains in hell;
Though one were fair as roses,
His beauty clouds and closes;
And well though love reposes,
In the end it is not well.

Pale, beyond porch and portal,
Crowned with calm leaves, she stands 50
Who gathers all things mortal
With cold immortal hands;
Her languid lips are sweeter
Than love's who fears to greet her
To men that mix and meet her
From many times and lands.

She waits for each and other,
She waits for all men born;
Forgets the earth her mother,

The life of fruits and corn; 60
And spring and seed and swallow
Take wing for her and follow
Where summer song rings hollow
And flowers are put to scorn.

There go the loves that wither,
The old loves with wearier wings;
And all dead years draw thither,
And all disastrous things;
Dead dreams of days forsaken,
Blind buds that snows have shaken, 70
Wild leaves that winds have taken,
Red strays of ruined springs.

We are not sure of sorrow,
And joy was never sure;
Today will die tomorrow;
Time stoops to no man's lure;
And love, grown faint and fretful,
With lips but half regretful
Sighs, and with eyes forgetful
Weeps that no loves endure. 80

From too much love of living,
From hope and fear set free,
We thank with brief thanksgiving
Whatever gods may be
That no life lives for ever;
That dead men rise up never;
That even the weariest river
Winds somewhere safe to sea.

Then star nor sun shall waken,
Nor any change of light: 90
Nor sound of waters shaken,
Nor any sound or sight:
Nor wintry leaves nor vernal,
Nor days nor things diurnal;

Only the sleep eternal
In an eternal night.

DRUMMER HODGE *

THOMAS HARDY

They throw in Drummer Hodge, to rest
Uncoffined—just as found:
His landmark is a kopje-crest
That breaks the veldt around:
And foreign constellations west
Each night above his mound.

Young Hodge the Drummer never knew—
Fresh from his Wessex home—
The meaning of the broad Karoo,
The Bush, the dusty loam,
And why uprose to nightly view
Strange stars amid the gloam.

Yet portion of that unknown plain
Will Hodge forever be;
His homely Northern breast and brain
Grow to some Southern tree,
And strange-eyed constellations reign
His stars eternally.

NEUTRAL TONES

THOMAS HARDY

We stood by a pond that winter day,
And the sun was white, as though chidden of God,
And a few leaves lay on the starving sod;
They had fallen from an ash, and were gray.

* The poems by Thomas Hardy are from *Collected Poems of Thomas Hardy.*

Your eyes on me were as eyes that rove
Over tedious riddles solved years ago;
And some words played between us to and fro
  On which lost the more by our love.

The smile on your mouth was the deadest thing
Alive enough to have strength to die;
And a grin of bitterness swept thereby
  Like an ominous bird a-wing. . . .

Since then, keen lessons that love deceives,
And wrings with wrong, have shaped to me
Your face, and the God-curst sun, and a tree,
  And a pond edged with grayish leaves.

¶ DURING WIND AND RAIN

THOMAS HARDY

They sing their dearest songs—
He, she, all of them—yea,
Treble and tenor and bass,
  And one to play;
With the candles mooning each face . . .
  Ah, no; the years O!
How the sick leaves reel down in throngs!

They clear the creeping moss—
Elders and juniors—aye,
Making the pathways neat
  And the garden gay;
And they build a shady seat. . . .
  Ah, no; the years, the years;
See, the white storm-birds wing across!

They are blithely breakfasting all—
Men and maidens—yea,
Under the summer tree,
  With a glimpse of the bay,

While pet fowl come to the knee. . . .
  Ah, no; the years O!
And the rotten rose is ript from the wall.

They change to a high new house,
He, she, all of them—aye,
Clocks and carpets and chairs
  On the lawn all day,
And brightest things that are theirs. . . .
  Ah, no; the years, the years;
Down their carved names the rain-drop ploughs.

THE OXEN

THOMAS HARDY

Christmas Eve, and twelve of the clock,
  "Now they are all on their knees,"
An elder said as we sat in a flock
  By the embers in hearthside ease.

We pictured the meek mild creatures where
  They dwelt in their strawy pen,
Nor did it occur to one of us there
  To doubt they were kneeling then.

So fair a fancy few would weave
  In these years! Yet, I feel,
If someone said on Christmas Eve,
  "Come; see the oxen kneel

"In the lonely barton by yonder coomb
  Our childhood used to know,"
I should go with him in the gloom,
  Hoping it might be so.

CHANNEL FIRING

THOMAS HARDY

That night your great guns unawares,
Shook all our coffins as we lay,
And broke the chancel window squares,
We thought it was the Judgment-day

And sat upright. While drearisome
Arose the howl of wakened hounds:
The mouse let fall the altar-crumb,
The worms drew back into the mounds,

The glebe cow drooled. Till God called, "No;
It's gunnery practice out at sea
Just as before you went below;
The world is as it used to be:

"All nations striving strong to make
Red war yet redder. Mad as hatters
They do no more for Christès sake
Than you who are helpless in such matters.

"That this is not the judgment-hour
For some of them's a blessed thing,
For if it were they'd have to scour
Hell's floor for so much threatening . . .

"Ha, ha. It will be warmer when
I blow the trumpet (if indeed
I ever do; for you are men,
And rest eternal sorely need)."

So down we lay again. "I wonder,
Will the world ever saner be,"
Said one, "than when He sent us under
In our indifferent century!"

And many a skeleton shook his head.
"Instead of preaching forty year,"
My neighbor Parson Thirdly said,
"I wish I had stuck to pipes and beer."

Again the guns disturbed the hour,
Roaring their readiness to avenge,
As far inland as Stourton Tower,
And Camelot, and starlit Stonehenge.

GOD'S GRANDEUR

GERARD MANLEY HOPKINS

The world is charged with the grandeur of God.
  It will flame out, like shining from shook foil;
  It gathers to a greatness, like the ooze of oil
Crushed. Why do men then now not reck his rod?
Generations have trod, have trod, have trod;
  And all is seared with trade; bleared, smeared with toil;
  And wears man's smudge and shares man's smell: the soil
Is bare now, nor can foot feel, being shod.

And for all this, nature is never spent;
  There lives the dearest freshness deep down things;
And though the last lights off the black West went
  Oh, morning, at the brown brink eastward, springs—
Because the Holy Ghost over the bent
  World broods with warm breast and with ah! bright wings.

THE CAGED SKYLARK *

GERARD MANLEY HOPKINS

As a dare-gale skylark scanted in a dull cage
  Man's mounting spirit in his bone-house, mean house, dwells—

* "The Caged Skylark" and "Felix Randal" from *Poems of Gerard Manley Hopkins*. Copyright by Oxford University Press. Reprinted by permission of the publisher.

That bird beyond the remembering his free fells;
This in drudgery, day-laboring-out life's age.

Though aloft on turf or perch or poor low stage,
Both sing sometimes the sweetest, sweetest spells,
Yet both droop deadly sometimes in their cells
Or wring their barriers in bursts of fear or rage.

Not that the sweet-fowl, song-fowl, needs no rest—
Why, hear him, hear him babble and drop down to his nest,
But his own nest, wild nest, no prison.

Man's spirit will be flesh-bound when found at best,
But uncumbered: meadow-down is not distressed
For a rainbow footing it nor he for his bones risen.

FELIX RANDAL

GERARD MANLEY HOPKINS

Felix Randal the farrier, O he is dead then? my duty all ended,
Who have watched his mould of man, big-boned and hardy-handsome
Pining, pining, till time when reason rambled in it and some
Fatal four disorders, fleshed there, all contended?

Sickness broke him. Impatient he cursed at first, but mended
Being anointed and all; though a heavenlier heart began some
Months earlier, since I had our sweet reprieve and ransom
Tendered to him. Ah well, God rest him all road ever he offended!

This seeing the sick endears them to us, us too it endears.
My tongue had taught thee comfort, touch had quenched thy tears,
Thy tears that touched my heart, child, Felix, poor Felix Randal;

How far from then forethought of, all thy more boisterous years,
When thou at the random grim forge, powerful amidst peers,
Didst fettle for the great grey drayhorse his bright and battering
sandal!

NIGHTINGALES *

ROBERT BRIDGES

Beautiful must be the mountains whence ye come,
And bright in the fruitful valleys the streams wherefrom
Ye learn your song:
Where are those starry woods? O might I wander there,
Among the flowers, which in that heavenly air
Bloom the year long!

Nay, barren are those mountains and spent the streams:
Our song is the voice of desire, that haunts our dreams,
A throe of the heart,
Whose pining visions dim, forbidden hopes profound,
No dying cadence nor long sigh can sound,
For all our art.

Alone, aloud in the raptured ear of men
We pour our dark nocturnal secret; and then,
As night is withdrawn
From these sweet-springing meads and bursting boughs of May,
Dream, while the innumerable choir of day
Welcome the dawn.

I PRAISE THE TENDER FLOWER

ROBERT BRIDGES

I praise the tender flower,
That on a mournful day
Bloomed in my garden bower
And made the winter gay.
Its loveliness contented
My heart tormented.

* The poems by Robert Bridges are from *The Poetical Works of Robert Bridges.* Reprinted by permission of The Clarendon Press, Oxford.

I praise the gentle maid
Whose happy voice and smile
To confidence betrayed
My doleful heart awhile:
And gave my spirit deploring
Fresh wings for soaring.

The maid for very fear
Of love I durst not tell:
The rose could never hear,
Though I bespake her well:
So in my song I bind them
For all to find them.

LOW BAROMETER

ROBERT BRIDGES

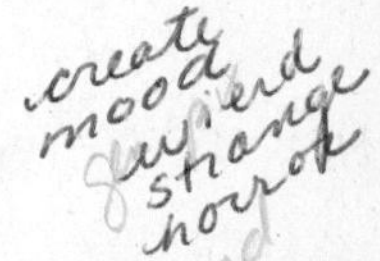

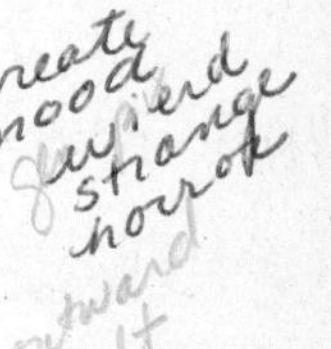

The south-wind strengthens to a gale,
Across the moon the clouds fly fast,
The house is smitten as with a flail,
The chimney shudders to the blast.

On such a night, when Air has loosed
Its guardian grasp on blood and brain,
Old terrors then of god or ghost
Creep from their caves to life again;

And Reason kens he herits in
A haunted house. Tenants unknown
Assert their squalid lease of sin
With earlier title than his own.

Unbodied presences, the pack'd
Pollution and remorse of Time,
Slipp'd from oblivion reënact
The horrors of unhouseled crime.

Some men would quell the thing with prayer
Whose sightless footsteps pad the floor,

Whose fearful trespass mounts the stair
Or bursts the lock'd forbidden door.

Some have seen corpses long inter'd
Escape from hallowing control,
Pale charnel forms—nay ev'n have heard
The shrilling of a troubled soul,

That wanders till the dawn hath cross'd
The dolorous dark, or Earth hath wound
Closer her storm-spread cloke, and thrust
The baleful phantoms under ground.

ΕΡΩΣ
(EROS)

ROBERT BRIDGES

Why hast thou nothing in thy face?
Thou idol of the human race,
Thou tyrant of the human heart,
The flower of lovely youth that art;
Yea, and that standest in thy youth
An image of eternal Truth,
With thy exuberant flesh so fair,
That only Pheidias might compare,
Ere from his chaste marmoreal form
Time had decayed the colours warm;
Like to his gods in thy proud dress,
Thy starry sheen of nakedness.

Surely thy body is thy mind,
For in thy face is nought to find,
Only thy soft unchristen'd smile,
That shadows neither love nor guile,
But shameless will and power immense,
In secret sensuous innocence.

O king of joy, what is thy thought?
I dream thou knowest it is nought,

And wouldst in darkness come, but thou
Makest the light where'er thou go.
Ah yet no victim of thy grace,
None who e'er long'd for thy embrace,
Hath cared to look upon thy face.

THE KINGDOM OF GOD

FRANCIS THOMPSON

"In no Strange Land"

O world invisible, we view thee,
O world intangible, we touch thee,
O world unknowable, we know thee,
Inapprehensible, we clutch thee!

Down the fish soar to find the ocean,
The eagle plunge to find the air—
That we ask of the stars in motion
If they have rumour of thee there?

Not where the wheeling systems darken,
And our benumbed conceiving soars!—
The drift of pinions, would we hearken,
Beats at our own clay-shuttered doors.

The angels keep their ancient places;—
Turn but a stone and start a wing!
'Tis ye, 'tis your estranged faces,
That miss the many-splendoured thing.

But (when so sad thou canst not sadder)
Cry;—and upon thy so sore loss
Shall shine the traffic of Jacob's ladder
Pitched betwixt Heaven and Charing Cross.

Yea, in the night, my Soul, my daughter,
Cry,—clinging Heaven by the hems;

And lo, Christ walking on the water
Not of Gennesareth, but Thames!

TO AN ATHLETE DYING YOUNG *

A. E. HOUSMAN

The time you won your town the race
We chaired you through the market-place;
Man and boy stood cheering by,
And home we brought you shoulder-high.

To-day, the road all runners come,
Shoulder-high we bring you home,
And set you at your threshold down,
Townsman of a stiller town.

Smart lad, to slip betimes away
From fields where glory does not stay,
And early though the laurel grows
It withers quicker than the rose.

Eyes the shady night has shut
Cannot see the record cut,
And silence sounds no worse than cheers
After earth has stopped the ears.

Now you will not swell the rout
Of lads that wore their honors out,
Runners whom renown outran
And the name died before the man.

So set, before its echoes fade,
The fleet foot on the sill of shade,

* The poems by A. E. Housman are from *A Shropshire Lad* by A. E. Housman. Reprinted by permission of Henry Holt and Company, Inc., and The Society of Authors as the literary representative of the Trustees of the estate of the late A. E. Housman, and Messrs. Jonathan Cape Ltd., publishers of A. E. Housman's *Collected Poems.*

And hold to the low lintel up
The still-defended challenge-cup.

And round that early-laurelled head
Will flock to gaze the strengthless dead,
And find unwithered on its curls
The garland briefer than a girl's.

❡ 1887

A. E. HOUSMAN

From Clee to heaven the beacon burns,
  The shires have seen it plain,
From north and south the sign returns
  And beacons burn again.

Look left, look right, the hills are bright,
  The dales are light between,
Because 'tis fifty years tonight
  That God has saved the Queen.

Now, when the flame they watch not towers
  About the soil they trod,
Lads, we'll remember friends of ours
  Who shared the work with God.

To skies that knit their heartstrings right,
  To fields that bred them brave,
The saviors come not home tonight:
  Themselves they could not save.

It dawns in Asia, tombstones show
  And Shropshire names are read;
And the Nile spills his overflow
  Beside the Severn's dead.

We pledge in peace by farm and town
  The Queen they served in war.

And fire the beacons up and down
The land they perished for.

"God save the Queen" we living sing,
From height to height 'tis heard;
And with the rest your voices ring,
Lads of the Fifty-third.

Oh, God will save her, fear you not:
Be you the men you've been,
Get you the sons your fathers got,
And God will save the Queen.

BREDON HILL

A. E. HOUSMAN

In summertime on Bredon
The bells they sound so clear;
Round both the shires they ring them
In steeples far and near,
A happy noise to hear.

Here of a Sunday morning
My love and I would lie,
And see the colored counties,
And hear the larks so high
About us in the sky.

The bells would ring to call her
In valleys miles away:
"Come all to church, good people;
Good people, come and pray."
But here my love would stay.

And I would turn and answer
Among the springing thyme,
"Oh, peal upon our wedding,

And we will hear the chime,
And come to church in time."

But when the snows at Christmas
On Bredon top were strown,
My love rose up so early
And stole out unbeknown
And went to church alone.

They tolled the one bell only,
Groom there was none to see,
The mourners followed after,
And so to church went she,
And would not wait for me.

The bells they sound on Bredon,
And still the steeples hum.
"Come all to church, good people,—"
Oh, noisy bells, be dumb;
I hear you, I will come.

ON WENLOCK EDGE

A. E. HOUSMAN

On Wenlock Edge the wood's in trouble;
His forest fleece the Wrekin[1] heaves;
The gale, it plies the saplings double,
And thick on Severn snow the leaves.

'Twould blow like this through holt and hanger[2]
When Uricon the city stood:
'Tis the old wind in the old anger,
But then it threshed another wood.

Then, 'twas before my time, the Roman
At yonder heaving hill would stare:

[1] Wrekin—*a hill in Shropshire, by a town called Wenlock in English and Uricon in Roman usage* [2] holt and hanger—*steep wooded hills*

The blood that warms an English yeoman,
 The thoughts that hurt him, they were there.

There, like the wind through woods in riot,
 Through him the gale of life blew high;
The tree of man was never quiet:
 Then 'twas the Roman, now 'tis I.

The gale, it plies the saplings double,
 It blows so hard, 'twill soon be gone:
To-day the Roman and his trouble
 Are ashes under Uricon.

⁋ THE SECOND COMING*

WILLIAM BUTLER YEATS

Turning and turning in the widening gyre
The falcon cannot hear the falconer;
Things fall apart; the centre cannot hold;
Mere anarchy is loosed upon the world,
The blood-dimmed tide is loosed, and everywhere
The ceremony of innocence is drowned;
The best lack all conviction, while the worst
Are full of passionate intensity.

Surely some revelation is at hand;
Surely the Second Coming is at hand.
The Second Coming! Hardly are those words out
When a vast image out of *Spiritus Mundi*
Troubles my sight: somewhere in sands of the desert
A shape with lion body and the head of a man,
A gaze blank and pitiless as the sun,
Is moving its slow thighs, while all about it

Reel shadows of the indignant desert birds.
The darkness drops again; but now I know
That twenty centuries of stony sleep
Were vexed to nightmare by a rocking cradle,
And what rough beast, its hour come round at last,
Slouches towards Bethlehem to be born?

SAILING TO BYZANTIUM

WILLIAM BUTLER YEATS

THAT is no country for old men. The young
In one another's arms, birds in the trees,
—Those dying generations—at their song,
The salmon-falls, the mackerel-crowded seas,
Fish, flesh, or fowl, commend all summer long
Whatever is begotten, born, and dies.
Caught in that sensual music all neglect
Monuments of unaging intellect.

An aged man is but a paltry thing,
A tattered coat upon a stick, unless
Soul clap its hands and sing, and louder sing
For every tatter in its mortal dress,
Nor is there singing school but studying
Monuments of its own magnificence;
And therefore I have sailed the seas and come
To the holy city of Byzantium.

O sages standing in God's holy fire
As in the gold mosaic of a wall,
Come from the holy fire, perne in a gyre,
And be the singing-masters of my soul.
Consume my heart away; sick with desire
And fastened to a dying animal
It knows not what it is; and gather me
Into the artifice of eternity.

Once out of nature I shall never take
My bodily form from any natural thing,

But such a form as Grecian goldsmiths make
Of hammered gold and gold enameling
To keep a drowsy Emperor awake;
Or set upon a golden bough to sing
To lords and ladies of Byzantium
Of what is past, or passing, or to come.

AMONG SCHOOL CHILDREN

WILLIAM BUTLER YEATS

1

I walk through the long schoolroom questioning;
A kind old nun in a white hood replies;
The children learn to cipher and to sing,
To study reading-books and history,
To cut and sew, be neat in everything
In the best modern way—the children's eyes
In momentary wonder stare upon
A sixty year old smiling public man.

2

I dream of a Ledaean body, bent
Above a sinking fire, a tale that she 10
Told of a harsh reproof, or trivial event
That changed some childish day to tragedy—
Told, and it seemed that our two natures blent
Into a sphere from youthful sympathy,
Or else, to alter Plato's parable,
Into the yolk and white of the one shell.

3

And thinking of that fit of grief or rage
I look upon one child or t'other there
And wonder if she stood so at that age—

For even daughters of the swan can share 20
Something of every paddler's heritage—
And had that colour upon cheek or hair,
And thereupon my heart is driven wild:
She stands before me as a living child.

4

Her present image floats into the mind—
Did Quattrocento finger fashion it
Hollow of cheek as though it drank the wind
And took a mess of shadows for its meat?
And I though never of Ledaean kind
Had pretty plumage once—enough of that, 30
Better to smile on all that smile, and show
There is a comfortable kind of scarecrow.

5

What youthful mother, a shape upon her lap
Honey of generation had betrayed,
And that must sleep, shriek, struggle to escape
As recollection or the drug decide,
Would think her son, did she but see that shape
With sixty or more winters on its head,
A compensation for the pang of his birth,
Or the uncertainty of his setting forth? 40

6

Plato thought nature but a spume that plays
Upon a ghostly paradigm of things;
Solider Aristotle played the taws
Upon the bottom of a king of kings;
World-famous golden-thighed Pythagoras
Fingered upon a fiddle-stick or strings
What a star sang and careless Muses heard:
Old clothes upon old sticks to scare a bird.

7

Both nuns and mothers worship images,
But those the candles light are not as those 50
That animate a mother's reveries,
But keep a marble or a bronze repose.
And yet they too break hearts—O Presences
That passion, piety or affection knows,
And that all heavenly glory symbolize—
O self-born mockers of man's enterprise;

8

Labour is blossoming or dancing where
The body is not bruised to pleasure soul,
Nor beauty born out of its own despair,
Nor blear-eyed wisdom out of midnight oil. 60
O chestnut tree, great rooted blossomer,
Are you the leaf, the blossom or the bole?
O body swayed to music, O brightening glance,
How can we know the dancer from the dance?

TWO SONGS FROM A PLAY

WILLIAM BUTLER YEATS

I

I saw a staring virgin stand
Where holy Dionysus died,
And tear the heart out of his side,
And lay the heart upon her hand
And bear that beating heart away;
And then did all the Muses sing
Of Magnus Annus at the spring,
As though God's death were but a play.

Another Troy must rise and set,
Another lineage feed the crow,

Another Argo's painted prow
Drive to a flashier bauble yet.
The Roman Empire stood appalled:
It dropped the reins of peace and war
When that fierce virgin and her Star
Out of the fabulous darkness called.

2

In pity for man's darkening thought
He walked that room and issued thence
In Galilean turbulence;
The Babylonian starlight brought
A fabulous, formless darkness in;
Odor of blood when Christ was slain
Made all Platonic tolerance vain
And vain all Doric discipline.

Everything that man esteems
Endures a moment or a day.
Love's pleasure drives his love away,
The painter's brush consumes his dreams;
The herald's cry, the soldier's tread
Exhaust his glory and his might:
Whatever flames upon the night
Man's own resinous heart has fed.

¶ FOR ANNE GREGORY

WILLIAM BUTLER YEATS

"Never shall a young man,
Thrown into despair
By those great honey-coloured
Ramparts at your ear,
Love you for yourself alone
And not your yellow hair."

"But I can get a hair-dye
And set such colour there,

Brown, or black, or carrot,
That young men in despair
May love me for myself alone
And not my yellow hair."

"I heard an old religious man
But yesternight declare
That he had found a text to prove
That only God, my dear,
Could love you for yourself alone
And not your yellow hair."

MINIVER CHEEVY *

EDWIN ARLINGTON ROBINSON

Miniver Cheevy, child of scorn,
Grew lean while he assailed the seasons;
He wept that he was ever born,
And he had reasons.

Miniver loved the days of old
When swords were bright and steeds were prancing;
The vision of a warrior bold
Would set him dancing.

Miniver sighed for what was not,
And dreamed, and rested from his labors;
He dreamed of Thebes and Camelot,
And Priam's neighbors.

Miniver mourned the ripe renown
That made so many a name so fragrant;
He mourned Romance, now on the town,
And Art, a vagrant.

Miniver loved the Medici,
  Albeit he had never seen one;
He would have sinned incessantly
  Could he have been one.

Miniver cursed the commonplace
  And eyed a khaki suit with loathing;
He missed the mediæval grace
  Of iron clothing.

Miniver scorned the gold he sought,
  But sore annoyed was he without it;
Miniver thought, and thought, and thought,
  And thought about it.

Miniver Cheevy, born too late,
  Scratched his head and kept on thinking;
Miniver coughed, and called it fate,
  And kept on drinking.

¶ MR. FLOOD'S PARTY

EDWIN ARLINGTON ROBINSON

Old Eben Flood, climbing alone one night
Over the hill between the town below
And the forsaken upland hermitage
That held as much as he should ever know
On earth again of home, paused warily.
The road was his with not a native near;
And Eben, having leisure, said aloud,
For no man else in Tilbury Town to hear:

"Well, Mr. Flood, we have the harvest moon
Again, and we may not have many more; 10
The bird is on the wing, the poet says,
And you and I have said it here before.
Drink to the bird." He raised up to the light

The jug that he had gone so far to fill,
And answered huskily: "Well, Mr. Flood,
Since you propose it, I believe I will."

Alone, as if enduring to the end
A valiant armor of scarred hopes outworn,
He stood there in the middle of the road
Like Roland's ghost winding a silent horn. 20
Below him, in the town among the trees,
Where friends of other days had honored him,
A phantom salutation of the dead
Rang thinly till old Eben's eyes were dim.

Then, as a mother lays her sleeping child
Down tenderly, fearing it may awake,
He set the jug down slowly at his feet
With trembling care, knowing that most things break;
And only when assured that on firm earth
It stood, as the uncertain lives of men 30
Assuredly did not, he paced away,
And with his hand extended paused again:

"Well, Mr. Flood, we have not met like this
In a long time; and many a change has come
To both of us, I fear, since last it was
We had a drop together. Welcome home!"
Convivially returning with himself,
Again he raised the jug up to the light;
And with an acquiescent quaver said:
"Well, Mr. Flood, if you insist, I might. 40

"Only a very little, Mr. Flood—
For auld lang syne. No more, sir; that will do."
So, for the time, apparently it did,
And Eben evidently thought so too;
For soon amid the silver loneliness
Of night he lifted up his voice and sang,
Secure, with only two moons listening,
Until the whole harmonious landscape rang—

"For auld lang syne." The weary throat gave out,
The last word wavered; and the song being done, 50
He raised again the jug regretfully
And shook his head, and was again alone.
There was not much that was ahead of him,
And there was nothing in the town below—
Where strangers would have shut the many doors
That many friends had opened long ago.

FOR A DEAD LADY

EDWIN ARLINGTON ROBINSON

No more with overflowing light
Shall fill the eyes that now are faded,
Nor shall another's fringe with night
Their woman-hidden world as they did.
No more shall quiver down the days
The flowing wonder of her ways,
Whereof no language may requite
The shifting and the many-shaded.

The grace, divine, definitive,
Clings only as a faint forestalling;
The laugh that love could not forgive
Is hushed, and answers to no calling;
The forehead and the little ears
Have gone where Saturn keeps the years;
The breast where roses could not live
Has done with rising and with falling.

The beauty, shattered by the laws
That have creation in their keeping,
No longer trembles at applause,
Or over children that are sleeping;
And we who delve in beauty's lore
Know all that we have known before
Of what inexorable cause
Makes Time so vicious in his reaping.

EROS TURANNOS

EDWIN ARLINGTON ROBINSON

She fears him, and will always ask
What fated her to choose him;
She meets in his engaging mask
All reasons to refuse him;
But what she meets and what she fears
Are less than are the downward years,
Drawn slowly to the foamless weirs
Of age, were she to lose him.

Between a blurred sagacity
That once had power to sound him, 10
And Love, that will not let him be
The Judas that she found him,
Her pride assuages her almost,
As if it were alone the cost.
He sees that he will not be lost,
And waits and looks around him.

A sense of ocean and old trees
Envelops and allures him;
Tradition, touching all he sees,
Beguiles and reassures him; 20
And all her doubts of what he says
Are dimmed with what she knows of days—
Till even prejudice delays
And fades, and she secures him.

The falling leaf inaugurates
The reign of her confusion;
The pounding wave reverberates
The dirge of her illusion;
And home, where passion lived and died,
Becomes a place where she can hide, 30
While all the town and harbor-side
Vibrate with her seclusion.

We tell you, tapping on our brows,
  The story as it should be,
As if the story of a house
  Were told, or ever could be;
We'll have no kindly veil between
Her visions and those we have seen,—
As if we guessed what hers have been,
  Or what they are or would be. 40

Meanwhile we do no harm; for they
  That with a god have striven,
Not hearing much of what we say,
  Take what the god has given;
Though like waves breaking it may be,
Or like a changed familiar tree,
Or like a stairway to the sea
  Where down the blind are driven.

THE SHEAVES

EDWIN ARLINGTON ROBINSON

Where long the shadows of the wind had rolled,
Green wheat was yielding to the change assigned;
And as by some vast magic undivined
The world was turning slowly into gold.
Like nothing that was ever bought or sold
It waited there, the body and the mind;
And with a mighty meaning of a kind
That tells the more the more it is not told.

So in a land where all days are not fair,
Fair days went on till on another day
A thousand golden sheaves were lying there,
Shining and still, but not for long to stay—
As if a thousand girls with golden hair
Might rise from where they slept and go away.

AFTER APPLE-PICKING *

ROBERT FROST

My long two-pointed ladder's sticking through a tree
Toward heaven still,
And there's a barrel that I didn't fill
Beside it, and there may be two or three
Apples I didn't pick upon some bough.
But I am done with apple-picking now.
Essence of winter sleep is on the night,
The scent of apples: I am drowsing off.
I cannot rub the strangeness from my sight
I got from looking through a pane of glass 10
I skimmed this morning from the drinking trough
And held against the world of hoary grass.
It melted, and I let it fall and break.
But I was well
Upon my way to sleep before it fell,
And I could tell
What form my dreaming was about to take.
Magnified apples appear and disappear,
Stem end and blossom end,
And every fleck of russet showing clear. 20
My instep arch not only keeps the ache,
It keeps the pressure of a ladder-round.
I feel the ladder sway as the boughs bend.
And I keep hearing from the cellar bin
The rumbling sound
Of load on load of apples coming in.
For I have had too much
Of apple-picking: I am overtired
Of the great harvest I myself desired.
There were ten thousand thousand fruit to touch, 30
Cherish in hand, lift down, and not let fall.
For all

That struck the earth,
No matter if not bruised or spiked with stubble,
Went surely to the cider-apple heap
As of no worth.
One can see what will trouble
This sleep of mine, whatever sleep it is.
Were he not gone,
The woodchuck could say whether it's like his 40
Long sleep, as I describe its coming on,
Or just some human sleep.

(THE OVEN BIRD

ROBERT FROST

There is a singer everyone has heard,
Loud, a mid-summer and a mid-wood bird,
Who makes the solid tree trunks sound again.
He says that leaves are old and that for flowers
Mid-summer is to spring as one to ten.
He says the early petal-fall is past
When pear and cherry bloom went down in showers
On sunny days a moment overcast;
And comes that other fall we name the fall.
He says the highway dust is over all.
The bird would cease and be as other birds
But that he knows in singing not to sing.
The question that he frames in all but words
Is what to make of a diminished thing.

(STOPPING BY WOODS ON A SNOWY EVENING

ROBERT FROST

Whose woods these are I think I know.
His house is in the village though;
He will not see me stopping here
To watch his woods fill up with snow.

My little horse must think it queer
To stop without a farmhouse near
Between the woods and frozen lake
The darkest evening of the year.

He gives his harness bells a shake
To ask if there is some mistake.
The only other sound's the sweep
Of easy wind and downy flake.

The woods are lovely, dark and deep.
But I have promises to keep,
And miles to go before I sleep,
And miles to go before I sleep.

⁅ DESERT PLACES

ROBERT FROST

Snow falling and night falling fast oh fast
In a field I looked into going past,
And the ground almost covered smooth in snow,
But a few weeds and stubble showing last.

The woods around it have it—it is theirs.
All animals are smothered in their lairs.
I am too absent-spirited to count;
The loneliness includes me unawares.

And lonely as it is, that loneliness
Will be more lonely ere it will be less—
A blanker whiteness of benighted snow
With no expression, nothing to express.

They cannot scare me with their empty spaces
Between stars—on stars where no human race is.
I have it in me so much nearer home
To scare myself with my own desert places.

⸿ COME IN

ROBERT FROST

As I came to the edge of the woods,
Thrush music—hark!
Now if it was dusk outside,
Inside it was dark.

Too dark in the woods for a bird
By sleight of wing
To better its perch for the night,
Though it still could sing.

The last of the light of the sun
That had died in the west
Still lived for one song more
In a thrush's breast.

Far in the pillared dark
Thrush music went—
Almost like a call to come in
To the dark and lament.

But no, I was out for stars:
I would not come in.
I meant not even if asked;
And I hadn't been.

⸿ PETER QUINCE AT THE CLAVIER *

WALLACE STEVENS

I

Just as my fingers on these keys
Make music, so the self-same sounds
On my spirit make a music too.

Music is feeling then, not sound;
And thus it is that what I feel,
Here in this room, desiring you,

Thinking of your blue-shadowed silk,
Is music. It is like the strain
Waked in the elders by Susanna:

Of a green evening, clear and warm, 10
She bathed in her still garden, while
The red-eyed elders, watching, felt

The basses of their being throb
In witching chords, and their thin blood
Pulse pizzicati of Hosanna.

2

In the green water, clear and warm,
Susanna lay.
She searched
The touch of springs,
And found 20
Concealed imaginings.
She sighed
For so much melody.

Upon the bank, she stood
In the cool
Of spent emotions.
She felt, among the leaves,
The dew
Of old devotions.

She walked upon the grass, 30
Still quavering.
The winds were like her maids,
On timid feet,

Fetching her woven scarves,
Yet wavering.

A breath upon her hand
Muted the night.
She turned—
A cymbal crashed,
And roaring horns. 40

3

Soon, with a noise like tambourines,
Came her attendant Byzantines.

They wondered why Susanna cried
Against the elders by her side:

And as they whispered, the refrain
Was like a willow swept by rain.

Anon their lamps' uplifted flame
Revealed Susanna and her shame.

And then the simpering Byzantines,
Fled, with a noise like tambourines. 50

4

Beauty is momentary in the mind—
The fitful tracing of a portal;
But in the flesh it is immortal.

The body dies; the body's beauty lives.
So evenings die, in their green going,
A wave, interminably flowing.
So gardens die, their meek breath scenting
The cowl of Winter, done repenting.
So maidens die to the auroral
Celebration of a maiden's choral. 60

Susanna's music touched the bawdy strings
Of those white elders; but, escaping,
Left only Death's ironic scraping.
Now in its immortality, it plays
On the clear viol of her memory,
And makes a constant sacrament of praise.

SUNDAY MORNING

WALLACE STEVENS

1

Complacencies of the peignoir, and late
Coffee and oranges in a sunny chair,
And the green freedom of a cockatoo
Upon a rug mingle to dissipate
The holy hush of ancient sacrifice.
She dreams a little, and she feels the dark
Encroachment of that old catastrophe,
As a calm darkens among water-lights.
The pungent oranges and bright, green wings
Seem things in some procession of the dead, 10
Winding across wide water, without sound.
The day is like wide water, without sound,
Stilled for the passing of her dreaming feet
Over the seas, to silent Palestine,
Dominion of the blood and sepulchre.

2

Why should she give her bounty to the dead?
What is divinity if it can come
Only in silent shadows and in dreams?
Shall she not find in comforts of the sun,
In pungent fruit and bright, green wings, or else 20
In any balm or beauty of the earth,
Things to be cherished like the thought of heaven?
Divinity must live within herself:

Passions of rain, or moods in falling snow;
Grievings in loneliness, or unsubdued
Elations when the forest blooms; gusty
Emotions on wet roads on autumn nights;
All pleasures and all pains, remembering
The bough of summer and the winter branch.
These are the measures destined for her soul. 30

3

Jove in the clouds had his inhuman birth.
No mother suckled him, no sweet land gave
Large-mannered motions to his mythy mind.
He moved among us, as a muttering king,
Magnificent, would move among his hinds,
Until our blood, commingling, virginal,
With heaven, brought such requital to desire
The very hinds discerned it, in a star.
Shall our blood fail? Or shall it come to be
The blood of paradise? And shall the earth 40
Seem all of paradise that we shall know?
The sky will be much friendlier then than now,
A part of labor and a part of pain,
And next in glory to enduring love,
Not this dividing and indifferent blue.

4

She says, "I am content when wakened birds,
Before they fly, test the reality
Of misty fields, by their sweet questionings;
But when the birds are gone, and their warm fields
Return no more, where, then, is paradise?" 50
There is not any haunt of prophecy,
Nor any old chimera of the grave,
Neither the golden underground, nor isle
Melodious, where spirits gat them home,
Nor visionary south, nor cloudy palm
Remote on heaven's hill, that has endured

As April's green endures; or will endure
Like her remembrance of awakened birds,
Or her desire for June and evening, tipped
By the consummation of the swallow's wings. 60

5

She says, "But in contentment I still feel
The need of some imperishable bliss."
Death is the mother of beauty; hence from her,
Alone, shall come fulfilment to our dreams
And our desires. Although she strews the leaves
Of sure obliteration on our paths,
The path sick sorrow took, the many paths
Where triumph rang its brassy phrase, or love
Whispered a little out of tenderness,
She makes the willow shiver in the sun 70
For maidens who were wont to sit and gaze
Upon the grass, relinquished to their feet.
She causes boys to pile new plums and pears
On disregarded plate. The maidens taste
And stray impassioned in the littering leaves.

6

Is there no change of death in paradise?
Does ripe fruit never fall? Or do the boughs
Hang always heavy in that perfect sky,
Unchanging, yet so like our perishing earth,
With rivers like our own that seek for seas 80
They never find, the same receding shores
That never touch with inarticulate pang?
Why set the pear upon those river-banks
Or spice the shores with odors of the plum?
Alas, that they should wear our colors there,
The silken weavings of our afternoons,
And pick the strings of our insipid lutes!
Death is the mother of beauty, mystical,
Within whose burning bosom we devise
Our earthly mothers waiting, sleeplessly. 90

7

Supple and turbulent, a ring of men
Shall chant in orgy on a summer morn
Their boisterous devotion to the sun,
Not as a god, but as a god might be,
Naked among them, like a savage source.
Their chant shall be a chant of paradise,
Out of their blood, returning to the sky;
And in their chant shall enter, voice by voice,
The windy lake wherein their lord delights,
The trees, like serafin, and echoing hills, 100
That choir among themselves long afterward.
They shall know well the heavenly fellowship
Of men that perish and of summer morn.
And whence they came and whither they shall go
The dew upon their feet shall manifest.

8

She hears, upon that water without sound,
A voice that cries, "The tomb in Palestine
Is not the porch of spirits lingering.
It is the grave of Jesus, where he lay."
We live in an old chaos of the sun, 110
Or old dependency of day and night,
Or island solitude, unsponsored, free,
Of that wide water, inescapable.
Deer walk upon our mountains, and the quail
Whistle about us their spontaneous cries;
Sweet berries ripen in the wilderness;
And, in the isolation of the sky,
At evening, casual flocks of pigeons make
Ambiguous undulations as they sink,
Downward to darkness, on extended wings. 120

❡ THE LOVE SONG OF J. ALFRED PRUFROCK *

T. S. ELIOT

S'io credesse che mia risposta fosse
A persona che mai tornasse al mondo,
Questa fiamma staria senza piu scosse.
Ma perciocche giammai di questo fondo
Non torno vivo alcum, s'i'odo il vero,
Senza tema d'infamia ti rispondo.

Let us go then, you and I,
When the evening is spread out against the sky
Like a patient etherized upon a table;
Let us go, through certain half-deserted streets,
The muttering retreats
Of restless nights in one-night cheap hotels
And sawdust restaurants with oyster-shells:
Streets that follow like a tedious argument
Of insidious intent
To lead you to an overwhelming question. . . . 10
Oh, do not ask, "What is it?"
Let us go and make our visit.

In the room the women come and go
Talking of Michelangelo.

The yellow fog that rubs its back upon the window-panes,
The yellow smoke that rubs its muzzle on the window-panes
Licked its tongue into the corners of the evening,
Lingered upon the pools that stand in drains,
Let fall upon its back the soot that falls from chimneys,
Slipped by the terrace, made a sudden leap, 20
And seeing that it was a soft October night,
Curled once about the house, and fell asleep.

And indeed there will be time
For the yellow smoke that slides along the street,
Rubbing its back upon the window-panes;
There will be time, there will be time
To prepare a face to meet the faces that you meet;
There will be time to murder and create,
And time for all the works and days of hands
That lift and drop a question on your plate; 30
Time for you and time for me,
And time yet for a hundred indecisions,
And for a hundred visions and revisions,
Before the taking of a toast and tea.

In the room the women come and go
Talking of Michelangelo.

And indeed there will be time
To wonder, "Do I dare?" and, "Do I dare?"
Time to turn back and descend the stair,
With a bald spot in the middle of my hair— 40
(They will say: "How his hair is growing thin!")
My morning coat, my collar mounting firmly to the chin,
My necktie rich and modest, but asserted by a simple pin—
(They will say: "But how his arms and legs are thin!")
Do I dare
Disturb the universe?
In a minute there is time
For decisions and revisions which a minute will reverse.

For I have known them all already, known them all:
Have known the evenings, mornings, afternoons, 50
I have measured out my life with coffee spoons;
I know the voices dying with a dying fall
Beneath the music from a farther room.
So how should I presume?

And I have known the eyes already, known them all—
The eyes that fix you in a formulated phrase,
And when I am formulated, sprawling on a pin,

When I am pinned and wriggling on the wall,
Then how should I begin
To spit out all the butt-ends of my days and ways? 60
 And how should I presume?

And I have known the arms already, known them all—
Arms that are braceleted and white and bare
(But in the lamplight, downed with light brown hair!)
Is it perfume from a dress
That makes me so digress?
Arms that lie along a table, or wrap about a shawl,
 And should I then presume?
 And how should I begin?

Shall I say, I have gone at dusk through narrow streets 70
And watched the smoke that rises from the pipes
Of lonely men in shirt-sleeves, leaning out of windows? . . .

I should have been a pair of ragged claws
Scuttling across the floors of silent seas.

And the afternoon, the evening, sleeps so peacefully!
Smoothed by long fingers,
Asleep . . . tired . . . or it malingers,
Stretched on the floor, here beside you and me.
Should I, after tea and cakes and ices,
Have the strength to force the moment to its crisis? 80
But though I have wept and fasted, wept and prayed,
Though I have seen my head (grown slightly bald) brought in upon
 a platter,
I am no prophet—and here's no great matter;
I have seen the moment of my greatness flicker,
And I have seen the eternal Footman hold my coat, and snicker,
And in short, I was afraid.

And would it have been worth it, after all,
After the cups, the marmalade, the tea,

Among the porcelain, among some talk of you and me,
Would it have been worth while, 90
To have bitten off the matter with a smile,
To have squeezed the universe into a ball
To roll it toward some overwhelming question,
To say: "I am Lazarus, come from the dead,
Come back to tell you all, I shall tell you all"—
If one, settling a pillow by her head,
  Should say: "That is not what I meant at all;
  That is not it, at all."

And would it have been worth it, after all,
Would it have been worth while, 100
After the sunsets and the dooryards and the sprinkled streets,
After the novels, after the teacups, after the skirts that trail along the
    floor—
And this, and so much more?—
It is impossible to say just what I mean!
But as if a magic lantern threw the nerves in patterns on a screen:
Would it have been worth while
If one, settling a pillow or throwing off a shawl,
And turning toward the window, should say:
  "That is not it at all,
  That is not what I meant, at all." 110

No! I am not Prince Hamlet, nor was meant to be;
Am an attendant lord, one that will do
To swell a progress, start a scene or two,
Advise the prince; no doubt, an easy tool,
Deferential, glad to be of use,
Politic, cautious, and meticulous;
Full of high sentence, but a bit obtuse;
At times, indeed, almost ridiculous—
Almost, at times, the Fool.

I grow old. . . . I grow old. . . . 120
I shall wear the bottoms of my trousers rolled.

Shall I part my hair behind? Do I dare to eat a peach?
I shall wear white flannel trousers, and walk upon the beach.
I have heard the mermaids singing, each to each.

I do not think that they will sing to me.

I have seen them riding seaward on the waves
Combing the white hair of the waves blown back
When the wind blows the water white and black.

We have lingered in the chambers of the sea
By sea-girls wreathed with seaweed red and brown 130
Till human voices wake us, and we drown.

GERONTION

T. S. ELIOT

Thou hast nor youth nor age
But as it were an after dinner sleep
Dreaming of both.

Here I am, an old man in a dry month,
Being read to by a boy, waiting for rain.
I was neither at the hot gates
Nor fought in the warm rain
Nor knee deep in the salt marsh, heaving a cutlass,
Bitten by flies, fought.
My house is a decayed house,
And the jew squats on the window sill, the owner,
Spawned in some estaminet of Antwerp,
Blistered in Brussels, patched and peeled in London. 10
The goat coughs at night in the field overhead;
Rocks, moss, stonecrop, iron, merds.
The woman keeps the kitchen, makes tea,
Sneezes at evening, poking the peevish gutter.
I an old man,
A dull head among windy spaces.

Signs are taken for wonders. "We would see a sign!"
The word within a word, unable to speak a word,
Swaddled with darkness. In the juvescence of the year
Came Christ the tiger 20

In depraved May, dogwood and chestnut, flowering judas,
To be eaten, to be divided, to be drunk
Among whispers; by Mr. Silvero
With caressing hands, at Limoges
Who walked all night in the next room;
By Hakagawa, bowing among the Titians;
By Madame de Tornquist, in the dark room
Shifting the candles; Fräulein von Kulp
Who turned in the hall, one hand on the door.
  Vacant shuttles 30
Weave the wind. I have no ghosts,
An old man in a draughty house
Under a windy knob.

After such knowledge, what forgiveness? Think now
History has many cunning passages, contrived corridors
And issues, deceives with whispering ambitions,
Guides us by vanities. Think now
She gives when our attention is distracted
And what she gives, gives with such supple confusions
That the giving famishes the craving. Gives too late
What's not believed in, or if still believed, 40
In memory only, reconsidered passion. Gives too soon
Into weak hands, what's thought can be dispensed with
Till the refusal propagates a fear. Think
Neither fear nor courage saves us. Unnatural vices
Are fathered by our heroism. Virtues
Are forced upon us by our impudent crimes.
These tears are shaken from the wrath-bearing tree.
The tiger springs in the new year. Us he devours. Think at last
We have not reached conclusion, when I
Stiffen in a rented house. Think at last 50
I have not made this show purposelessly

And it is not by any concitation
Of the backward devils
I would meet you upon this honestly.
I that was near your heart was removed therefrom
To lose beauty in terror, terror in inquisition.
I have lost my passion: why should I need to keep it
Since what is kept must be adulterated?
I have lost my sight, smell, hearing, taste and touch:
How should I use them for your closer contact? 60

These with a thousand small deliberations
Protract the profit of their chilled delirium,
Excite the membrane, when the sense has cooled,
With pungent sauces, multiply variety
In a wilderness of mirrors. What will the spider do,
Suspend its operations, will the weevil
Delay? De Bailhache, Fresca, Mrs. Cammell, whirled
Beyond the circuit of the shuddering Bear
In fractured atoms. Gull against the wind, in the windy
Of Belle Isle, or running on the Horn,
White feathers in the snow, the Gulf claims,
And an old man driven by the Trades
To a sleepy corner.

Tenants of the house,
Thoughts of a dry brain in a dry season.

JOURNEY OF THE MAGI

T. S. ELIOT

"A cold coming we had of it,
Just the worst time of the year
For a journey, and such a long journey:
The ways deep and the weather sharp,
The very dead of winter."
And the camels galled, sore-footed, refractory,
Lying down in the melting snow.
There were times we regretted

The summer palaces on slopes, the terraces,
And the silken girls bringing sherbet. 10
Then the camel men cursing and grumbling
And running away, and wanting their liquor and women,
And the night-fires going out, and the lack of shelters,
And the cities hostile and the towns unfriendly
And the villages dirty and charging high prices:
A hard time we had of it.
At the end we preferred to travel all night,
Sleeping in snatches,
With the voices singing in our ears, saying
That this was all folly. 20

Then at dawn we came down to a temperate valley,
Wet, below the snow line, smelling of vegetation;
With a running stream and a water-mill beating the darkness,
And three trees on the low sky,
And an old white horse galloped away in the meadow.
Then we came to a tavern with vine-leaves over the lintel,
Six hands at an open door dicing for pieces of silver,
And feet kicking the empty wine-skins.
But there was no information, and so we continued
And arrived at evening, not a moment too soon 30
Finding the place; it was (you may say) satisfactory.

All this was a long time ago, I remember,
And I would do it again, but set down
This set down
This: were we led all that way for
Birth or Death? There was a Birth, certainly,
We had evidence and no doubt. I had seen birth and death,
But had thought they were different; this Birth was
Hard and bitter agony for us, like Death, our death.
We returned to our places, these Kingdoms, 40
But no longer at ease here, in the old dispensation,
With an alien people clutching their gods.
I should be glad of another death.

BIOGRAPHICAL NOTES

P. *1.* GEOFFREY CHAUCER. 1340?–1400. Son of a vintner, Geoffrey Chaucer spent most of his life in royal and public service, as page, soldier, squire, court reporter, magistrate, member of Parliament, and ambassador. His work varies from translations and adaptations of the prominent Continental literature of the Middle Ages, to the great scope of *The Canterbury Tales.*

P. *24.* SIR THOMAS WYATT. 1503?–1542. Wyatt, a famous courtier of his day, lived several years upon the Continent in the service of King Henry VIII. He brought to England translations and original compositions in the "new style" of Petrarch, Marot, and other Renaissance writers. This work included the sonnet form, but Wyatt's own work was more notable in the serious and song lyric.

P. *27.* THOMAS, LORD VAUX. 1510–1556. Contemporary of Wyatt and also a courtier, Vaux wrote poems in the new fashion established by Wyatt and Surrey and was particularly successful for his more didactic or moralistic pieces. His work, as well as that of Wyatt and Surrey, appeared in the first "anthology" of the English Renaissance—*Tottel's Miscellany,* 1557.

P. *29.* HENRY HOWARD, EARL OF SURREY. 1516?–1547. Surrey was of royal blood, descended from Edward the Confessor and Edward III. He was several times imprisoned for quarreling and riotous behavior; but he performed important military service. He was accused of treason and beheaded just a week before the death of Henry VIII. His important technical contribution was blank verse.

P. *34.* GEORGE TURBERVILLE. 1540?–1610? Born of an ancient family, the De Turvervilles of Dorset, George Turberville sought his fortunes chiefly in the Inns of Court and as a courtier. He held several political positions under Queen Elizabeth and went on a mission, as secretary to Thomas Randolph, to Russia. His work included many translations and a treatise on hawking and on hunting, as well as briefer poems.

P. *34.* EDMUND SPENSER. 1552?–1599. Although of an ancient family, Edmund Spenser was born into more modest and middle-class surroundings than many of his contemporaries. He served as secretary and clerk to several important noblemen, including Lord Grey of Wilton, Lord Deputy of Ireland, where Spenser lived much of his life. Although sponsored by Sir Walter Ralegh, Spenser was disappointed in securing substantial recognition at court with *The Faerie Queene.*

P. *44*. SIR WALTER RALEGH. 1552?–1618. One of the most colorful and famous of the Elizabethan courtiers, Ralegh performed important service as a soldier, leader of many expeditions to the New World, and writer. He wrote important works in history, exploration, and geography, as well as poems; he was noted for his skepticism. Ralegh was executed as a result of an unfair accusation of complicity in a plot against James I. The sentence was originally mitigated but was revived thirteen years later upon the insistence of the Spanish ambassador.

P. *48*. SIR PHILIP SIDNEY. 1554–1586. Sidney was considered the ideal courtier of the Renaissance pattern. He traveled widely, gave important military and diplomatic service, and was mortally wounded on the battlefield. He wrote a pastoral romance, *Arcadia,* as well as his sonnet sequence, *Astrophel and Stella,* and other lyric poetry.

P. *52*. FULKE GREVILLE, LORD BROOKE. 1554–1628. Greville was an early associate of Sir Philip Sidney. Also a courtier, his work as a poet is particularly interesting for the development of Calvinist thinking in the Petrarchan and religious poetic traditions of his day.

P. *55*. JOHN LYLY. 1553?–1606. Member of Parliament and university wit, Lyly was most noted for his prose romances. Chief of these is *Euphues,* written in a self-conscious, elaborate style; the title of this work added the term *euphuism* to critical vocabulary to designate the rhetorical method used.

P. *56*. ROBERT DEVEREUX, EARL OF ESSEX. 1566–1601. Like Sidney and Ralegh, a courtier in the grand manner, but of nobler birth, Essex was one of the most important political figures of the Renaissance and for many years enjoyed the special favor of Queen Elizabeth. He was a patron of the arts and paid for the burial of Spenser, who had died in poverty, near Chaucer in Westminster Abbey.

P. *56*. GEORGE PEELE. 1558?–1597? Like Lyly, Peele was a university wit, an early dramatist of the Elizabethan theatre who composed plays in both verse and prose. His best-known poems are lyrics from his plays.

P. *57*. GEORGE CHAPMAN. 1559?–1634. Poet and dramatist, Chapman was best known for his verse translations of the Homeric epics.

P. *58*. SAMUEL DANIEL. 1562–1619. Daniel was master of the Queen's Revels, 1603–1615, and minor courtier. His verse varied from the lyric and the sonnet cycle *Delia* to rhymed classical drama and rhymed epistles.

P. *58*. MICHAEL DRAYTON. 1563–1631. Drayton attempted many types of verse, frequently of great lengths, and he was buried in Westminster Abbey. He is chiefly remembered now for some of his sonnets and lyrics.

P. *62*. CHRISTOPHER MARLOWE. 1564–1593. Shakespeare's greatest predecessor in the drama, Marlowe had a strong influence upon the developing Elizabethan stage. Besides his plays (notably *Tamburlaine, Doctor Faustus, Jew of Malta,* and *Edward II*), Marlowe did a few minor translations, his famous lyric, The Passionate Shepherd to His Love, and the narrative poem *Hero and Leander*.

P. *63*. WILLIAM SHAKESPEARE. 1564–1616. Most famous English poet and dramatist, Shakespeare was born at Stratford-on-Avon. In 1586 he went to London and soon joined a company of actors, with whom he prospered as both actor and playwright. He enjoyed favor from the court and from his contemporaries and retired to Stratford to property he had purchased there. As a lyric poet, Shakespeare is known for the songs from his plays and for his sonnets.

P. *69*. THOMAS NASHE. 1567–1601. Among the university wits of his day, Nashe was chiefly known as pamphleteer, strong satirist, and writer of picaresque prose fiction which anticipated the development of the novel.

P. *71*. THOMAS CAMPION. 1567?–1619. Campion was perhaps the most famous composer and song-writer of the highly complex madrigal and song tradition of the English Renaissance. He was also a physician and literary critic.

P. *79*. BEN JONSON. 1572?–1637. Usually accorded the position of Shakespeare's greatest rival as dramatist and poet, Ben Jonson built much of his work upon the practice of classical writers. His critical work made him the outstanding literary critic of his time, and his influence upon other writers was profound.

P. *84*. JOHN DONNE. 1572?–1631. After his early years as satirist, lyric poet, and lawyer, during which time his fortunes varied almost from year to year, Donne was ordained in the Anglican Communion in 1615 and thereafter became Dean of St. Paul's, a writer of important religious poetry, and probably the greatest pulpit orator and sermon-writer of his time. He is considered the founder of the "metaphysical" school of poets of the seventeenth century.

P. *92*. JOHN FLETCHER. 1579–1625. Fletcher was best known

a dramatist, particularly as a collaborator. Much of his work was done with Francis Beaumont.

P. *93*. JOHN WEBSTER. 1580?–1625. Webster is usually regarded as the best tragic dramatist following Shakespeare. His two best-known plays are *The White Devil* and *The Duchess of Malfi*. Webster undoubtedly collaborated with many of the dramatists of his time.

P. *93*. ROBERT HERRICK. 1591–1674. Best-known of the "Sons of Ben" (Jonson), Herrick was an Anglican and a staunch Royalist. During the Civil War, he was ousted from his position as vicar of Dean Prior, Devonshire, but was restored to his living by Charles II.

P. *98*. GEORGE HERBERT. 1593–1633. An Anglican divine, Herbert led a life of saintly piety, from 1629 to 1633 as rector of Fuggleston St. Peter's at Bemerton, near Salisbury. His biography formed one of the famous *Lives* written by Izaak Walton.

P. *102*. THOMAS CAREW. 1595?–1639? A minor courtier and brilliant wit, a Cavalier and Royalist, Carew shows the influence of both Jonson and Donne.

P. *103*. JAMES SHIRLEY. 1596–1666. Shirley was one of the last of the great Jacobean dramatists to write just before the theaters were closed by the Puritans in 1642.

P. *104*. EDMUND WALLER. 1606–1687. Courtier and Royalist, Waller was apprehended in 1643 for his "Waller's Plot" to seize London for Charles II. He managed to save his life, was banished, and later secured a pardon. For a time after the Restoration, until his death, he was a member of Parliament.

P. *105*. JOHN MILTON. 1608–1674. Milton was the great Puritan writer of his time. Early abandoning his plan to take orders, he resolved to devote himself to literature. He studied and wrote at home for six years and then traveled on the Continent. As the break between King and Parliament became imminent, Milton returned home, where he supported himself as a private tutor and became the most important pamphleteer of the period. Under Cromwell he served as Latin (or Foreign) Secretary. During this time he became totally blind. Upon the Restoration he was imprisoned for a short time and thereafter lived in seclusion, writing his major and many of his minor poems.

P. *113*. SIR JOHN SUCKLING. 1609–1642. A Royalist and soldier, Suckling was implicated in an abortive army plot in 1641, fled to France and finally to Spain, where he was imprisoned for a time by the Spanish Inquisition. He died by taking poison. He is known not only for his verse but also as the inventor of cribbage.

P. *115*. RICHARD CRASHAW. 1612?–1649. Son of an anti-papistical preacher, Crashaw was ejected from Cambridge for refusal to subscribe to the Puritan's Covenant. He proceeded to Paris, where he adopted the Roman Catholic faith. After years of great financial distress, he became for a short time before his death secretary to Cardinal Palotto of Rome and sub-canon of Our Lady of Loretto.

P. *116*. ANDREW MARVELL. 1621–1678. Marvell served as secretary to Milton during Milton's period as Latin Secretary to Cromwell. He was a member of Parliament for a long period, both before and after the Restoration. Other than his lyrics, his best known works are his pastorals and his satires.

P. *121*. HENRY VAUGHAN. 1622–1695. Born in Wales, Vaughan was educated at Oxford and became a physician. He was apparently influenced by Hermetic and other mystical philosophies regarding the manifestation of God in nature.

P. *123*. JOHN DRYDEN. 1631–1700. Most famous dramatist, translator, satirist, and critic of the Restoration period, Dryden was born in Northamptonshire, in a Puritan family. Dryden changed his affiliations to become a Royalist, and later he became a Roman Catholic. He was made a fellow of the Royal Society and poet laureate; he held the latter appointment from 1670 to the year following the revolution of 1689. With the position as laureate had gone the appointment as historiographer royal.

P. *128*. ANNE, COUNTESS OF WINCHILSEA. 1661–1720. The poems of Lady Winchilsea appeared only after 1700, so that she has been known as a minor poet of the "age of reason." Although she successfully besought the acquaintance of Alexander Pope, he later stooped to satirize her as a female wit.

P. *129*. JONATHAN SWIFT. 1667–1745. Swift was born in Ireland and educated at Trinity College, Dublin, an Anglican institution. In 1695 Swift took holy orders and for some years held various positions both in Ireland and in England, until he became Dean of St. Patrick's Cathedral, Dublin, in 1713. Thenceforth he resided mainly in Ireland. A brain disease began to cloud his intellect about 1736, made him violently insane in 1741, and caused his death in 1745. He is chiefly known as a great prose satirist, author of *Gulliver's Travels*.

P. *133*. ALEXANDER POPE. 1688–1744. Born into a well-to-do Roman Catholic family in London, Pope at twelve years of age suffered a severe illness which left him dwarfish and in perpetual ill-health. He grew to know the leading literary persons of his day and soon became the most famous and successful poet of the "age of reason," living in affluence after the success of his translation of the *Iliad* in 1719. Admired as a poet, Pope seems to have been disliked, even feared, for his vanity, petty vindictiveness and snobbishness; his pen wielded tremendous power and influence over ideas and persons.

P. *157*. THOMAS GRAY. 1716–1771. A classical scholar, Gray spent much of his life in college and in traveling. He declined the position of poet laureate and for the last years of his life held an honorary professorship at Cambridge.

P. *161*. WILLIAM COLLINS. 1721–1759. Collins renounced church leanings and sought his literary career in London, was commonly in financial difficulties. During the last nine years of his life he was intermittently mentally deranged.

P. *164*. WILLIAM COWPER. 1731–1800. Educated in the public schools, Cowper was called to the bar and began a career as minor public official. Throughout his life he was subject to fits of melancholy and insanity.

P. *165*. PHILIP FRENEAU. 1752–1832. Freneau was for a time a seaman and was a strong satirist of the British during the Revolutionary War. Much of his professional career was spent as a liberal editor.

P. *167*. WILLIAM BLAKE. 1757–1827. Son of a London hosier, Blake was apprenticed to an engraver. He worked as an artist and invented a new method of printing from etched copper plates, illustrating many books besides his own.

P. *174*. ROBERT BURNS. 1759–1796. Son of a farmer and with fragmentary education, Burns caught social attention with his first published book and was considerably lionized. He farmed and later worked as an exciseman.

P. *183*. WILLIAM WORDSWORTH. 1770–1850. Wordsworth took a degree at Cambridge but seemed little interested in his studies. He made a walking tour through France and Switzerland and later returned to France again, where an illegitimate daughter was born to him. At this time he was much interested in the principles of the French Revolution. In 1795 he received a small legacy with the request that he devote himself wholly to poetry henceforth. He received many honors and was appointed poet laureate in 1843.

P. *193*. SAMUEL TAYLOR COLERIDGE. 1772–1834. Coleridge began a medical education but never took a degree. Much of his life was spent in journalism, lecturing, study, and travel, with little practical effect. He indulged in opium at various times in his life. Through annuities from the famous Thomas and Josiah Wedgwood and later through the kindness of Dr. Gillman, Coleridge managed to work both as poet and as critic.

P. *215.* WALTER SAVAGE LANDOR. 1775–1864. Landor early had strong republican feelings. In 1805 he inherited family property, part of which he expended in various plans on behalf of liberalism. He lived a number of years in Italy, particularly in Florence.

P. *216.* GEORGE GORDON, LORD BYRON. 1788–1824. Byron was congenitally lame. He early succeeded to the family title and became a member of the House of Lords. He traveled much and in 1816 left England never to return. He set out to join the Greek revolutionists and died of fever on the expedition.

P. *224.* PERCY BYSSHE SHELLEY. 1792–1822. Shelley was expelled from Oxford for writing the pamphlet "The Necessity of Atheism." In 1815 he inherited a large income from the estate of his grandfather and spent all but three of his remaining years abroad. He was drowned in the Bay of Spezzia on the shipwreck of his boat *Ariel.*

P. *230.* WILLIAM CULLEN BRYANT. 1794–1878. Bryant trained for the law and practised for ten years. He then became an editor and had a particularly distinguished career as an editor of the New York *Evening Post* from 1829 to 1878; in this position he held to a steady liberalism.

P. *231.* JOHN KEATS. 1795–1821. Trained in medicine, Keats abandoned the profession soon after receiving his certificate in 1816. For his remaining five years, Keats wrote industriously. He died in Italy of consumption soon after going there with his friend Joseph Severn.

P. *252.* RALPH WALDO EMERSON. 1803–1882. Emerson was educated at the Boston Latin School and at Harvard. After graduation he taught for a time and then became pastor of the Second Church of Boston. Unable to hold a belief in the sacrament of the Lord's Supper, he resigned his church. Subsequently, for three decades, he wrote, traveled twice to Europe, and lectured throughout the country. He founded the Transcendental Club. During the decade preceding the Civil War, Emerson was strongly anti-slavery. For the last decade of his life, he experienced a progressive break-up of his faculties and, finally, failure of memory.

P. *255.* ELIZABETH BARRETT BROWNING. 1806–1861. Mrs. Browning's confined parental life and betrothal to Robert Browning have been treated in the famous play *The Barretts of Wimpole Street.* Her marriage to Browning and encouragement by him led to the publication of her most famous work, *Sonnets from the Portuguese.*

P. *256.* HENRY WADSWORTH LONGFELLOW. 1807–1882. Longfellow was educated at Bowdoin College, in Maine, and afterwards became a distinguished professor of modern languages there and at Harvard. His fame came comparatively early and remained with him throughout his life. In 1854 he resigned his professorship and continued privately his life as poet and translator.

P. *258.* ALFRED, LORD TENNYSON. 1809–1892. Tennyson attended Cambridge, but did not take a degree. The group known as "Twelve Apostles," a student group, convinced him of the sacredness of his poetic calling. Reception of his first works was spotty, with one devastating attack upon his 1832 volume, *Poems,* which made the poet almost an object of ridicule. However, by 1850 he had earned his public, received a pension, and been appointed poet laureate.

P. *271.* EDGAR ALLAN POE. 1809–1849. Poe was born in Boston to parents who were actors. In 1811 he was taken into the home of John Allan of Richmond, Virginia, although not legally adopted. He was educated in England and for a brief time at the University of Virginia. For his living, he chiefly depended upon editorial work and his writing; much of the time he lived in poverty. He is well known as a critic and short story writer as well as a poet.

P. *273.* EDWARD FITZGERALD. 1809–1883. Fitzgerald was educated at Cambridge and lived a retired life in Suffolk. Friend of Carlyle, Thackeray, and Tennyson, he translated many works, but the *Rubaiyat* provided his chief reputation.

P. *274.* ROBERT BROWNING. 1812–1889. Browning was of a Dissenting family, and he was educated largely in his father's fine library. During his marriage, he lived in Italy, returning to England after the death of Elizabeth Barrett Browning in 1861. He was immensely productive during the latter part of his life and became greatly admired during his lifetime. The Browning Society became a symbol of nineteenth-century culture, also during his lifetime.

P. *283.* EMILY BRONTË. 1818–1848. Emily Brontë was born in a parsonage on the edge of the Yorkshire moors and lived a retired life for almost all of her thirty years. She is best known for her novel *Wuthering Heights.*

P. *284.* ARTHUR HUGH CLOUGH. 1819–1861. Like Matthew Arnold, and opposed in this position to Browning and Tennyson,

Clough was a leading poet of doubt in mid nineteenth-century England.

P. *284.* HERMAN MELVILLE. 1819–1891. Melville was born in New York City. He sailed as a seaman for a number of years, picturing the seaman's life and the South Seas in several books. For twenty years he was a customs inspector in New York. His most famous work is his novel *Moby-Dick*.

P. *285.* WALT WHITMAN. 1819–1892. Born into a Quaker family, Whitman was for thirty years in printing and editorial work and hand-set the type for his own first book of poems. During the Civil War he worked as a nurse in Washington hospitals and then for some years as a clerk in governmental offices. Stricken by paralysis, he spent the last twenty years of life in gradual recovery, travel, and retired residence at Camden, New Jersey.

P. *295.* MATTHEW ARNOLD. 1822–1888. Son of a famous educator, Arnold was educated at Rugby and Oxford. He taught for a time at both schools, and in 1851 he was appointed inspector of schools, a post he held for many years. He won a great reputation as a critic as well as a poet.

P. *298.* DANTE GABRIEL ROSSETTI. 1828–1882. Son of an exiled Italian poet and patriot, Rossetti was born in London. He was impatient of formal instruction and at twenty years of age became a pupil of the artist Ford Madox Brown. Rossetti became one of the original Pre-Raphaelites, a brotherhood which aimed "to divest art of conventionality, to work with sincerity of purpose, to reproduce with fidelity." Following the tragic death of his wife—for which Rossetti blamed himself—Rossetti declined rapidly.

P. *299.* GEORGE MEREDITH. 1828–1909. Meredith was born in Portsmouth the son of a tailor. After an unsystematic education, he tried his hand at several efforts, including the study of law, editorial work in the periodical field, and war correspondent. For thirty-five years he earned his living as a publisher's reader. In late life he was crippled by paralysis but had then won literary fame, chiefly for his novels.

P. *300.* CHRISTINA ROSSETTI. 1830–1894. Christina was the youngest of the four Rossetti children. For a time she shared the work of her brother Dante Gabriel in the beginnings of the Pre-Raphaelite movement. During her life she endured much suffering, both physical and mental, and remained devout according to the standards of that part of the Church of England which had been regenerated by the Oxford Movement.

P. *301.* EMILY DICKINSON. 1830–1886. Emily Dickinson was born in Amherst, Massachusetts, the daughter of a prominent lawyer and treasurer of Amherst College. She was educated at Amherst Academy and for a year at South Hadley Female Seminary, now Mount Holyoke College. She had a number of literary friendships, but she seldom left home after she was twenty-six years old and after the death of her father became a recluse. With three minor exceptions, her poems were published after her death.

P. *305.* ALGERNON CHARLES SWINBURNE. 1837–1909. Swinburne was born in London in a distinguished and aristocratic family. His education was at home, under his mother and grandfather, and, for a time, at Oxford. He embarked on a career of writing, marked also by self-indulgence and self-wreckage. For the last thirty years of his life his practical affairs were managed by Theodore Watts-Dunton.

P. *308.* THOMAS HARDY. 1840–1928. Hardy spent his childhood in Dorsetshire. He worked as an ecclesiastical architect. He first wrote poetry almost exclusively; then, to earn more money, he turned to fiction, which he abandoned in 1895 at the height of his powers to return again to poetry. Hardy and Meredith are the English writers who have achieved first-rank reputations as both poets and novelists.

P. *312.* GERARD MANLEY HOPKINS. 1844–1889. Hopkins was trained at Oxford. His conversion to Catholicism occurred in 1866, and eleven years later he entered the Jesuit priesthood. He served as a missionary in the slums of Liverpool; later he had charge of a church at Oxford and taught Greek in the University of Dublin. His poems were published by his friend Robert Bridges in 1918.

P. *314.* ROBERT BRIDGES. 1844–1930. Educated at Eton and Oxford, Bridges for a time studied and then practised medicine. In 1913 he was appointed poet laureate. For a number of years he was associated with the Oxford University Press, and he wrote a number of prose critical works.

P. *317.* FRANCIS THOMPSON. 1859–1907. Thompson was born in Lancashire and was first intended for the priesthood. He failed to qualify and shortly thereafter failed again, this time in his father's profession of medicine. For three years he lived the life of an outcast in London, his torture aggravated by the opium habit. Wilfrid Meynell and his wife Alice gave him the means of working out his salvation as man and as artist. He spent some time in a priory and in a monastery and died of tuberculosis.

P. *318.* A. E. HOUSMAN. 1859–1936. Housman was born in Shropshire, which he made the scene of many poems. He studied at Oxford and became, for ten years, a clerk in the British Patent Office. Then he became a teacher, first at University College, London, and later at Cambridge, as professor of Latin.

P. *322.* WILLIAM BUTLER YEATS. 1865–1939. Yeats was born near Dublin of a distinguished family of artists. He attended school in London and in Dublin. He helped found the Irish literary theater and was a leader in the Irish literary renaissance. He served the Free State as a Senator, 1922–1928, and his influence grew as folklorist, playwright, poet, champion of new tendencies, and seer.

P. *328.* EDWIN ARLINGTON ROBINSON. 1869–1935. Although born in Head Tide, Maine, Robinson grew up in Gardiner, on the Kennebec River. He was obliged to terminate his formal education on the death of his father, after he had attended Harvard for two years. Subsequent years were difficult, but he was given a clerical governmental position at the instigation of President Theodore Roosevelt. He later occupied himself steadily with the writing of poetry.

P. *334.* ROBERT FROST. 1875–. Frost was born in San Francisco but at the age of ten was taken to New England, where his ancestors had lived for generations. He attended Dartmouth briefly and Harvard for two years; thereafter he took up teaching, shoemaking, and farming. In 1912 he sold his farm and settled with his family in a village in England, and his first two books of poems were published in London. He returned to America in 1915 and has since divided his time between farming and various connections as a "poet in residence" or lecturer at various institutions of learning.

P. *337.* WALLACE STEVENS. 1879–. Born in Reading, Pennsylvania, Stevens studied at Harvard and at the New York Law School. He was admitted to the bar in 1904, and practiced in New York until 1916, when he became associated with the Hartford Accident and Indemnity Company, of which he has been a vice-president since 1934.

P. *344.* T. S. ELIOT. 1888–. Eliot was born in St. Louis and received both B.A. and A.M. degrees from Harvard. He subsequently studied at the Sorbonne and at Oxford. In 1914 he settled in London where he became a teacher, lecturer, editor, and publisher. In 1927 he became a naturalized British subject.

INDEX OF AUTHORS

Rinehart Editions